Praise for *Sex Trafficking*

"Siddharth Kara possesses that rare and valuable combination of passion for his subject, insight, and rigorous research. His analysis is persuasive and his descriptions heartbreaking in their clarity. Human trafficking in all forms is slavery, no matter how you cut it, and in this book Kara brings a modern-day scourge to the light of day."

—ERICA STONE, PRESIDENT, AMERICAN HIMALAYAN FOUNDATION

"A disturbing and illuminating study." —*IRISH TIMES*

"I approached this book with a certain weariness. Having worked on the subject of sex trafficking for many years, I was unenthusiastic about yet another exposé or cri de coeur from a business executive turned anti-slavery advocate. I could not have been more wrong. This is a unique and inspiring book—an honest, lucid, and immensely intelligent account of a devastating yet pervasive aspect of contemporary globalization. It deserves to be widely read by anyone who wants to understand one of the most persistent and complex human rights violations of our times."

—JACQUELINE BHABHA, HARVARD LAW SCHOOL

"As an experienced investigator of human trafficking offences, I was not expecting to discover anything new from this book. The reality was the opposite—this book offers unique and invaluable insight into the whole subject of human trafficking. The global financial perspective was especially helpful, and I have found the analysis and recommendations extremely useful in my work as an investigator and policy adviser. I strongly recommend it to others involved in the fight against human trafficking."

—STEPHEN WILKINSON, SENIOR INVESTIGATING OFFICER ON HUMAN TRAFFICKING, UNITED KINGDOM

"This book could not be more important. After years of witnessing slavery and meeting with slaves, Siddharth Kara illuminates one of our most pressing human rights issues. He offers brand-new research and reliable facts, shattering the myths and sensationalism that tend to surround this topic. Everyone should read this book: it will change the way we think about our world." —ZOE TRODD, HARVARD UNIVERSITY

SEX TRAFFICKING

Inside the Business of Modern Slavery

Siddharth Kara

Columbia University Press New York

Columbia University Press
Publishers Since 1893
New York Chichester, West Sussex

A Caravan book. For more information, visit
www.caravanbooks.org.

Library of Congress Cataloging-in-Publication Data

Kara, Siddharth.
Sex trafficking : inside the business of modern slavery / Siddharth Kara.
p. cm.
Includes bibliographical references and index.
ISBN 978-0-231-13960-1 (cloth : alk. paper)—
ISBN 978-0-231-13961-8 (pbk. : alk. paper)—
ISBN 978-0-231-51139-1 (e-book)
1. Human trafficking. 2. Human trafficking—Prevention. 3. Minorities—Crimes against. 4. Minorities—Social conditions. 5. Minorities—Economic conditions. 6. Globalization—Economic conditions. 7. Prostitution. 8. Slavery. 9. Sex-oriented businesses. I. Title.

HQ281.K37 2009
364.15—dc22

2008021988

Columbia University Press books are printed on permanent and durable acid-free paper.
This book is printed on paper with recycled content.
Printed in the United States of America

c 20 19 18 17 16 15 14 13 12 11
p 20 19 18 17 16 15 14 13 12 11

Their vessels now had made th' intended land,
And all with joy descend upon the strand;
When the false tyrant seiz'd the princely maid,
And to a lodge in distant woods convey'd;
Pale, sinking, and distress'd with jealous fears,
And asking for her sister all in tears.
The letcher, for enjoyment fully bent,
No longer now conceal'd his base intent;
But with rude haste the bloomy girl deflow'r'd,
Tender, defenceless, and with ease o'erpower'd.
Her piercing accents to her sire complain,
And to her absent sister, but in vain:
In vain she importunes, with doleful cries,
Each unattentive godhead of the skies.

—Ovid, *Metamorphoses*

Contents

Preface

After my third research trip into the global sex trafficking industry, I brooded for twenty-four hours on a flight from Mumbai to Los Angeles, wondering how to write this book. Countless faces of torture, savagery, and abject slavery swirled in my mind. I did not know how I would convey these stories; I knew only that the truths of the scores of sex slaves I met in brothels, massage parlors, street corners, and apartments across the world must be told, however unpalatable those truths may be. Though I originally intended this book as a systematic narration of my journey into the sex trafficking industry, a much broader intention began to form in my mind. I realized I wanted to recount a life-altering journey, one that motivated in me a newfound mission to contribute to more successful international efforts to abolish sex trafficking and all other forms of contemporary slavery.

That slavery still exists may surprise some readers, but the practice of violently coerced labor continues to thrive in every corner of the globe. There were 28.4 million slaves in the world at the end of 2006, and there will most likely be a greater number by the time you read this book (see table A.1 for detail). Some are child slaves in India, stolen from their homes and worked sixteen hours a day to harvest the tea that middle-class consumers drink or sew the carpets that adorn their sitting rooms. Others are bonded laborers in South Asia, Latin America, and Africa, who accrue or inherit debts that can never be repaid, no matter how long they work. Slaves in the United States harvest agricultural products: onions, avocados, and corn in Texas, California, Florida, and the Carolinas. Up to 5 percent of the world's cocoa beans are picked by slave hands in the Ivory Coast. Slaves continue to harvest coffee in Kenya and Ethiopia, and they burn wood in hellish furnaces in Brazil to produce charcoal that is used to temper the steel in everything from garden shears to car axles. Approximately 1.2 million of these 28.4 million slaves are young women and children, who were deceived, abducted, seduced, or sold by families to be prostituted across the globe. These sex slaves are forced to service hundreds, often thousands of men before they are discarded, forming the backbone of one of the most profitable illicit enterprises in the world. Drug trafficking generates greater dollar revenues, but trafficked women are far more profitable. Unlike a drug, a human female does not have to be grown, cultivated, distilled, or packaged. Unlike a drug, a human female can be used by the customer again and again.

The brutalities associated with sex slavery are perverse, violent, and utterly destructive. Whips, cigarette burns, broken bones, starvation—every slave has suffered these tortures, but sex slaves suffer each of these as well as innumerable counts of rape - ten, fifteen, twenty or more times per day. In brothels across the globe, I met women and children who suffered unspeakable acts of barbarity. Meeting these victims was not easy. With each interview, I became increasingly filled with heartbreak, sorrow, and rage. Nothing I write can possibly convey the sensation of peering into the moribund eyes of a broken child who has been forced to have sex with hundreds of men before the age of sixteen.

I am often asked how I first became "interested" in the topic of sex trafficking. The seeds of my research were sown years ago when I was an undergraduate at Duke University. A story on CNN spotlighted a young Croatian girl, fourteen years old, from a well-to-do family in Zagreb. She was breaking swimming records across Europe and intended to swim for Croatia in the 1996 Summer Olympics in Atlanta. Hopes were high that she would bring home more than one gold medal to the fledgling country. One night, as she slept, a bomb sent shrapnel flying into her bedroom, shattering her legs. She would never swim again.

As I watched this story in the midst of stressful first-semester examinations, I was filled with indignation. This young girl's talent put her in the top 0.001 percent of swimmers in the world, and mindless violence had ruined her life. Who was I to bemoan having too many papers to write when there were far more exceptional individuals than I whose lives were destroyed at the age of fourteen? I resolved to travel to the former Yugoslavia and do what I could to help. I joined forces with two Duke graduate students and procured a faculty sponsor, interviewed a handful of students to join us, found one student at Duke from the former Yugoslavia and met weekly to learn Bosnian from her, procured a grant from the Duke board of directors, contacted the United Nations High Commissioner for Refugees (UNHCR) to get placements in refugee camps, and spent eight weeks volunteering in those camps in Summer 1995.

My camp was located in Novo Mesto, Slovenia, about sixty kilometers west of the Croatian border. The camp was populated by five hundred former occupants of a town in northwest Bosnia called Velika Kladusa. In late 1991, Serb soldiers raided the village, executed the men, burned down the homes, and told the survivors—mostly elderly and children—that they would kill them if they stayed. The survivors walked for days to reach the Croatian border, where UN personnel sent them to the camp in Slovenia. They were not sent to camps in Croatia, which were much closer, because those camps were full.

In the Novo Mesto camp, the refugees lived six to a room, shared the same filthy outdoor toilets, and were served two meals a day of stale bread, oily soup, and rotting brown salad. We three Duke students lived just as the refugees did. That summer, I lost eighteen pounds, struggled to have any sort of positive effect on the refugees' lives, and learned that all they really wanted was to have someone listen. So I listened—to a father who was once an engineer for Boeing in Sarajevo, who spoke of the destruction of his home and the sorrow that his children had not been in school for almost four years; to the elderly women who had outlived their children and watched their grandchildren rot from malnourishment; to the teenagers who drowned their sorrows in alcohol and self-hatred. Last, but far from least, I heard stories of Serb soldiers who raped and trafficked young Bosnian Muslim women by the truckloads to brothels across Europe.

It took me a few years to process my experiences in Slovenia. In early 2000, I was in the midst of an MBA degree at Columbia University when the stories of the trafficked women in Bosnia resurfaced in my mind. I had little appetite for a return to corporate life, but I was equally unsure what to do with the trafficking tales I had heard in the refugee camp. I considered the paths before me and made a radical decision: The time had come to tell this story.

The research that commenced that summer proved the single greatest challenge of my life. When I began, few people knew what sex trafficking was, so I decided the only way to find out was to go into the field and learn for myself. Beginning in Summer 2000, I used the money saved from my business career to take three separate trips to visit brothels, shelters, towns, borders, and villages in India, Nepal, Burma, Thailand, Vietnam, Italy, Moldova, Albania, the Netherlands, the United Kingdom, Mexico, and the United States. I was slowed only by the necessity of getting a job and saving more money to take more research trips. I conducted over 150 interviews with sex trafficking victims in brothels and shelters. I conducted another 120 interviews with the families of victims, the men who purchased them, shelter and NGO workers, trafficking police, trafficking attorneys, one brothel owner, and one trafficker. I walked into brothels, massage parlors, and sex clubs to see for myself how the industry functioned. I journeyed to the villages and towns from which the victims originated to understand the conditions that gave rise to their exploitation. I traveled to borders between India and Nepal, Nepal and China, Moldova and Transdniestr, Moldova and Romania, Italy and Austria, Italy and Slovenia, Albania and the Adriatic Sea, Albania and Serbia, the United States and Mexico, Thailand and Burma, Thailand and Laos, and Vietnam and China to understand how the movement of victims was accomplished. I interviewed victims who had been trafficked for purposes other than sexual exploitation, and I interviewed over two hundred individuals in other forms of contemporary slavery, including bonded laborers, forced laborers, and child slaves.

I conducted more research in India than other countries, as I could get by with rudimentary Hindi and was familiar with the lay of the land. In other countries, I hired guides and translators to help. I stayed in hostels, slept in village huts, and journeyed by plane, train, bus, car, motorbike, bullock cart, and on foot through steaming jungles to arrive at my destinations. Word of mouth and hustling with locals were my best tools for finding the sex trafficking underbelly in each country. In cities like Chiang Mai or Mumbai, finding sex slaves was easy—the brothels were in plain view, even though they were illegal. In Moldova, sex clubs were numerous and prostitutes came right to my hotel door the evening I arrived. In other countries, such as Italy, where the laws against illegal brothels are more strictly enforced, it took time to track down sex slaves. Eventually, I learned that in most countries, taxi drivers almost always knew where to find cheap sex, and cheap sex was almost always provided by slaves.

Most of my interviews were conducted in one of two venues: inside a sex establishment or at a shelter for trafficking victims. The interviews inside sex establishments were extremely hit or miss. I searched out individuals who appeared to speak English and might be willing to converse. I never took a tape recorder or camera into a brothel because patrons were often searched and I did not want to put myself or the slaves at risk. For the same reasons, I never went back to the same brothel more than once, whether I managed to interview someone or not. When soliciting conversations, I had to make a split-second judgment as to whether a request might lead to harm to the slave. Brothels owners and pimps often devised ways to test the loyalties of their slaves, who in turn received positive treatment if they passed or severe punishments if they failed. These tests, such as planting a fake human-rights worker promising freedom for information, created overwhelming distrust in the victims. As a result, most conversations I attempted ended very quickly. I was always honest about who I was, but most slaves did not trust me. Of the numerous victims' stories shared in this book, only a handful derive from successful conversations inside a sex establishment, and those represent a small fraction of conversations I attempted in such venues.

Conditions were more favorable in shelters and I was able to record or transcribe most of my interviews. When I first began my research, many shelters allowed supervised interviews with victims, but within a few years, they rightfully began declining such interviews, as the individuals often felt forced to discuss matters they would rather forget, and many interviewers carelessly published information without protecting the identity and security of the former slave. Thankfully, I had spent considerable time establishing trust with shelters in various countries and could conduct interviews with volunteers, gather data, and speak with victims who were willing to speak. Most sex trafficking victims, however, did not want to speak. They did not want to relive their agonies, and they feared the shame that would be forced upon them if people in their home towns learned of their ordeals. They feared that their families would be harmed by traffickers, who had warned them never to utter a word, and they feared deportation. Most victims I interviewed were under the age of twenty-five, and most suffered debilitating physical injuries, malnutrition, psychological traumas, posttraumatic stress disorder, and infection by a scourge of sexually transmitted diseases, including HIV/AIDS. On more than one occasion, I had to reschedule a conversation because the individual could not continue. The memories were painful and the courage required to relive them was extraordinary. Three victims in this book shared their stories for the first time during my interview. One of them was a child.

Because of the extreme sensitivity and potential danger in discussing trafficking ordeals, I established two ground rules to ensure that I never, ever made a victim's life worse than it already was. First, I was determined to do no harm. I never forced a conversation and I never solicited one where the victim would have suffered for speaking to me. In shelters, I did not approach interviewees with a list of questions that I expected to be answered; each encounter was a conversation. I informed the individual that she could share whatever information she desired. The results were often long, honest, detailed discussions, in which the victims poured their hearts out. Second, when visiting sex establishments, I was always equipped with information on nearby shelters and health services, just in case a sex slave requested assistance. In most cases, I did not offer the information unless asked, as many sex slaves had convinced themselves that they were not slaves and suggesting otherwise could only distress them. Nevertheless, I occasionally left the information behind, hoping it would prove beneficial to someone, at some point.

After conducting three research trips in and out of brothels and shelters across the globe, it became clear to me that sex trafficking is a heinous crime against humanity. It generates immense profits through the vulgar and wanton destruction of female lives. Attempting to describe that destruction was not easy for me. The first drafts of this book were composed as a narrative journey, into which I wove a general description of the functioning of contemporary sex trafficking. This initial approach did not work. It was better suited to capture a broad readership, but it did not serve the more crucial imperative of portraying with as much accuracy as possible the origins of the sex trafficking industry, how it operates worldwide, and how best to eradicate it. To accomplish these ends, the first chapter became dedicated to an analytical exposition of the key aspects of the contemporary sex trafficking industry, concluding with an argument on how to abolish it. The final chapter explores this argument in full, which can be summarized as follows: the most effective measures to eradicate the global sex trafficking industry are those that reduce the aggregate demand for sex slaves by slave owners and consumers through an attack on the industry's immense profitability. A new brand of global abolitionist movement is suggested, wherein governments, nonprofit organizations, key international organizations, and individual citizens alike take more surgical steps designed to dismantle the business of sex trafficking. This book is a call to such action, motivated by my personal witness of unconscionable suffering, to be conveyed in a less restrained tone during the narrative chapters of this book. I promise you, the reader, that if you will carry through the foundational analysis in Chapter 1, you will be all the better equipped to undertake the transnational journey into the global sex trafficking industry that follows. Along the way, you will meet numerous slaves as well as a handful of courageous people dedicated to the abolition of sex trafficking and the assistance of its victims. I hope that this book will motivate greater efforts to assist them.

Acknowledgments

I am forever grateful to all of the individuals who shared their stories with me. I am in awe of their strength and humbled by their courage. One by one, they placed their faith in me, solely upon the dream that their voices might be heard. I hope I did not let them down.

Numerous people across the world offered invaluable goodwill, assistance, and insights throughout my research. I would like to thank each of them: Supriya Awasti, Manju Vyas, Bhanuja Saran, Ranjana Gaur, Father Raymond, Devika Mahadevan, Deepak Kumar, Kanhiya Singh, the staff of Gramin Mahila Srijansil Pariwar, Anu Tamang, Sunita Danuwar, Sushila Mahato, Januka Bhattarai, Shama Chhetri, Bhola Dhungana, Lhwang Lama, Superintendent Sushila Singh, the staff of the U.S. embassy in Kathmandu, Daniela Mannu, Rosanna Paradiso, Isabella Orfano, Francesco Cachediti, Paola Monzini, Morena, Nayla, and Shpresa from the Parsec Street Unit Team, Claudio Donadel, "Michael," Cristina Bianconi, Monika Peruffo, Suzanne Hoff, Maria de Cock, Klara Skrivankova, Liliana Rotaru, Stella Rotaru, Daniela Gutu, Lily Moka, Alina Budeci, "Peter," Olga Colomeet, Olga Patlati, Angela Bulat, Holly Wiseman, Victor Lutenco, Susanne Jalbert, Ludmila Bilevschi, Antonia De Meo, Matthias Kalush, Ledia Beci, Ruth Rosenberg, Donika Curraj, Brikena Puka, Arian Giantris, Bernadette Roberts, Vincent Tournecuillert, Artur Marku, Bruce

Hintz, Michael Robinson, Melissa Stewart, Panadda Changmanee, Karen Smith, Mimi, Lieutenant Colonel Suchai Chindavanich, the translators in Mae Sot, Kit Ripley, and Sister Judy.

Kevin Bales has been a mentor, guide, and friend since the day we met for sushi at the town square in Oxford, Mississippi. He taught me more than anyone about modern slavery, and he set the example I have strived to emulate.

My agent Susan Cohen placed her faith in a young man with little more than a proposal and youthful idealism. Her tireless efforts found a home for this book. Along the way, she became a very cherished friend.

Peter Dimock is so much more than an editor. He championed this book every step of the way and pushed me to find the only voice that could tell this story. When I was rattled, he was steady. When I could not write any better, he taught me how.

My mother, father, and brother I thank for their unconditional encouragement. The good in me comes from my parents, and I could not have completed this book without everything they sacrificed to raise me, educate me, and facilitate this mission.

Above all, there is Aditi. My inspiration, my endless all. Your love and friendship carried me through the most difficult days of this journey. With more gratitude than words can convey, I thank you for your guidance, support, and unwavering faith. I could not navigate this world without you.

1 Sex Trafficking

An Overview

Men can co-exist on condition that they recognize each other as being all equally, though differently, human, but they can also co-exist by denying each other a comparable degree of humanity, and thus establishing a system of subordination. —*Claude Lévi-Strauss,* Tristes Tropiques

Untamed Desire

My father once told me the story of how the world was created. In between each cycle of time, he said, there is emptiness. The god Brahma slumbers and another god, Shiva, meditates over why the world of man invariably degrades from a realm of "generosity, self-restraint, gentleness, and truth" into a miasma of "greed, lust, violence, and deceit." Because Shiva must swallow this poisonous cosmos at the end of time, he meditates on a way to prevent man's degradation. At the cusp of the answer, he is disturbed by Brahma, who grows restless and prematurely seeks to initiate creation by taking the form of a bull and mounting his own daughter. Furious, Shiva hurls his trident at the god-bull, who pulls out of his daughter in an effort to dodge the weapon. In doing so, Brahma's seed spills across the heavens, and Shiva's trident strikes the seed where it lands, thereby igniting creation. At that moment, Shiva drops his head in sorrow. He recognizes that once again, the world of man will be suffused with greed, suffering, and pain, for it has been initiated upon the seed of untamed desire. The sequence is undeniable—desire leads to suffering, suffering leads to anger, anger leads to violence, and violence destroys the world.[1]

I never truly understood this story until I first laid my eyes on Maya. Gaunt and distressed, she was nineteen when I interviewed her, after almost four years as a sex slave in each of Mumbai's two main red-light districts, Kamathipura and Falkland Road. She was born in the Sindhupalchok region of Nepal, one of the poorest stretches of land on the planet, with an annual per capita income of $180, or fifty cents per day. Desperate to make ends meet, her parents sold her to a local agent for $55 on the promise that she would have a good job at a carpet factory, from which she could send home up to $10 per month. The night Maya left home, the agent resold her to a *dalal* (trafficker), who took her to Butwal, a border town with India, where they spent the night with another girl. The next day, Maya, the other girl, and the *dalal* crossed the border into India by foot. A few days later, they were in Mumbai.

This is what Maya told me happened next:

> Once I came to Mumbai, the *dalal* sold me to a *malik* [brothel boss] in Kamathipura. The *malik* told me I owed him thirty-five thousand rupees [$780], and I must have sex with any man who chooses me until this debt is repaid. I refused, and his men raped me and did not feed me. When I agreed to do sex, they gave me medicines because I had a urine infection. I was in that bungalow two years and made sex to twenty men each day. There were hundreds of girls in this bungalow, many from Nepal. One time I tried to escape. I complained to the police, but they did nothing. A few days later the *malik*'s men found me on the streets and took me back to the brothel. The *malik* put chili paste on a broomstick and pushed it inside me. Then he broke my ribs with his fist. The *gharwali* [house manager, madam] tended my wounds for a short time, and after this time I went with clients again, even though my ribs pained very badly. The *gharwali* gave me opium to make the pain less. After two years, the *malik* sold me to another *malik* on Falkland Road. During this time I lived in a *pinjara* [cage] with one other woman. It was very small and it was on the street, so it was very noisy at night. I was pregnant two times, and the *gharwali* gave me pills to kill the baby. The second time I became very ill. When I was strong I ran away. I went to a shelter near Falkland Road. They told me I have HIV. They helped me contact my father, but he told me not to come home. He said I can never be married and because I have HIV, I can only bring shame.

Maya's story is emblematic of the hundreds of thousands of women and children trafficked and forced into prostitution each year. As with each victim in this book, I have not used Maya's real name, and in a few instances in which discussing precise geographic locations might result in danger to the individual, I have provided an alternate setting. Like most sex trafficking victims, Maya and her family were vulnerable to deceit due to economic desperation. Once Maya arrived at the brothel, she was swiftly broken down through physical and psychological torture. While her journey to Mumbai was direct, other victims endure multiple stops in several countries, where they are exploited, resold, and tortured. At each destination, victims are told they must work off the "debt" of trafficking them by having sex with up to twenty men per day. The accounting of these debts is invariably exploitive, involving deductions for food, clothing, rent, alcohol, and exorbitant interest rates. The false promise of attaining freedom is a powerful tool that brothel owners utilize to control their victims. As time passes, some slaves accept their fates, and in a Stockholm Syndrome–like transformation, they might be "freed" to serve as working prostitutes who mentor new slaves upon arrival. In Maya's case, when her brothel owner decided she had worked off her debt, she was resold and given a new debt. If she had not escaped, the cycle of slavery might never have ended.

Civilization at a Crossroads

The global magnitude of victimization of young women like Maya is staggering. Every minute of every day, the most vulnerable women and children in the world are raped for profit with impunity, yet efforts to combat sex trafficking remain woefully inadequate and misdirected. There are several reasons for this insufficiency. First, despite increased media attention, sex trafficking remains poorly understood. Second, the organizations dedicated to combating sex trafficking are underfunded and uncoordinated internationally. Third, the laws against sex trafficking are overwhelmingly anemic and poorly enforced. Finally, despite numerous studies and reports, a systematic business and economic analysis of the industry, conducted to identify strategic points of intervention, has not yet been undertaken.

This book is dedicated to the task of addressing each of these key impediments to an effective global response to sex trafficking. The book's central argument is that the enormity and pervasiveness of sex trafficking is a direct result of the immense profits to be derived from selling inexpensive sex around the world. The structures of Western capitalism, as spread through the process of economic globalization, contribute greatly to the destruction of lives this profitability entails. Sex trafficking is one of the ugliest contemporary actualizations of global capitalism because it was directly produced by the harmful inequalities spread by the process of economic globalization: deepening of rural poverty, increased economic disenfranchisement of the poor, the net extraction of wealth and resources from poor economies into richer ones, and the broad-based erosion of real human freedoms across the developing world.[2] Ending sex trafficking requires an attack on the industry's immense profitability and a radical shift in the conduct of economic globalization.

What Is Sex Trafficking?

Many policy makers are still debating what the term "trafficking" means. The 2000 United Nations Trafficking Protocol established a generally accepted definition of trafficking as the following:

> the recruitment, transportation, transfer, harbouring or receipt of persons by means of threat or use of force or other forms of coercion, of abduction, of fraud, of deception, of the abuse of power, or of a position of vulnerability or of the giving or receiving of payments or benefits to achieve the consent of a person having control over another person, for the purpose of exploitation. Exploitation shall include, at a minimum, the exploitation of prostitution of others or other forms of sexual exploitation, forced labour services, slavery or practices similar to slavery, servitude or the removal of organs.

The primary confusion relates to whether the definition of trafficking, as the process of "recruitment, transportation, [and] transfer . . . for the purpose of exploitation" includes the exploitation itself.[3] The wording connotes only the movement portion of the trafficking chain, which explains why so many laws and programs against trafficking focus on movement more than exploitation. However, trafficking is not about movement; it is about slavery. The transatlantic slave trade from the sixteenth to the eighteenth centuries involved the trafficking of eleven million Africans across thousands of miles to work as slaves on plantations.[4] Why is this historical practice termed a slave trade and the same practice today termed trafficking? This linguistic attenuation scrambles global attention and blunts abolitionist policies. More focus is placed on thwarting movement across borders than on shutting down the modern plantations to which those individuals are being moved. Such tactics have proved overwhelmingly futile because the modes of transport are numerous (by ship, vehicle, plane, train, foot), the costs of transport are miniscule, and the sources of potential slave labor are nearly limitless. Despite the shifts in ease and inexpensiveness of human transportation, current anti-trafficking efforts primarily seek to crack down on modern-day slave traders, resulting in little more than adjustments in routes, larger bribes to border guards, and the procurement of false travel documents. Such minor increases in costs make a very small economic dent in today's slave trade. A much clearer understanding of sex trafficking is required—wherein the movement and the purpose of the movement are disaggregated as criminal acts—to achieve greater abolitionist effectiveness. To promote this understanding, I offer two definitions that should prove more useful when formulating policies and initiatives intended to abolish acts of sex trafficking:

- *Slave trading* can be defined as the process of acquiring, recruiting, harboring, receiving, or transporting an individual, through any means and for any distance, into a condition of slavery or slave-like exploitation.
- *Slavery* can be defined as the process of coercing labor or other services from a captive individual, through any means, including exploitation of bodies or body parts.[5]

These definitions are not meant to replace the long-established, more complex articulations of the crimes, but a disaggregation of the criminal acts constituent to sex trafficking should prove more effective when formulating efforts to combat those crimes.

Anatomy of Sex Trafficking

All sex trafficking crimes have two components: slave trading and slavery. Slave trading represents the supply side of the sex trafficking industry. Slavery represents the demand side. Within these two components, there are three steps: acquisition, movement, and exploitation. The interrelationship among these elements reveals the anatomy of sex trafficking, as figure 1.1 shows.

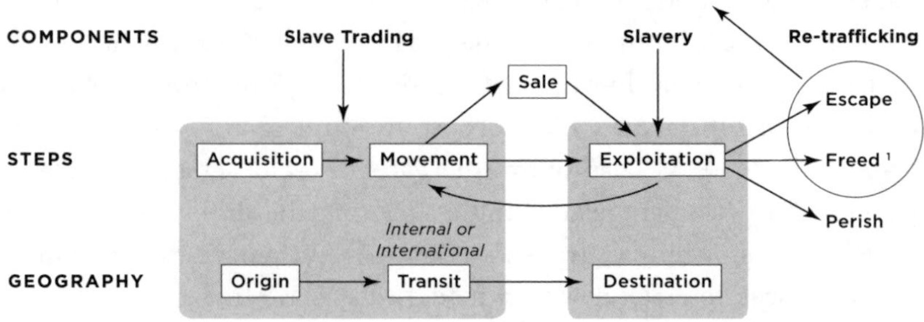

[1] "Freed" slaves might be released for various reasons. Those who "graduate" to paid sex work would not be re-trafficked.

FIGURE 1.1 Anatomy of Sex Trafficking

Imagine that sex trafficking is a disease infecting human civilization. To eradicate a disease requires an understanding of its molecular anatomy. This molecular understanding, in turn, reveals a broader knowledge of how the disease functions. With this broader understanding, the disease's vulnerable points are revealed and a treatment can be devised to eradicate it. To keep the disease from returning, the host organism must also be understood. The conditions that initially gave rise to the disease must be altered, lest the disease return. This rudimentary analogy provides the framework for my approach to the abolition of sex trafficking. The molecular anatomy of sex trafficking—acquisition, movement, and exploitation—must be understood to elucidate its broader functioning as a criminal business. The details of how the business functions reveal the industry's vulnerable points, namely, the drivers of profits and the market force of demand. Analyzing these forces allows us to derive the best tactics to treat the infection. To ensure that the business of sex trafficking is eradicated in the long term, the conditions in the "host organism," that first gave rise to the infection—namely, poverty and economic globalization—must also be addressed.[6]

Acquisition of sex slaves primarily occurs in one of five ways: deceit, sale by family, abduction, seduction or romance, or recruitment by former slaves. Each of these means was utilized in almost every country I visited; however, local factors promoted certain means over others.

Deceit

Deceit entails the false offer of a job, travel, or other income-generating opportunity for the purpose of acquiring a slave. It can also include false marriage offers. When people are desperate due to a lack of economic opportunity, displacement due to war or other civil strife, or bias against participation in the workplace (for females and minorities), the allure of a steady, high-paying job in a rich nation proves impossible to resist. Throughout the former Soviet bloc, job offers in newspapers, such as *Makler* in Moldova, successfully recruit thousands of sex slaves each year with promises of lucrative jobs in countries as close as Italy and as far away as the United States and Japan. People know that many such job offers are false, but as many interviewees told me, they are so desperate that they accept them hoping that "nothing bad will happen to me."

In countries where marriage is the only way for a female to secure social acceptance, basic rights, and avoid a lifetime of persecution, false marriage offers are a particularly effective way to acquire new slaves. In rural Albania, the gender prescriptions of the *Kanun I Lekë Dukaginit* (Code of Lekë Dukagjini) render life extremely difficult for unmarried women. A former sex slave named Pira told me that the night she was married, her husband sold her to slave traders who transported her to Kosovo and sold her to the owners of a sex club, where she was forced to have sex with hundreds of men before she escaped. Similarly, throughout South Asia and East Asia, the false promise of marriage to a wealthy man leads to trafficking of thousands of women each year. In Nepal, such offers have become highly sophisticated, as slave traders recruit Indian men to act as prospective grooms, provide testimonials, have phone conversations, and offer pledges of a fairy-tale life. After the young girl is sold to a brothel, many slave traders send small remittances to parents with letters in the handwriting of the slave, providing assurances that the daughter is enjoying her marriage.

Perhaps the most effective location for the use of deceit in recruiting slaves is in refugee camps. Across the globe, 32.9 million people are displaced due to genocide, civil war, environmental disaster, or other major crises.[7] Approximately 9.9 million of these individuals, 72 percent of whom are women and children, reside in refugee camps.[8] I visited refugee camps in Thailand where tens of thousands of members of the Karen hill tribe from Burma have fled military oppression, rape, incarceration, and murder. The conditions in the camps were filthy, crowded, and depressing, and the refugees were not allowed to leave or seek employment in the host country. Because the refugees were trapped, slave traders who offered job opportunities met with high success rates in acquiring new slaves. Every refugee I met knew the risks, but like the desperate citizens of Moldova, they felt they had no choice.

Sale by Family

The same conditions of poverty, desperation, and displacement lead many families to sell a child into slavery. Such sales are almost always heartbreaking decisions that parents are forced to make due to extremes of destitution few Westerners can imagine. Slave traders sniff out the most despondent individuals and make job offers for a child in exchange for a payment that might be as little as twenty or thirty dollars. In some parts of the world, this sum represents one or two months' income, in addition to the monthly remittances the job is meant to provide. In rare cases, parents sell their children out of greed. These parents become accustomed to the remittances sent back by slave owners, who use these paltry payments to entice more families to sell their children. A jittery young woman named Bridgitte, who was pressured to remain in sex slavery for years because of remittances sent to her parents, told me, "We are like slot machines to our families."

Abduction

Abduction is not as frequent a means of acquiring slaves as the mainstream media would have us believe. False job offers or sale by a family are much more common because abduction renders transportation much more challenging. Not only is the abducted victim inherently unwilling to travel, but also she will try to escape at any opportunity. Nonetheless, abduction does occur. One of the most unbelievable tales of sex trafficking I heard involved a young woman named Ines from the town of Vlora in Albania. She was abducted by three men in broad daylight and exploited in numerous brothels and sex clubs in several West European countries from 1995 to 2003.

Seduction or Romance

Many victims of forced prostitution are originally acquired through promises of love. In Central and Eastern Europe, "loverboys" are agents who approach attractive and vulnerable young girls, offering them undying love, treating them to extravagant gifts, and seducing them to migrate to a rich country where they can build a life together. False documents are provided for travel, and the loverboy usually sends the young woman in advance by train or plane and tells her to meet a friend upon arrival. That friend is almost always a slave trader or brothel owner. While more common in Europe, seduction is also used to traffic Latin American women into the United States. One of the most startling examples of seduction involved the Carreto family of Mexico, in which several men spent years courting women, marrying them, and sometimes fathering children before transporting the victims to apartments in Queens, New York, where they were forced into sexual enslavement.

Recruitment by Former Slaves

The last mode of acquisition was the most difficult for me to accept. When I first interviewed sex slaves who told me they had been recruited by former slaves, I found it hard to believe. However, as I learned more about the complex psychology of sexual enslavement, I began to understand. Sex slaves employ numerous adaptive mechanisms to survive their ordeals, including drug and alcohol abuse and the morose acceptance that the life of a slave is the best life they deserve. Throughout my travels, I met several slaves who had spent years in sexual enslavement and ultimately became allies of the slave owners. Silpa, a former Kamathipura slave turned *gharwali*, assisted me with client interviews as well as the only interview I conducted with a brothel owner. I also met former slaves who returned to their home villages to recruit new slaves. These women were dressed in the finest clothes, given a great deal of money, and promised commissions for each new slave they recruited. After extolling to their prospective targets the benefits of working as an entertainer in Mumbai or Bangkok, they often returned with several new slaves.

One final means of acquisition is unique to a single ethnicity in a single country: the Edo of Nigeria. Women from this ethnic group are recruited through elaborate juju rituals that bind the individual's spirit to an obligation to repay exorbitant debts after transport to the destination country. Failure to meet these debts results in deep spiritual affliction as well as harm to loved ones. I describe this means of acquisition in more detail in chapter 3.

Movement

Sex slaves are moved from countries of origin through transit countries into destination countries. In the case of internal trafficking, the same country acts as origin, transit, and destination. This movement is achieved by almost any conveyance imaginable. I met victims who were transported by car, bus, train, plane, speedboat, ferry, and raft. Some spent days marching by foot over mountainous border regions. Some are moved from a village to a nearby urban center, or across distances as far as Thailand to the United States, or from Peru to Japan. Bribes are paid to border guards and false passports are used to transport individuals almost anywhere in the world. When victims are abducted, or if they learn that the job offer is false, they are often drugged or beaten into silence for the duration of a journey. One former sex slave named Sushila was given ice cream laced with opiates during her three-day bus journey from Nepal to Mumbai. She slept for the entire journey, waking up the morning she was sold as a slave.

The macro-movement of sex slaves involves transit from poor areas and countries to richer areas and countries. Trafficking routes in South Asia primarily start in rural Nepal, Bangladesh, or India and end in Indian urban centers such as Mumbai, New Delhi, Chennai, or Kolkata. From India, some victims are re-trafficked to the Middle East and West Europe. Trafficking routes in East Asia primarily involve movement from the poorer Mekong Subregion nations of Burma, Cambodia, Laos, and Vietnam into Thailand, as well as movement of Thai and other East Asian slaves to Malaysia, China, Japan, Australia, Western Europe, the Middle East, and the United States. Victims from Africa are transported into Western Europe, the Middle East, East Asia, and the United States. Similar destinations also receive slaves from Latin America and the Caribbean.

Of all the regions I explored, none was more complex than Europe. The flow of victims typically involved movement from poorer nations (Central and Eastern Europe) into richer nations (Western Europe, as well as Turkey and the Middle East), but the proximity of poor Europe to rich Europe and the ease of travel to almost any country in the European Union made the movement of sex slaves throughout Europe a high-frequency operation almost impossible to thwart. Numerous victims I met were transported from Eastern Europe and forced into sex slavery for months at a time in several West European countries. Others were transported from Eastern Europe to the Middle East, then back to Western Europe. Attempts to contravene the movement of victims along one route resulted in shifts to other routes or the increased use of false documents to render victims invisible to border control or law enforcement. As more countries joined the European Union, the black market in false identification cards and passports exploded across Central and Eastern Europe, allowing sophisticated organized crime groups to move human slaves with ease.

One of the most recent trends I observed during my research was a two-step process of movement from a rural area into an urban center in the same country, followed by the international transportation of a select number of slaves for exploitation internationally. The purpose of this two-step process was to break slaves more completely before transporting them abroad. The more broken a slave's spirit was, the more accepting she was of the life of a slave. This meant that the slave was less likely to escape, and traffickers could charge higher prices at sale to brothel owners. Further, sophisticated market assessments could be made regarding which ethnicity was demanded in certain brothels or certain countries. A Russian organized crime group might acquire slaves from rural Russia, exploit those slaves in Moscow, then receive orders from brothel owners across Europe for more Russian slaves. The Russian crime group could then select the slaves most likely to service the slave owners' needs most effectively—whether for commercial sex, manufacturing, forced begging—and transport them accordingly. The evolution of this two-step process in the movement and exploitation of slaves demonstrates the alarming efficiency and sophistication of the business of modern slavery.

Exploitation

Exploitation of sex slaves primarily indicates the violent coercion of unpaid sex services, though in essence, exploitation begins the moment the slave is acquired. Slaves are raped, tortured, starved, humiliated, and drugged during transportation, both for the pleasure of traffickers and also to break the slaves to make them more submissive upon sale. As a young woman named Tatyana, who accepted a job offer through *Makler,* told me, "When I left home with the agents, they raped me and they did not feed me for days. They forced me to urinate in my clothes." Another sex trafficking victim was taken to a hotel by her alleged job agent and raped by six German men for several days in a row. Another was dumped in the trunk of a car for a four-day journey from Poland to Italy, beaten daily, and given nothing to eat.

Many trafficking victims are never actually sold because they are acquired, transported, and exploited by a single crime network. Albanian mafias acquire women throughout Eastern Europe, transport them to Western Europe, and force them into sex slavery in clubs or brothels operated by the same crime group. Other victims, such as Tatyana, are acquired and sold several times en route to a final point of exploitation. Such sales take place at established buyers' markets, where victims are forced to strip naked to be inspected by potential buyers for deformities, venereal diseases, and overall attractiveness. Agents representing numerous establishments and crime groups will purchase slaves in a similar fashion to slave auctions in the antebellum American South. With individual agents or small trafficking operations that acquire slaves, the slaves are transported to red-light districts and sold to brothel owners with whom the agents have established contacts.

Breaking the spirits of slaves begins during transportation and continues once the slave is sold. More torture, rape, and humiliation await slaves as their owners do everything possible to ensure they will service clients submissively and never try to escape. In Falkland Road in Mumbai, a former sex slave turned working prostitute named Mallaika told me that sex slaves were tortured and murdered every day. She told me that minors were mercilessly abused when they first arrived and that they were given opium so they would have sex with clients. If they misbehaved, arms were broken. If they tried to escape, they might have their throats cut in front of other slaves, who were subsequently required to clean up the slaughter as a visceral lesson in the fate that awaited them should they try to escape.

Sex slaves are exploited in six primary types of venue, and I tracked down some or all in almost every country I visited: brothels, clubs, massage parlors, apartments, hotels, and streets. In red-light districts, brothels are the most common venues. Some are immense, such as the bungalow brothels in Kamathipura and Falkland Road, which can posses up to two or three hundred prostitutes, up to one half of whom might be minors and slaves. Brothels in Thailand typically hold between twenty and fifty slaves, each awaiting selection behind a pane of glass in a room called an "aquarium." Other brothels are smaller, such as the clandestine villa brothels in Italy. I visited a villa brothel halfway between Turin and Milan that housed no more than twenty sex slaves from several European countries. In addition to the slaves, it had a plush entry room and fully stocked bar.

Club brothels are found primarily in Europe and East Asia. They are dance clubs in which sex slaves are provided for purchase. Sex services are usually transacted in back rooms or a basement. The slaves live in the club brothels and are never allowed to leave. Several slaves I met were first exploited in club brothels before being moved to hotels or street prostitution, once they accepted life as a prostitute. Most of the clubs looked exactly the same as any normal club, with bouncers at the front door and music, dancing, alcohol, and drugs inside. Other clubs were unflinching in their debauchery, such as a sex club I visited in Chisinau, Moldova that was filled with men from several countries engaging in depravities with drugged young girls. Many were barely pubescent.

Throughout my journeys, massage parlors led to some of the most awkward exchanges I had. From Kathmandu to Mestre to Chiang Mai to Los Angeles, massage parlors were used as front organizations for prostitution, and because prostitution was illegal in each of these cities (closed-door prostitution in the case of Mestre), I was never actually told I could buy sex, but only that massages were not available. I purposefully acted as obtuse as possible when entering massage parlors and insisted that I wanted a massage, only to receive blank stares, irritated responses, or excuses that there was no hot water so massages could not be provided. When I eventually hinted that I would pay for another type of service, I was led to a back room or up a flight of stairs, where a handful of young women were offered for my selection.

Most common in Europe and the United States, apartment brothels are essentially miniature brothels operated by a small organization or group of people with no more than six to eight slaves. I typically found the apartment brothels through newspaper advertisements in the relationship sections of local newspapers. In Mestre, an advertisement in the Find a Friend section of the newspaper resulted in directions to a particular street corner, where I was instructed to make a second call for specific directions to the apartment. While I was unable to find an apartment brothel in the United States, I received victim testimonials from sex slaves who had been exploited in apartments. A handful of U.S. federal cases against human traffickers—including the Carreto case—have also revealed that apartments are often used as venues of exploitation. The Carretos even advertised in their neighborhood with postcards and streetpole pin-ups to secure clientele.

Hotels are less frequently used as venues to exploit sex slaves because the environments are not secure. Prostitutes who work for pimps or crime networks in hotels are usually former slaves who have accepted a life of prostitution and seek to make as much money as possible. Pimps typically split up to half the payment for sex with hotel prostitutes. Hotel prostitution was more prevalent in Thailand than in any other country I visited. At every hotel I stayed in, I was immediately solicited by agents just outside the front door, offering "young" and "fresh" girls who could be delivered to my room for as little as ten dollars. In Moldova, Turkish businessmen invested heavily in creating a burgeoning sex-tourist industry that provided prostitutes in hotels, clubs, bars, and restaurants for any male visitor. Not five minutes after I checked into my hotel near the southern end of Chisinau, I received a knock on the door from a young woman who told me that when a group of men or a single man checked in, the hotel rang her pimp, who sent a girl to the room to solicit sex.

Similar to hotels, street prostitution offers ample contact with the outside world and ample opportunity to escape. Pimps choose only those women they can trust to service clients without hassle. The prostitutes are given quotas each night for the number of men they must service. If they meet their quotas, they receive extra food or gifts. If they do not, they are starved and tortured. Escape from the streets is unlikely because the slaves are far from home in a country the language of which they do not know. In addition, they do not have money or passports, so they risk incarceration or deportation. Going to the police is rarely an option because in almost every country I visited, the police were purchasers of sex slaves. Corrupt police accept bribes to allow brothels and clubs to function, turn the other way when sex slaves work the streets, or warn brothel owners if an investigation is being planned. They also take sexual favors from slaves as part of the bargain. In Italy, where street prostitution is legal, pimps bribe the police to ignore the exploitation of minors. On the Salaria in Rome, I saw dozens of teenage girls huddled every few blocks, half-naked and shivering in the winter air. The pace of purchase was rapid, almost like a drive-in window at a fast-food restaurant. Julia, a teenager from Romania, was still working the streets in bra and panties even though she was pregnant.

The Fate of Sex Slaves

The contemporary sex trafficking industry involves the systematic rape, torture, enslavement, and murder of millions of women and children, whether directly through homicide or indirectly through sexually transmitted diseases and drugs. Because the laws in most countries against rape, torture, and homicide are more punishing and better enforced than those against sex trafficking—which can be construed as the aggregation of rape, torture, and homicide—the fate of the world's sex slaves remains terribly grim. First and foremost, escape is rarely an option for a sex slave. The slaves I met in victim shelters were the bare few who had managed to escape, and even then their lives offered little hope. Most were infected with HIV, suffered acute drug and alcohol addictions, had been shunned by families, and had little prospects for employment or any form of self-sufficiency upon departure from the shelters, which invariably had to limit their duration of residence due to resource shortages. Slaves rarely attempt escape because brothel owners terrorize them regarding the consequences and also threaten violence against family members back home. Few studies have been conducted on the life expectancies of sex slaves, but Manju Vyas, a local expert on Mumbai's red-light districts, informed me that most victims rarely survived past their mid-thirties.

Specific cultural factors also ensnare victims into extended sex slavery. Parents often send young Thai women to work in the entertainment industry to earn money to provide for them into old age. A strict sense of obligation to parents constituent to Thai culture, *bhun kun*, inculcates the youngest daughter with a duty to provide material support to aging parents. One of the most heartbreaking encounters I experienced with a sex slave was in a brothel in Chiang Mai, where a brave young Thai girl named Panadda told me that even though she hated the men who came to the brothel and harmed her, she was proud to fulfill her duty to her parents in the form of tiny payments that the brothel owner sent to her father after her trafficking debts were repaid.

Similar sociocultural aspects of the Edo culture in Nigeria, related to juju rituals, ensnare sex slaves for years. On pain of extreme physical and spiritual affliction, Edo women swear to repay debts and never to discuss their situation with anyone. Because the spiritual hold is so strong, the debt obligations are exorbitant—sometimes up to fifty thousand euros, or five to ten times the debt obligations imposed on slaves from other countries. Nigerian sex slaves suffer extreme abuse, and only the tiniest fraction muster the courage to escape. The few I met in Turin refused to speak of their ordeals and shelter personnel told me that they also refused to speak to attorneys seeking to press charges against the exploiters. Because Italy only allows victims to remain in shelters if they sign a contract stipulating cooperation with the authorities, such women eventually found themselves in trials in which they were forced to testify. Some suffered epileptic fits or entered catatonic trances rather than break their juju vows.

The fates of an increasing number of sex slaves involve re-trafficking, two, three, or more times. Because most victims who escape are forced to return to the same conditions of poverty, domestic violence, social bias, or lack of economic opportunity that precipitated their initial trafficking, many return to the slave traders who originally deceived them in search of a better deal the second time around. Alternatively, many repatriated victims are recruited, deceived, seduced, or abducted into a second or third round of slavery, each time by a different slave trader. At the same shelter in Albania in which I met Ines, I met another victim named Nadia who had been re-trafficked five times. A simple lack of shelter and a wage-paying job had consigned her to repeated counts of slavery for the majority of her adult life.

The Business of Sex Slavery

The acquisition, movement, and exploitation of sex slaves form an industry that generates billions of dollars in profits each year, at a profit margin greater than almost any industry in the world, illicit or otherwise. My analysis of the business of sex slavery is broken into three parts: the overall size and growth of the industry by number of slaves, the revenues and profits generated by the sale of trafficked slaves to their exploiters, and the revenues and profits generated by the exploitation of sex slaves. Examples of the modes, means, and economics of the movement and exploitation of sex slaves in each region explored in this book appear in appendix B.

By my calculation,[9] the total annual number of individuals trafficked for commercial sexual exploitation is between five hundred thousand and six hundred thousand, out of a total number of annual human trafficking victims of 1.5 to 1.8 million. These numbers include individuals trafficked within their home countries as well as across international borders. In addition to sexual exploitation, humans are trafficked for domestic servitude, forced agricultural work, begging, manufacturing, construction, and organ harvesting. There is a jumbled history of estimates of human trafficking going back to 1998,[10] but the number most often quoted by governments and nongovernmental organizations (NGOs) is that of the U.S. State Department: six hundred thousand to eight hundred thousand individuals trafficked each year across international borders and "millions" trafficked internally.[11] A separate number for sex trafficking is not provided. The numbers in this book indicate that one woman or child is trafficked for the purpose of sexual exploitation every sixty seconds, dispersed across the globe as shown in table 1.1.

Table 1.1 offers a snapshot of the size and growth of the current sex trafficking industry: 1.2 million trafficked sex slaves at the end of 2006, with five hundred thousand to six hundred thousand new victims during 2007, representing an annual gain of approximately forty-three thousand new slaves when netted against the slaves who escape, are freed, or perished during 2007. Asian countries have the highest total number of sex slaves, but on a per capita basis, Europe has the highest levels of sex slavery in the world. Overall, the sex trafficking industry is growing at a modest annual rate, with Eastern Europe and the Middle East showing the fastest growth and only North America relatively flat. This current growth rate is much lower than the rate fifteen years earlier, when the industry exploded concurrently with the rise of economic globalization. At present, the sex trafficking industry is akin to a mature, multinational corporation that has achieved steady-state growth and produces immense cash flows. Assuming a 3.5 percent growth rate for the next five years, there would be 1.48 million sex slaves at the end of 2012.

From the number of sex slaves, one derives a measure of the profits generated by their exploitation. Two numbers have been suggested for the annual profits generated by the entire human trafficking industry: $9.5 billion by the U.S. State Department and $31.7 billion by the International Labour Organization (ILO).[12] The ILO number is generally

TABLE 1.1

Sex Trafficking: Size and Growth Rate, 2006–2007

	Estimated Trafficked Sex Slaves, End of 2006	Estimated Sex Trafficking Victims,[1] 2007	Estimated Sex Slaves Escaped, Freed, or Deceased, 2007	Implied Trafficked Sex Slaves, End of Year 2007 (mean)	Percent Growth (mean)
South Asia	335,000	120,000–150,000	110,000–135,000	347,500	*3.7*
East Asia and Pacific	315,000	125,000–145,000	113,000–135,000	326,000	*3.5*
Western Europe	180,000	82,500–96,000	78,000–88,000	186,250	*3.5*
Central and Eastern Europe	125,000	62,500–74,000	60,000–66,500	130,000	*4.0*
Latin America	90,000	40,000–50,000	40,000–44,000	93,000	*3.3*
Middle East	80,000	40,000–50,000	40,000–43,500	83,250	*4.1*
Africa	65,000	25,000–30,000	24,000–27,000	67,000	*3.1*
North America	10,000	5,000	4,700–5,200	10,050	*0.5*
Total	**1,200,000**	**500,000–600,000**	**470,000–544,000**	**1,243,050**	***3.6***

[1] Includes internal slave trading.

regarded as more reliable than the U.S. State Department's figure, which never specified whether it represents the sale of human trafficking victims, their exploitation, or both. Adding to the confusion, sometimes the numbers are quoted as revenues and other times as profits. Transparency into the underlying metrics used to derive these figures has been limited, and neither group has yet provided specific profit quantifications of the sex trafficking portion of the human trafficking industry.

Tables 1.2 and 1.3 offer my best assessment of the current revenues and profits generated by the sex trafficking industry. In all cases, I have skewed toward smaller unit assumptions to present conservative numbers.

In the tables, I have disaggregated the regional profits generated by slave trading and slavery, the two components of the sex trafficking chain.[13] This disaggregation offers important revelations. First, the sale of trafficked sex slaves to brothel owners and pimps generated revenues of $1.0 billion in 2007, or a global average sale price of $1,895 per slave. After costs, these sales generated approximately $600 million in profits. Second, the commercial exploitation of trafficked sex slaves generated $51.3 billion in revenues in 2007, the result of millions of men purchasing sex from slaves every day. After costs, the slaves' exploiters cleared $35.7 billion in profits, or a global average of $29,210 per slave. The total revenue generated by the exploitation of all victims of human trafficking in 2007 was $58.6 billion, with profits of $39.7 billion. The total revenue generated by all forms of contemporary slavery in 2007 was a staggering $152.3 billion, with profits of $91.2 billion (see table A.2 for detail). Figure 1.2 summarizes these numbers.

The profit numbers in this graph indicate that trafficked sex slaves are by far the most lucrative slaves in the world. Only 4.2 percent of the world's slaves are trafficked sex slaves, but they generate 39.1 percent of slaveholders' profits. To benchmark the astounding profits generated by the exploiters of sex slaves, one need look no further than the fact that the global weighted average net profit margin of almost 70 percent makes it one of the most profitable enterprises in the world. By comparison, Google's net profit margin in 2006 was 29.0 percent, and it is one of the most profitable companies in the United States. The same figure for Microsoft was 28.5 percent; for Intel, 14.3 percent. General Electric posted a 12.8 percent profit margin; AT&T, 11.7 percent; and Exxon Mobil, 10.8 percent.

It may seem like a stretch to make direct comparisons between multinational corporations and ramshackle brothels, but the superficial point

TABLE 1.2

Sex Trafficking: Slave-Trading Revenues and Profits, 2007[1]

	Weighted Average Purchase Price per Slave (U.S. dollars)[2]	Revenues from Slave Trading (millions of U.S. dollars)	Estimated Slave-Trading Profit Margin (percent)	Profits from Slave Trading (millions of U.S. dollars)
South Asia	660	89	*57.6*	51
East Asia and Pacific	750	101	*58.7*	59
Western Europe	4,800	428	*56.7*	243
Central and Eastern Europe	2,600	177	*60.8*	108
Latin America	1,500	68	*57.9*	39
Middle East	3,000	135	*57.0*	77
Africa	630	17	*58.1*	10
North America	5,250	26	*45.0*	12
	Weighted Average Price			
Total	**1,895**	**1,042**		**599**

[1] Based on mean projections of new sex trafficking victims from table 1.1.

[2] The weighted average purchase price includes values derived in 2006 and held constant in 2007, calculated as follows: South Asia is given a ratio of one-fifth international origin and four-fifths internal origin; East Asia and Pacific, a ratio of two-thirds international origin and one-third internal origin; Western Europe, all international origin; Central and Eastern Europe, a ratio of two-thirds international origin and one-third internal origin; Latin America and Africa, a ratio of one-third international origin and two-thirds internal origin; Middle East and North America, all international origin. The final sale price of a slave is used rather than adding multiple sales during movement.

TABLE 1.3

Sex Trafficking: Slavery Revenues and Profits, 2007

	Weighted Average Retail Price per Sex Act (U.S. dollars)[1]	Average Annual Revenues per Trafficked Sex Slave (U.S. dollars)	Revenues from Trafficked Sex Slaves (millions of U.S. dollars)[2]	Weighted Average Profit Margin per Trafficked Sex Slave (percent)	Average Annual Profits per Trafficked Sex Slave (U.S. dollars)	Profits from Trafficked Sex Slaves (millions of U.S. dollars)
South Asia	4.15	16,705	5,701	*71.5*	11,942	4,075
East Asia and Pacific	4.40	18,749	6,009	*70.5*	13,222	4,238
Western Europe	33.00	114,129	20,900	*68.5*	78,196	14,320
Central and Eastern Europe	16.00	55,905	7,128	*70.0*	39,110	4,987
Latin America	9.00	35,640	3,261	*70.5*	25,126	2,299
Middle East	20.00	78,120	6,377	*69.5*	54,293	4,432
Africa	4.00	15,984	1,055	*71.0*	11,349	749
North America	27.50	90,648	909	*64.0*	57,975	581
		Weighted Average Revenue			*Weighted Average Profit*	
Total		**42,030**	**51,339**		**29,210**	**35,680**

[1] The weighted average price of a sex act includes values derived in 2006 and held constant in 2007, calculated from the six primary venues of sex slavery found in each region.

[2] Based on the average of starting and ending number of sex slaves in each region during 2007.

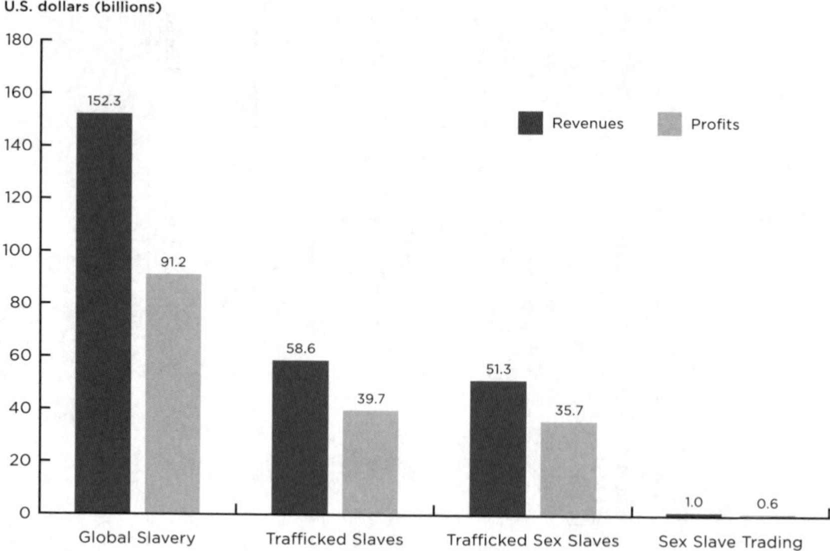

FIGURE 1.2 Slavery and Trafficking Revenues and Profits, 2007

should be clear: Slave labor makes profits soar. As a result, sex trafficking has captivated both small-time criminals and sophisticated organized crime groups across the globe. The level of complexity and coordination among these crime groups is astounding. In Italy, international mafias from Nigeria, Moldova, Romania, and Albania are responsible for the majority of trafficking victims transported to and from the country. These groups collaborate seamlessly with local Italian mafias, which have a well-established system of leasing certain territories for exploitation of victims in exchange for a share of the revenues that the exploitation generates. In South Asia and East Asia, sex trafficking is conducted more by small groups and individual agents that operate as freelance criminals. Nonetheless, mafias do traffic individuals from Mekong Subregion countries into Thailand, or from Nepal, Bangladesh, and Pakistan into the red-light districts of major Indian cities. Some of the profits of these sales are invested or laundered into legitimate industries, such as Bollywood films, as was claimed by a man I interviewed named MB, who owns several brothels in Mumbai.

Other organized crime groups, such as the Red Mafia and the Aleski Network, are well known to traffic drugs, women, and weapons across Europe, generating tens of millions of dollars in annual profits. In Japan, the Yamaguchi-Gumi, Inagawakia, and Sumiyoshikai organized crime groups traffic women, drugs, and weapons from countries as close as China and as far as Peru. The triple play of trafficking drugs, humans, and weapons in the same shipment has become increasingly popular, especially in war-torn regions such as Africa, Afghanistan, and the former Yugoslavia, into which organized crime groups trafficked sex slaves during the 1990s to meet the demand for sex services by thousands of peacekeeping troops and foreign workers. It has been well documented that U.S. and other foreign military personnel purchased trafficked women in brothels in the former Yugoslavia during this time; some bought and sold sex slaves like regular slave traders. In the current U.S. occupation of Iraq, thousands of South Asians and Middle Easterners have been allegedly trafficked for forced labor on U.S. military bases, their passports confiscated and wages unpaid.[14]

The Economics of Sex Slavery

Business analysis can tell us how an industry makes money and how much money it makes. Economic analysis can tell us how an industry functions through the factors of supply and demand. Certain market forces create a demand for a product; other market forces create a supply to meet that demand. An industry cannot exist without both forces. Understanding the market forces that gave rise to the contemporary sex trafficking industry and the implications that these forces have for the industry's trajectory will reveal the optimal interventions required to erode or abolish sex trafficking. We begin with the supply side of the dynamic.

Supply Side: Why the Supply of So Many Sex Slaves?

Several factors have contributed to the supply of potential slave labor throughout history, including poverty, bias against gender or ethnicity, lawlessness, military conflict, social instability, and economic breakdown. Each factor was important to the accretion of the supply of contemporary sex slaves. Each factor was also directly exacerbated by the sweeping phenomenon of economic globalization—that is, those aspects of globalization related to the increased economic integration of the world through the unfettered profusion of American-style capitalism.

When the Berlin Wall fell in November 1989, it released pent-up pressure across the Soviet bloc. Revolutions were spawned as rapidly as people could mobilize them, demanding democratic reforms. In the years that followed, a transition from state-run Soviet republics to Western-style democracies and capitalist systems swept the region, inspiring similar revolutions in countries as far away as Nepal. Capitalism and democracy are almost always[15] more desirable than oppressive, state-controlled regimes, but during this fragile transition period, many postcommunist countries became sources of trafficked sex slaves.

Joseph Stiglitz, a Nobel Prize–winning economist, defines globalization as

> the closer integration of the countries and peoples of the world which has been brought about by the enormous reduction costs of transportation and communication, and the breaking down of artificial barriers to the flows of goods, services, capital, knowledge, and (to a lesser extent) people across borders.[16]

While the global economic integration that began in the early 1990s[17] led to several benefits, such as expanding international trade, foreign investment, and acceleration of the transfer of knowledge among countries, globalization's corresponding ills resulted in a rapid increase in global slavery by deepening rural poverty, widening the chasm between rich and poor, promoting social instability, and eroding real human freedoms, all of which compromised the very democratic transitions that enabled the transformation in the first place. As the process of economic globalization unfolded, it essentially manifested a singular dynamic: the net transfer of wealth, raw materials, commodities, and other assets from newly opened, developing nations into richer, developed ones. The resulting social strife and economic collapse, coupled with the same advances that promoted the freer exchange of goods, services, capital, knowledge, and people, catalyzed the ascent of human trafficking and contemporary slavery.

Globalization helped make present-day slaves easy to procure, easy to transport, and easy to exploit in an increasing number of industries. Maintaining slaves requires minimal effort, especially sex slaves, who can be sold for sex services literally thousands of times before being replaced. Today's slaves thus represent a quantum leap in profitability over slaves in the Old World.[18] A modern-day brothel owner can purchase a slave for between $200 and $1,000 in Asia, or $2,000 and $8,000 in Western Europe, and generate returns of well over 1,000 percent a year.

Acquisition costs are low because there are hundreds of millions of poor, disenfranchised, and vulnerable individuals who are desperate to find a better life. The cost of transportation is also at historic lows.[19] Even if a victim is trafficked from one side of the globe to the other, plane tickets are an inconsequential expense compared to the profits that sex slaves generate.

While sex trafficking has thrived everywhere across the world, three primary origin regions emerged in the 1990s: South Asia, Central and Eastern Europe, and East Asia. Historic factors in each of these geographic regions helped promote sex slavery, namely: extreme poverty, severe gender bias, and acute minority disenfranchisement. Globalization-related crises exacerbated these factors, leaving tens of millions of individuals vulnerable to exploitation, particularly women and children. This vulnerability, coupled with pervasive male demand to purchase sex, provided the perfect environment for the proliferation of sex trafficking. The intricacies of how economic globalization unfolded during the 1990s have been well documented, but the link between that process and the ascent of sex trafficking has not.

ECONOMIC GLOBALIZATION In the depths of the Great Depression, John Maynard Keynes wrote: "The decadent international but individualistic capitalism in the hands of which we found ourselves after the war is not a success. It is not intelligent. It is not beautiful. It is not just. It is not virtuous. And it doesn't deliver the goods."[20] During the 1990s, the aggressive spread of extreme market-economy principles and corporate-centered American-style capitalism was equally unintelligent, un-virtuous, and unjust. Economic globalization unleashed catastrophic increases in poverty levels and civil strife, most directly in Central and Eastern Europe and East Asia. In South Asia, the negative effects were less immediate, but equally pernicious in catalyzing the ascent of contemporary human trafficking. One of the primary institutions that facilitated economic globalization was the International Monetary Fund (IMF),[21] the policies and actions of which, during the 1990s, exacerbated the economic collapses of most of the former Soviet republics, as well as the so-called tiger economies of East Asia. The combined crises led to the worst global economic recession since the Great Depression.

Shortly after the fall of the Berlin Wall, the IMF offered a rigid formula of market-economy measures to former Soviet republics to assist their transition to Western-style market economies. This formula involved the rapid adoption of a package of monetary and fiscal policies, regardless of country or context. First, the IMF mandated fiscal austerity measures, such as cutting government expenditures on health care, education, unemployment benefits, and other social services. The logic was to promote efficiency, though the net result was to worsen the destitution of those who depended on such government programs. Second, the IMF advocated that the prices of products, services, and commodities should be dictated by market forces rather than a central authority, as had occurred under socialism. The logic was to promote efficiency and competition, though the net result was massive inflation that eroded the value of local currencies. Third, the IMF pushed for rapid market liberalization, opening local markets to foreign commercial and financial interests. The logic was to promote the free flow of capital and economic growth, though the net result was wild flows of hot money that devastated local markets. Fourth, the IMF insisted on rapid privatization, selling government-run companies to the private sector. The logic was, again, to increase efficiency and competition, though the net result was the transfer of billions of dollars in wealth and assets to Western economic interests and a handful of corrupt politicians and businessmen. Finally, the IMF required massive interest rate increases. The logic was to attract foreign money seeking strong returns, which would support local currencies and lower inflation, though the net result was pervasive default on loans, bank foreclosures, and deepening economic recession.

The IMF's prescription of shock therapy to former Soviet republics in the early 1990s yielded cataclysmic results. Most Soviet republics suffered precipitous economic collapse, which, coupled with IMF-mandated cutbacks in social protections, led to unprecedented levels of destitution and poverty. In the former Soviet Union, total gross domestic product from 1990 to 1998 fell by 44 percent[22] while during the same period it increased by 11 percent and 18 percent in the United Kingdom and United States, respectively.[23] In 1998, matters for the former Soviet Union worsened when the price of oil crashed to less than $10 per barrel, thanks in part to IMF-imposed conditions on East Asia. Because oil was Russia's top export commodity, the Russian economy collapsed, deepening recessions throughout East Asia and Latin America. Capital markets across the globe careened to multiyear lows and hundreds of millions of people fell below national poverty lines, resulting in severe levels of economic degradation, social upheaval, and historic levels of global unemployment. Not even the United States was spared, as the Dow Jones industrial average suffered its top three steepest one-day point declines in the ten months from October 1997 to August 1998.

Because Russia was the largest trading partner for most of its former republics, the collapse of the Russian economy in 1998 exacerbated the already corroding economies of the entire former Soviet bloc. By 1998, the Ukrainian economy was only 41 percent its size at the time the Berlin Wall fell. During that time, the country's population shrank by 1.6 million,[24] with over five hundred thousand individuals being trafficked abroad. Moldova suffered the steepest decline, as its economy shrank to 35 percent its size in 1990.[25] Not surprisingly, Moldova also suffered the worst population decrease of any former Soviet Republic—seven hundred and twenty thousand individuals, or 16.5 percent the population[26]—with more than one-half these individuals trafficked internationally. As economies cratered, poverty levels soared. In 1990, twenty-three million East Europeans lived on less than $2 per day;[27] by 2001 that number had grown to ninety-three million, or one out of four people in the region.[28] In 2001, two hundred and fifty million of the four hundred million people in Central and Eastern Europe lived in shrinking economies. Deepening poverty and crumbling economies meant that inflation rates soared, topping 3,000 percent per year in many former Soviet republics. If a carton of milk cost $3 at the beginning of the year, it cost $90 at the end of the year; if a car cost $20,000 at the beginning of the year, it cost $600,000 at the end of the year. Put another way, if an individual had $30,000 in personal savings at the beginning of the year, that same amount was worth only $1,000 at the end of the year. After a few years of such inflation, personal savings were obliterated, spurring mass migration to the more stable countries and currencies in Western Europe. Shrewd traffickers preyed on this desperation, duping millions into modern-day slavery. Because gender and minority disenfranchisement meant that women, children, and minorities were the hardest hit during times of socioeconomic crisis, these groups were the most heavily trafficked. To make matters worse, governments in Central and Eastern Europe provided almost no social assistance due to massive increases in debt obligations to Western creditors—especially the IMF—as a result of loans provided to try to stabilize their economies.[29] In 1990, Moldova had no external debt. By the end of 2006, Moldova's debt had escalated to $2.1 billion, almost the same size as the entire Moldovan economy. Much of this debt took the form of structural adjustment loans from the IMF, which mandated the sharp cutbacks in government spending discussed above. By the end of the decade, the poorest people in the former Soviet bloc had suffered tremendously at the IMF's hands. Perhaps nothing better captures this than the fact that life expectancies in the region declined from 1990 to 2000. The only other region in the world in which life expectancies declined during the same time period was sub-Saharan Africa, primarily as a result of the HIV pandemic.

In East Asia, similar IMF policies severely aggravated poverty levels and spurred the mass migration of millions of poor East Asians to their own Western Europe—Thailand, Malaysia, and Indonesia—in search of subsistence income. Before the arrival of economic globalization, the tiger economies of East Asia had grown steadily for thirty years without suffering a major recession. In the early 1990s, developing Asian countries, such as Thailand, sought capital from Western investors for continued growth and much-needed infrastructure development, but access to this capital required certification from the IMF that its specific brand of market-economy principles had been adopted. Similar to the former Soviet republics, accepting these shock-therapy principles resulted in disaster.[30]

Thanks to the rapidly opened capital markets mandated by the IMF, in the early 1990s, speculative investors and U.S. hedge funds poured hot money into East Asia's currency, capital, and real-estate markets, creating several market bubbles. When the bubble in the Thai real-estate market burst, those same investors feared currency devaluation and pulled out their money as fast as they could by selling the baht in exchange for the U.S. dollar. The Thai government could not cope with the massive levels of currency movement and used up all of its dollar reserves trying to keep its currency stable. When the government ran out of resources, the Thai baht crashed 25 percent in one night on July 2, 1997. Devaluation speculation and currency crashes spread rapidly to Malaysia, South Korea, Indonesia, and the Philippines. Economies that had not seen recessions in a generation were plunged into chaos, prompting Mahathir bin Mohammad, prime minister of Malaysia, to blast,

> We are told . . . we must open up, that trade and commerce must be totally free. Free for whom? For rogue speculators. . . . We had tried to comply with the wishes of the rich and mighty . . . but when the big funds use their massive weight in order to move the shares up and down at will and make huge profits by their manipulations then it is too much to expect us to welcome them, especially when

> their profits result in massive losses for ourselves . . . the currency traders have become rich, very very rich through making other people poor.[31]

Having initially precipitated the disaster with its policies, the IMF responded with a whopping $95 billion bailout and a set of privatization and interest-rate policies that turned a currency crisis into the worst global economic recession in living memory. High interest rates meant that businesses could not make loan payments or access new capital to maintain production, which led to massive job cuts. Unemployment throughout the region soared, tripling in Thailand from 1997 to 1998. Shortly after the IMF-imposed increase in interest rates—up to fifty times greater than they had been—one-half of bank loans in Thailand went into default. Some of the largest banks in East Asia, Japan, and Hong Kong collapsed, deepening recession throughout the region. As capital continued to flee East Asian countries, Western banks used the bailout money to sell their remaining currency positions and avoid exposure to further economic downturn.[32] Stock prices collapsed by as much as 90 percent throughout East Asia as the robust economies of Malaysia, Thailand, and Indonesia cratered 7 percent, 10 percent, and 13 percent, respectively, in just a few months,[33] leading to the 1998 crash in oil prices that worsened recessions throughout the Soviet bloc and the developing world. The IMF also imposed deep cuts on social welfare programs throughout East Asia. The prices of basic food and staples shot up by 50 to 80 percent, resulting in mass riots and starvation. In the Mekong Subregion, the sudden increase in rural poverty spurred mass migration from the hills of rural Thailand, Burma, Laos, and Cambodia into urban centers such as Chiang Mai and Bangkok, where Thailand's relatively more stable economy[34] allowed the country to weather the globalization storm more effectively. These desperate migrants were easily exploited in sweatshops, construction projects, manufacturing jobs, and brothels.

In South Asia, the negative effects of economic globalization were less immediate, but they equally fueled the ascent of sex trafficking. While the globalization-aligned market reforms that commenced in 1991 under then–finance minister Manmohan Singh led to stellar economic growth in India, that growth scarcely trickled down to the poorest people in the country. Approximately 850 million people in India—80 percent of the population and almost three times the entire population of the United States—still subsist on less than $2 per day.[35] In neighboring Nepal, an even greater percent of the population scrapes by on fewer than $2 a day: 82.5 percent, or 22 million people. Poverty levels in Pakistan and Bangladesh are equally unconscionable. Because incomes for the middle and upper classes of India have soared while the incomes of the region's poor have remained stagnant, the real incomes of South Asia's impoverished masses have declined due to inflationary pressures on basic goods and services. Today, there are more billionaires in India than there are in the United Kingdom, but there are also fourteen times more people living in poverty in India than the entire population of the United Kingdom. This expanding chasm between rich and poor has precipitated anger, a lack of faith in government, and the bulk migration of rural masses throughout South Asian countries into Indian urban centers in search of a piece of the country's swelling economic pie. Slave traders exploit this migration by recruiting individuals into low-paid or unpaid labor. Women and children are often trafficked into the clutches of India's deadly brothels, where males have more money than before with which to buy sex from slaves.

GENDER While IMF policies unleashed deadly global intensifications of human exploitation and suffering, those policies did not necessitate that sex slavery explode in South Asia, Central and Eastern Europe, and East Asia after the fall of the Berlin Wall. The particular ascension of sex slavery in these regions resides at the intersection of the socioeconomic bedlam promoted by economic globalization and a historic, deeply rooted bias against females.

Throughout my travels, no discovery shocked me more than the extreme level of bias and socioeconomic disenfranchisement that millions of women face across the globe. These factors contributed directly to female vulnerability to slave traders when the surrounding political and economic infrastructures disintegrated. Numerous reports provide an unequivocal sense of the enormous imbalance between male and female access to education, health care, and economic opportunities, particularly in developing countries. A UN report noted that, of the 115 million children around the world who are not in school, 70 million are girls, with particularly large numbers in South Asia and East Europe.[36] Another report revealed that 600 million of the 850 million illiterate adults in the world are women and that a lack of education is a key factor in promoting poverty, higher HIV infection rates, and vulnerability to exploitation and trafficking.[37] The effect of these and other socioeconomic imbalances is that 70 percent of the 985 million people living in extreme poverty in developing nations are women.[38] As the correlation between socioeconomic disenfranchisement and vulnerability to sex trafficking is undeniably high, every one of these extremely poor women—and the children in their care—is vulnerable to slavery.

Beyond systemic bias, the most alarming discovery of my research was the prevalence of violence against women, particularly in rural areas. From Moldova to Albania to Nepal to Thailand, rural women were regularly abused by men and local laws against domestic violence—if there were any—were not enforced at all.

In India, fifteen thousand women are murdered each year over dowry disputes, even though the dowry system is illegal.[39] The use of ultrasound in rural clinics has led to an estimated five hundred thousand abortions of female fetuses in India per year since 1981.[40] Apparently it is so terrible to be a female in parts of India that upward of 12.5 million future females have been destroyed in the last twenty-five years alone.[41] From battery acid thrown in the faces of Bangladeshi girls who spurn male advances to the Pakistani Hudood Ordinance of 1979, which stipulates that it is impossible for a woman to be raped unless there are four male witnesses to the attack, life for millions of women in South Asia is a process of terrible abuse. According to the Asian Development Bank,

> Women's low status is most dramatically reflected in the fact that in all seven countries in South Asia there are fewer women than there are men. The negative sex ratio can be attributed to excess mortality of women and girls resulting from both direct and indirect discrimination in the provision of food, medical treatment, education, and above all physical and sexual violence.[42]

In Africa, six thousand women are genitally mutilated each day, upwards of two million per year.[43] In South Africa, a woman is killed by her intimate partner every six hours. Worldwide, one-half of women murdered each year are killed by their current or former intimate partner.[44] Even in the West, violence against women persists. In the United Kingdom, two women per week are murdered by their intimate partners; in Spain, one women is killed by her intimate partner every five days; in

Italy, a woman is raped every seventeen minutes; and in the United States, a woman is raped every six minutes and battered every fifteen seconds.[45]

Throughout the world, millions of women are systematically discriminated against, denied education and employment, beaten, and treated as male sexual property. In regions where these abuses are most prevalent, I found the most active origins of trafficked sex slaves. In every rural pocket I visited, women cried of the abuses they suffered. Some were accused of being witches, some were raped while still children, and some were beaten daily by drunk, unemployed husbands. Many sex slaves explained that fleeing from these abuses delivered them into the hands of sex traffickers. When I asked these women why they thought men treated them so poorly, their answers invariably presupposed the necessity of male abuse of females. They pointed to culture, religion, a lack of rights, and bias in the law-enforcement and judicial systems as the reasons they were abused with impunity. A brave woman in Sindhupalchok summarized the truth of the lives of so many rural women in the world when she said, "Men want women as slaves."

ETHNICITY AND CASTE Similarly to gender, minority ethnicities and castes are disenfranchised from economic and educational opportunities as well as health care, social safety nets, and basic rights. In each of the three primary-origin regions of sex trafficking, minorities were the most heavily trafficked populations during the socioeconomic upheaval caused by economic globalization. *Dalits* in India, Tamang in Nepal, hill tribes in Thailand and Vietnam, Karen in Burma, Roma in Albania, and Gagauzes in Moldova were the most frequently trafficked and enslaved populations from their home countries. Lower-caste individuals rarely found justice when exploited because law enforcement and judicial systems were deeply biased against them. Majority ethnicities saw the minorities as ignorant and subhuman. Exploiting them for labor was similar to exploiting animals. Enslaving them for sexual exploitation was an unabashed statement of racial superiority.[46]

Demand Side: Why the Demand for So Many Sex Slaves?

While the supply of potential slaves erupted during the 1990s concurrent with the havoc wreaked by economic globalization, the demand side of the sex-slave industry can be isolated to three market forces: male sexual demand, profit (as related to the inverse relationship with labor costs), and the elasticity of demand.[47]

MALE SEXUAL DEMAND There could be no sex-slave industry without male demand for commercial sex. However, only a small segment of males are responsible for this demand. Some men purchase sex once in their lives; others purchase it once a week. By my calculation, only 0.5 percent of males over the age of eighteen are required to purchase commercial sex on any given day to maximize the capacity of today's 1.2 million trafficked sex slaves. Depending on assumptions related to frequency of purchase per consumer, anywhere from 6 percent to 9 percent of males in the world over the age of eighteen actually purchase sex from slaves at some point each year. While the preponderance of this book relates directly to the consequences of male depravity, greed, and sexual violence, I also believe that the preponderance of males do not condone these vulgarities. Nevertheless, male sexual demand has promoted the commercial sex industry for centuries and it will probably continue to do so for centuries to come. Whether for entertainment, violence, or other purposes, male sexual demand drives men into sex establishments in almost every country in the world. Beginning in the 1990s, those establishments were increasingly filled with slaves. The reason for this trend is the most important theme of this book: Sex slavery is the profit-maximizing version of prostitution.[48]

PROFIT The most effective way for any business to increase profits is to minimize costs. For most businesses, the largest operating cost is labor. Consider a brothel as a business. The owners of brothels filled with prostitutes "pay" their "laborers" with a portion of each purchase price that a male client pays. The owners of brothels filled with slaves pay almost nothing to their "laborers" from the retail price paid for sex. The only meaningful labor costs in sex slavery might be salary for staff and token payments to slaves or their families. When the mass migration trends unleashed during the 1990s created a windfall in potential slave labor, it did not take long for those in the sex industry to deduce that they could vastly increase profits by capitalizing on the desperation and vulnerability of dislocated women and children. Other industries—such as construction, agriculture, begging, and organ harvesting—subscribed to the same logic. Where lawlessness, chaos, and an inability to protect the rights of the most vulnerable prevailed, slavery soared, and as sex slavery in particular did so, the profitability of the business of commercial sex services also soared. The greater the profits, the greater the demand for slaves. The use of slaves also increased consumer demand because brothel owners could expand the potential market for their product—sex with a human female or child —by lowering the retail price of that product. The cheaper the cost of sex, the more men who could afford it, or afford it more often. This elasticity of demand is the most powerful driver of the demand side of the sex trafficking industry.

ELASTICITY OF DEMAND Just how little does sex from a slave cost? Assuming an eight-hour workday and 260 workdays a year, in India, the price of a sex act from a slave requires 2.5 hours of work at the 2006 national per capita income of $3,339.[49] Exclude the 850 million Indians who live on less than $2 per day, and the required hours of work drop by more than half. In Italy, 2.2 hours of work are required at the national per capita income of $30,921. In the United States, it is around 1.4 hours. Now imagine you are a day laborer, taxi driver, or garbage collector and you could trade two hours of work for one hour of sex. How often would you do it? If the current magnitude of the sex trafficking industry is any indication, the answer is: all the time.[50]

In most red-light districts I visited, I procured tangible evidence that the average price of a sex act was decreasing over time as a direct result of the increased use of slaves. These decreasing prices opened the market to low-wage consumers, such as day laborers and *tuk-tuk* (rickshaw) drivers. Such men could not previously afford sex with a prostitute, but as prices in some parts of Asia and Europe dropped by half, new consumers entered the market, and traditional consumers returned more often. The drop in the retail price of a sex act functions exactly the same as an increase in a consumer's disposable income, and as Keynes argues, "the fundamental psychological law . . . is that men are disposed, as a rule and on average, to increase their consumption as their income increases."[51] The logical question to ask is what would happen to consumer demand if the price instead required six or nine hours of work? What if the price were raised above the threshold of a consumer's monthly disposable income? An economic concept called the elasticity of demand can shed light on these questions.

When analyzing the elasticity of demand, economists use demand curves to determine the level of demand for a product at any given price. As price increases, demand decreases. The price elasticity of a product designates the percent decrease in demand for every 1 percent increase in price. Some products are very elastic; others are not. Gasoline is highly inelastic: Even when prices increase significantly, consumers purchase gasoline at almost the same levels. Demand remains high because consumers have already made the decisions that determine how much gasoline they require, including the type of car they drive and the distance between home and work. Also, there are no substitutes for gasoline. Consumers cannot fill their cars with water instead of petrol. Meanwhile, movie tickets are highly elastic. If the price of a movie ticket doubles, the demand for watching movies in cinemas drops appreciably, as consumers opt for substitutes, such as renting a DVD or watching cable television.

Using data from a group of eighteen friends (in 2005), I plotted rudimentary demand curves for gasoline and movie tickets. Though eighteen people is not nearly enough for a statistically defensible curve, the data nevertheless convey the general principle of price elasticity. Figure 1.3 shows that, even when the price of gasoline doubles, demand decreases very little. In my example, the price elasticity of gasoline is 0.09.[52] Price elasticities of less than 1.0 are considered inelastic. Movie tickets show much more elasticity (figure 1.4): As prices increase, demand drops noticeably. The price elasticity of movie tickets is 1.32.

Similarly, with data gathered from four customers during a visit to a brothel in Kamathipura operated by the aforementioned Silpa, I constructed a basic demand curve for sex services in this particular brothel. Much more data would need to be gathered to refine the numbers, and similar demand curves could be plotted for different cities and different types of sex venues. That said, the sex-service demand curve in this brothel shows that sex services are highly elastic (figure 1.5).

With Silpa's help, I pieced together the curve in figure 1.5 based on interviews with two day laborers, a shopkeeper, and a taxi driver who frequented the brothel. I also plotted the individuals' monthly income and expenses to determine the maximum monthly disposable income available to purchase sex. It should be noted that precise predictions of consumer purchase habits are highly speculative; during my interviews I had to prod and suggest answers more than once to extract the data. Nevertheless, based on these interviews, the price elasticity of sex

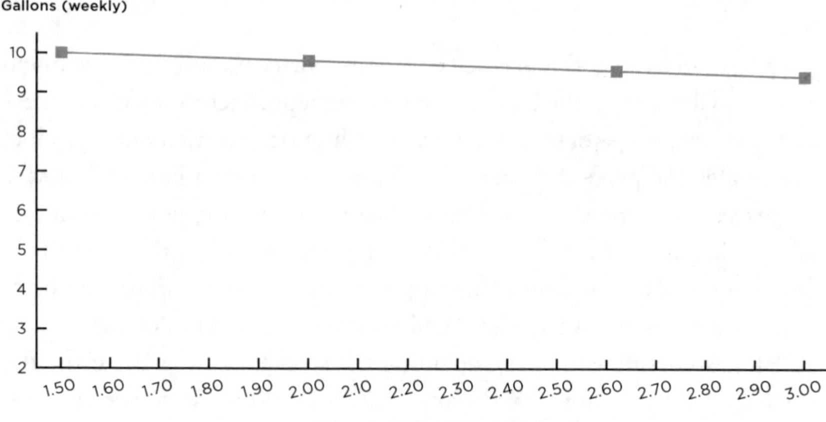

FIGURE 1.3 Demand Curve for Gasoline

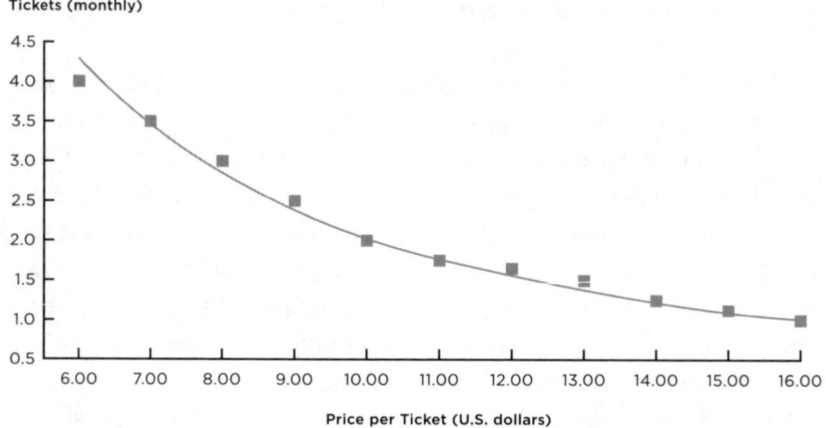

FIGURE 1.4 Demand Curve for Movie Tickets

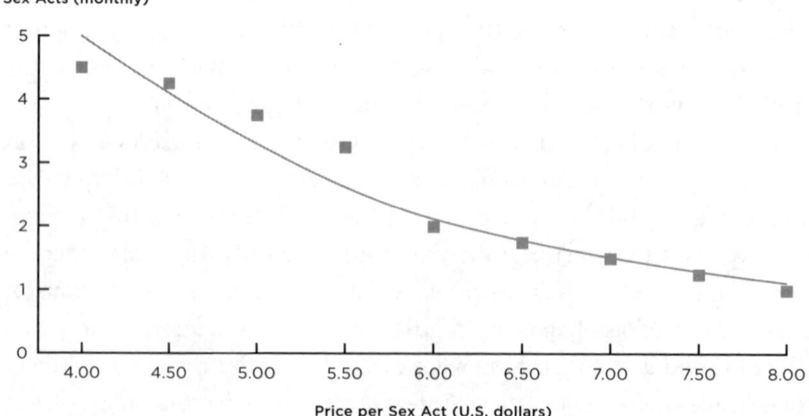

FIGURE 1.5 Demand Curve for Sex Acts: Kamathipura Brothel

services in Silpa's brothel is 1.9, much more elastic than a movie ticket. A key revelation is that when the price doubled from $4 to $8, aggregate demand dropped by almost 80 percent. A large part of the reduction was due to the fact that, when the price increased from $5.50 to $6.00, the two-day laborers were priced out of the market. They only had enough monthly disposable income to purchase one sex act per month up to $5.50, above which they indicated that they would opt for substitutes, such as alcohol or pornography. Even if the day laborers were not priced out of the market, basic economic theory suggests that any increase in retail price—which is economically the same as a drop income—would result in a greater than linear decrease in demand, because consumers always increase consumption, "by not as much as the increase in their income"[53] and they similarly decrease consumption by more than the decrease in their income. If real-world prices could be doubled and achieve a decrease in demand by even one-half the amount predicted by the data I gathered, the profitability of the sex trafficking industry would be severely compromised.

While highly rudimentary, this analysis strengthens the assertion that demand for sex services has increased as a result of the increased use of slaves. Men may not know they are purchasing sex from a slave, but they know they are paying much lower prices than before, and for the most part only slave labor can facilitate those lower prices. In Kamathipura, prices have decreased by over 50 percent during the last decade as a direct result of the increased traffic in slaves from Nepal, Bangladesh, and rural India. I believe that more analyses of the price elasticity of sex slaves will demonstrate similar results, indicating that the most effective strategy against sex trafficking would be to erode its profitability. As the costs of being a sex-slave retailer are elevated, the slave owner must either forfeit profit or raise price. In either scenario, demand drops.[54]

Why Does Sex Slavery Continue to Thrive?

Despite increased policy, law-enforcement, and media attention on sex trafficking, the industry continues to thrive. The reason for this persistence is simple: immense profitability with minimal risk. Sex slavery is illegal in every country in the world; therefore, there should be inherent risk in participating in the exploitation of sex slaves. However, the glaring absence of almost any measurable real risk related to sex-slave crimes directly contributes to the expansion and ongoing health of the sex trafficking industry. Until the market force of risk is increased radically, and as long as sex trafficking remains immensely profitable, the industry will flourish. Fortunately, the tactics that erode profitability are the same as those that increase real risk. To elevate real risk, it is necessary to understand why there is so little to begin with.

The absence of real risk can be distilled to a handful of failures in the philosophical, legal, and law-enforcement approaches to sex trafficking. Those failures include:

- confusion over the definition of trafficking, which results in more focus on movement than exploitation;
- corruption in law enforcement, border control, and judicial systems;
- lack of international coordination and cooperation in investigating and prosecuting trafficking crimes;
- lack of specific law-enforcement focus on slave-related crimes, or underfunded special law enforcement when it exists;
- feeble enforcement of the law and minimal prosecution of sex traffickers;
- insufficient protections for victims, whose testimony is required to convict sex traffickers;
- and ineffective laws that have little economic effect on sex traffickers.

Confusion over what trafficking is results in blunted purpose, diffracted focus, and the exclusion of important components of trafficking-related crimes. From a functional standpoint, these failures can be remedied by the disaggregated definitions of slave trading and slavery I provided at the beginning of the chapter. When utilized to formulate new abolitionist policies, I believe these definitions will help focus efforts on the discrete components and steps constituent to trafficking crimes—especially slavery and exploitation—yielding enhanced results.

Across the developing world, corruption in law enforcement, border control, and judicial systems allows traffickers to conduct business with minimal consequences. Police take bribes in every country I visited to allow sex-slave establishments to operate, warn brothel owners when investigations are imminent, and permit the exploitation of minors with impunity. Border guards do the same to allow traffickers to pass from one country to the next. Judges take bribes to lessen trafficking charges to minor infractions, such as pimping. In all cases, paltry civil wages allow traffickers to offer bribes that represent a rounding error in operational profits to them but a large increase in a civil servant's income.

Lack of coordination among origin and destination countries also hampers prosecution of trafficking crimes. Cristina Bianconi, a top trafficking prosecutor in Italy, told me that the single largest hurdle she faces in prosecuting sex traffickers is the paucity of cooperation between Italy and origin countries such as Albania, Moldova, and Romania, where attempts to gather information are met with jurisdictional wrangling and political delays. A trafficking prosecutor in Moldova who preferred to remain anonymous told me that when Russian traffickers are prosecuted in Moldova, they simply return to Russia, which lacks a bilateral extradition treaty with Moldova for human traffickers. While organized crime groups have globalized the crime of sex trafficking, the legal and governmental efforts to thwart them remain mired in nationalistic inertia and bureaucratic inefficiency.

To circumvent law-enforcement corruption and better investigate anti-trafficking crimes, a small number of countries have created special trafficking police units. These units are typically very small and underfunded. The heads of anti-trafficking police units in Nepal and Thailand that I spoke with were genuinely committed to abolishing trafficking, slavery, and other crimes against women, but they did not have enough money to train their officers or even provide them with uniforms. Foreign assistance was the primary means of funding, and those sources fell woefully short. The police units also were not permitted to conduct proactive investigations or raids on sex-slave establishments; they could only respond to complaints from the community or escaped slaves. Intimidation from traffickers and a lack of witness protection meant that complaints from victims were rare, and fewer than 10 percent of victims testified against their exploiters. Most important, the size in manpower and funding of the anti-trafficking units in these and other countries was typically 10 percent or less than the size and funding of anti–drug trafficking units. As long as drug trafficking receives ten times the law enforcement attention and resources that sex trafficking does, the latter will continue to flourish.

The absence of political will to enforce the law, as well as endemic corruption, allows trafficking and slavery to transpire in broad daylight. When criminals are not prosecuted, there is no penalty for committing a crime, and even as most countries have begun to tout increases in trafficking prosecutions and convictions, those (often trumped-up) numbers are immaterial when weighed against the total number of trafficking crimes committed each year. In the United States—where trafficking laws and enforcement are as strong as any country—140 traffickers were convicted in 91 human trafficking cases from 2001 to 2005.[55] Anywhere from seventy-five thousand to one hundred thousand new trafficking victims entered the United States during that same period of time. If one assumed an sizeable twenty victims per trafficker, that would imply that 3,750 to 5,000 individuals committed trafficking crimes from 2001 to 2005, of which 140 were convicted, or roughly 3 to 4 percent.[56] Faced with a minimal likelihood of being caught and a robust opportunity to generate hundreds of thousands of dollars in profits through exploiting sex slaves, it is no wonder that an increasing number of criminals are willing to take the "risk."

Other than the meager chance of being caught, there is almost no real risk to being a sex trafficker because of the anemic penalties prescribed in the law. Sex slavery is primarily a crime of economic benefit; that is, the slave owner exploits slaves to minimize labor costs and maximize profits. To make that crime riskier, there must be a measurable risk of economic detriment to committing the crime. Assessing the real risk of committing sex trafficking crimes is a matter I will take up in chapter 8, as part of a detailed discussion on tactics designed to thwart the profitability of sex trafficking, but the essential point can be relayed through one example. In India, there is no financial penalty for sex slavery, but the penalty for owning a brothel is approximately a $44 fine. Even if all of the owners of brothels in which sex slaves were exploited were convicted each and every year, sex trafficking would still be a high-profit, minimal-risk venture because the owner of one sex slave in a brothel can generate cash profits per year in excess of $12,900 (see table B.1), a sum equal to 291 times the financial penalty prescribed in the law. In Italy and Thailand, there is no financial penalty for sex trafficking. Jail terms are always a part of any trafficking conviction, but they are rarely more than a few years in duration, and in many countries, they can be lessened by paying small fines. Even in countries such as the United States, Albania, and the Netherlands, where the financial penalties against trafficking crimes are hefty, held up against the nominal prosecution and conviction rates, the real penalties remain immaterial.

Inverting the risk-reward economics of the sex trafficking industry should be the top priority of policy makers across the globe. While brighter minds will devise the best measures by which to do so, I hope to spur that analysis with a few suggestions of my own. The tactics I suggest are intended to erode the profitability of sex trafficking while increasing the risk of committing the crimes. These tactical interventions can be easily implemented in the short term. As the sex-slave equation shifts toward risk and away from reward, I have no doubt that the business of sexually exploiting women and children will diminish. For these and other slave-related crimes to be completely abolished in the long term, however, the conditions that first gave rise to the crime must also be remedied. These conditions are primarily the structural crime of poverty and the inimical asymmetries spread by the current process and governance of economic globalization, which in turn exacerbates poverty levels. The long-term abolition of sex trafficking and all other forms of contemporary slavery will require an elevation in global efforts to eradicate extreme poverty, as well as the reconception of economic globalization as a system for which ultimate legitimacy depends on promoting the social, political, and economic well-being of all members of humanity.

A Personal Mission

After writing this book, I hope to lobby the global community to adopt a targeted suite of tactical imperatives designed to invert the risk economics of committing sex trafficking crimes. Analysis and debate should be undertaken to determine the best measures to achieve this end, but the following seven tactics are a good place to start:

1. The creation of an international slavery and trafficking inspection force, operationally similar to the weapons inspectors utilized by the United Nations, charged with searching for establishments in which slaves are being exploited, freeing the victims, and detaining the criminals;
2. The creation of formally trained and paid community vigilance committees, consisting of members of the community, taxi and *tuk-tuk* drivers, business owners, and specially trained individuals who frequent sex establishments to seek out slaves, gather data, and report their findings to the inspection force or local law enforcement;

3. Targeted, proactive raids against establishments for which there is a strong suspicion of slave-like exploitation, with protections in place to minimize adverse effects against the individuals – slaves or otherwise - living in those establishments;
4. Funding to increase salaries for anti-trafficking police, prosecutors, and judges;
5. Special or fast-track courts to prosecute trafficking crimes, with international observers and participants as well as judicial review to minimize corruption;
6. Fully funded witness protection for slaves and their families for the duration of a trial and up to twelve months afterward;
7. A massive increase in the financial penalties associated with sex-slave crimes, which, along with increased prosecution and conviction levels achieved through the above, should elevate the real risk of sex trafficking to an economically detrimental level.

Each of these tactics merits additional explanation, which I undertake in chapter 8, including a preliminary quantification of the extent to which the combination of these seven tactics might erode the profitability and elevate the risk associated with sex trafficking crimes. Other tactics might prove more effective, but I believe these tactics will provide the best start.

The broader ills of poverty and the harmful governance of economic globalization will require far more challenging steps. Global efforts are already underway to remedy these issues, but I fear that too many of them rely on the consistent action of governments and institutions with interests that run counter to the measures required to redress the severe inequalities in the contemporary capitalist system. These same governments secure and maintain power by enacting policies that directly benefit themselves and their top constituents—modern multinational corporations—which almost entirely prioritize profits over any other measure of decency, sustainability, and basic human rights. The favoritism that governments show to these companies smacks of the ignoble charter monopolies that wreaked havoc across the developing world in the heyday of European mercantilism. Today, the corporations that are the rapacious successors to the East India trading companies exploit the labor and resources of billions of the poorest people in the world, siphoning the value of those human lives into the pockets of a relatively small number of obscenely wealthy owners (and less so, stockholders) of these companies. However, every participant in Western capitalism holds shares in the structural inequalities inherent to the system, and those inequalities can only be remedied by reallocating capital, production, profit participation, market access, and other primary goods to the poorest people in the world. To achieve these ends, policy makers at the highest levels will have to be convinced that the measures required are essential to the justice and sustainability of the modern world. The challenge is great, but the necessity to prevail is greater.

What Can One Person Do?

For far too long, contemporary slaves have endured increasing intensities of exploitation and suffering. With measured doses of hubris, contemporary abolitionists must do whatever it takes to bring those days to an end. Do not despair whether one person can have an impact. One person can listen, one person can learn, one person can draw a line in the sand, and one person can convince another person to act. If you are so inclined, I implore you to take the following five steps today:

1. Raising awareness: Read this book and share it with as many people as possible to elevate awareness of these crimes.
2. Financial support: Every anti-trafficking NGO in this book needs help. However small your donation, support as many as you can. Even if sex trafficking ended today, there would be over one million women and children in need of shelter, health care, counseling, and vocational training.
3. Community vigilance: Do not wait for the tactics suggested in this book to become a reality. You can do your part by establishing your own community vigilance committee today. I am currently working on a comprehensive educational, training, and resource packet on how to set up these committees. Follow me on Twitter.com @siddharthkara, where I will announce how you can access the packet once it is ready. Dedication, vigilance, and a passion to end slavery will be the most important requirements.

4. Write a letter: To initiate the process of elevating contemporary abolitionist efforts, write a letter to your national lawmakers. If all one hundred senators in the United States received thousands of letters demanding aggressive action to end modern slavery, I have no doubt that the requisite governmental and institutional remedies would soon be adopted.
5. Social media: Use the power of social media to make a statement about the importance of eradicating slavery. These communication tools are immensely powerful, and whether it is a short video, a blog, or a full-length documentary film, the ability to use media to spread knowledge and awareness, as well as to organize broader community movements to end slavery, will prove invaluable to modern-day abolitionists around the world.

Take these five steps today, and ask others to take them with you. The beginning of the end of slavery is in your hands.

2 India and Nepal

The happy days are gone, now there are horrors in store. Tomorrow after tomorrow, each day will be worse. The earth has lost its youth. —Mahabharata

The First Encounter

Walking the streets of Mumbai is like jumping into a blender and turning the dial straight to purée. The city is a manic tornado of oppressive heat, frenetic traffic, and legions of human beings panting down your neck. Your senses have to be as sharp as a sniper's or you will accidentally step in bovine fecal matter the same instant a delirious taxi driver runs you down. Every corner of the city brims with intensity, and the three-way intersection at the base of Falkland Road is no exception.

On my first visit to Falkland Road, I was nerve-wracked and drenched in sweat. I had spoken to sex trafficking victims in shelters, but nothing prepared me for the real-world encounter. Hundreds of prostitutes stood outside their four-foot-by-ten-foot *pinjaras* down the main vein of the street and thousands more filled the brothels in the *gallis* (alleys) that fanned out left and right from the road. The alleys were numbered one through nine.

The first solicitation took me by surprise. I stepped onto the sidewalk to circumnavigate a parked truck and was immediately grabbed by a young woman dressed in a tan blouse with tiny mirrors sewn into it. Amid the dingy street-dwellers and filth-caked buildings, she appeared

Pinjaras on Falkland Road

like an oasis. She offered sex for one hundred fifty rupees ($3.33). I stammered. The *pinjaras* were located directly on the street and anyone could see who entered. I was not ready. I walked off the sidewalk, kept my head low, and ambled a few blocks down the road. I surmised that the privacy of a brothel might be easier for me to handle, so I entered one on the sixth *galli*. After passing through the front door, I found myself inside a ramshackle sitting room with torn couches and filth-caked chairs. Several prostitutes lounged in the entry room while rag-tag men chewed *paan*,[1] spat, and belched. A *tout* (solicitor, hawker) sold crisps, cigarettes, and alcohol amid a cacophony of female voices echoing from the floors above. Dust and grime were everywhere.

A middle-aged *gharwali* named Bipasha sat in a chair near the front door, chewing betel nut. She handled my request. The conversation was in Hindi.

"What do you need?" she asked when I entered.

"You have Nepalese?"

"Yes."

"Young ones?"

"Yes, very young. How young you like?"

"Fourteen or fifteen?"

"Yes, brother. I have this."

She called upstairs with a banshee shriek. At least two-dozen girls gathered in the foyer. They were teenagers. They folded their hands and

Bungalow brothel I visited on Falkland Road

averted their eyes. Several had bruises on their arms. One had a long scar transecting her forehead. Their clothes were clean, but their skin was desiccated and filthy. They looked exhausted. Older prostitutes watched from the hallway.

I pointed to one of the girls and asked, "How much?"

"Four hundred rupees."

"I am not a tourist," I told her, "Tell me the proper price."

Bipasha grinned, revealing a mouth of yellow, black-rimmed teeth.

"Okay brother, okay. Two hundred rupees. You can have fun with this one."

"What is her name?" I asked.

"Sita."

I paid the *gharwali* and followed Sita up the stairs.

On the way up, I rubbed my palms against my pants to dry the accumulating sweat. I felt as if a huge neon arrow were flashing over my head with the word *spy* painted on my face. The brothel was filled with hundreds of women of all ages. Some snickered, some flashed their privates, some pinched Sita's arm as she passed. Laundry was hung to dry on the staircase rails. Children played amid the filth. One girl drew pictures of flowers with pink chalk on the floor; another girl tied pigtails into a younger girl's hair. "Dishoom! Dishoom!" two boys yelled, as they formed guns with their hands and chased each other in and out of prostitutes' rooms. A few *touts* roamed the halls, selling goods to customers and prostitutes alike. From behind closed doors, the sounds of grunting men seeped into the halls.

On the third floor, I arrived at Sita's room near a makeshift altar of the god Ganesha. The room was small with a tiny cot. Sita's clothes were folded on a shelf in the corner, next to a steel urn filled with water. Dead insects floated on the surface. A small steel-grated window allowed four dusty spears of light into the room. Pin-ups of bikini girls adorned the walls.

Sita removed her slippers at the door and sat on her cot. I noticed several scars on her legs that looked like cigarette burns. I did not feel comfortable closing the door, so I kept it ajar as I tried to speak to Sita in Hindi, which she understood.

"Where are you from?" I asked.

"Nepal."

"Which region?"

"Makwanpur"

"How long have you been here?"

She shrugged.

"How many years do you have?"

"Fourteen."

Several women in the hall peeked into the room. One of them called downstairs. I did not know if they had overhead our conversation, but I did not want trouble. I could feel my back sticking to my shirt from sweat, and I decided I had seen enough. I pushed the volume button on my mobile phone to fabricate the sound of a phone call. I answered, acted as if it were important, and left Sita a one-hundred-rupee note and the address of a local shelter before hurrying downstairs. The *gharwali* called for me as I rushed through the entry room, but I maintained the false conversation until I was back on Falkland Road.

The Children Are Suffering

In the course of multiple forays into Falkland Road and Kamathipura—literally, "place of pleasure"—I met dozens of sex slaves from Nepal, Bangladesh, and the Indian states of Kerala, Uttar Pradesh, Bihar, Punjab, Andhra Pradesh, Maharastra, and Karnataka. The enormity of suffering was unbearable. Every day, thousands of slaves were violated ten or twenty times each. They were starved, beaten, and treated like animals. In almost every brothel I visited, I heard at least one scream resonate down a dingy brothel corridor.

As often as I entered Mumbai's brothels, there was only so much I could see in quick jaunts in and out of harm's way. In shelters, I learned more. A young woman named Mallaika painted a bleak picture of the corrosive inner workings of Mumbai's sex industry. I met her with the help of Manju Vyas, director of the Aapne Aap ("Your Way") Women's Shelter, a five-minute walk from Falkland Road.

Pulling no punches, Mallaika told me the women in Falkland Road were tortured, drugged, and murdered every day. She said every year the number of trafficking victims increased, especially minors:

> Minors are starved and beaten when they first arrive. The *gharwali* gives them opium so they will have sex. If they do not behave, the *malik* makes the radio high and beats them until they go unconscious. Just a few days back a minor came from my village and was sold by her parents for twenty thousand rupees [$444]. She refused to have sex, so the *malik* broke her arm.

Mallaika was a former sex slave who had been working in Mumbai's red-light districts for twelve years, since she was sixteen years old. At thirteen, she was forced to marry her uncle, but after two stillborn deliveries her uncle-husband sold her to a *dalal,* who sold her to a *gharwali* in Mumbai. Several years later, the *gharwali* informed her she had repaid her debt. Mallaika graduated from slave to the *adhiya* system, by which she split half her earnings with the brothel owner. Even though she accepted life as a prostitute, Mallaika knew her days were numbered. She had HIV, just like another former sex slave I met named Seema. During our conversation, Seema clung tightly to her six-year-old daughter, Hasina, and told me:

> For twenty-one years I have been at Falkland Road. I was too young when I was sold to do this work. I did not know any better. I only do it now because I have no choice. Now that I have HIV, I do not know how much longer I will live. Who will protect my daughter when I am gone?

Seema was right to be concerned. Not only is HIV among prostitutes and sex slaves the single largest contributing factor to India's rapid increase in HIV infections,[2] but the escalating incidence of HIV among sex workers has elevated the demand for younger prostitutes, who are deemed more likely to be disease free. From my first visit to the Mumbai red-light districts in 2000 to my last visit in late 2005, I was told by local experts that there had been an appreciable increase in the number of girls under the age of fourteen engaged in commercial sex on Falkland Road and Kamathipura. Mallaika, Seema, and other prostitutes I interviewed reported that clients increasingly asked for *kali* ("unblossomed") girls, usually ten to twelve years of age. Sometimes they were the daughters of sex slaves who never broke free, a fate Seema rightfully feared for her daughter Hasina.

Even though Seema and Mallaika continued in sex work, both blasted the trafficking of children to brothels. They said the police came every day to collect bribes, but they did nothing to help the children. When the odd police raid was conducted to search for minors, Mallaika said:

> I have seen them take bribes to leave the minors behind. Also the medical officers take bribes to provide certificates that the girls are not minors. No one is helping these children. No one knows how they suffer. Something must be done to prevent trafficking and forced prostitution. So many women are dying; the children are suffering.

Daughters of Nepal

Of all the children suffering in the brothels of India, perhaps none suffer more frequently than the daughters of Nepal. Up to twenty thousand Nepalese girls are trafficked to India each year and up to thirty thousand of the one hundred thousand prostitutes in Mumbai are Nepalese. In each brothel I visited, one or two floors were dedicated strictly to Nepalese women and children. Men in brothels told me they preferred the small, thin figures of Nepalese females. One brothel regular told me he preferred Nepalese prostitutes to Indians and Bangladeshis because they were more demure and did not try to hustle him once he entered their rooms. Nepalese prostitutes were generally more timid because they were thousands of miles from home and spoke broken Hindi at best. Also, the older Nepalese prostitutes inculcated new slaves with habits of good customer service. Many took pride in being more frequented than other nationalities. At a brothel in Kamathipura, one Nepalese girl named Urmila even offered me a cup of tea when I entered her room. After I declined, she lay down on her back and stared upward at the ceiling, as if preparing for surgery. I lifted her to a seated position and assured her that my intentions were benign. She told me that she had been in the brothel for only three weeks, after two weeks in a brothel in Varanasi en route from Nepal.

"The *dalals* have brought hundreds of Tamang[3] girls from my district in Sindhupalchok," Urmila told me, "The first stop is always Varanasi."

Urmila was the eighth female from Sindhupalchok whom I met inside a Mumbai brothel, and each one of them spoke of hundreds of women being trafficked from the region. Many had also spent time in Varanasi before continuing to Mumbai. The woman I met right before Urmila was also from Sindhupalchok, and she opened a rare vista into the lives of Nepalese sex slaves. Her name was Ṣilpa, and she was the exact opposite of Urmila. She had been in Kamathipura for sixteen years and was the *gharwali* of Urmila's brothel. Thirty-two-years old with raccoon-like circles under her eyes, Silpa spoke excellent English and was sipping a whiskey in the sitting room of the brothel when I met her. She first offered me a "fresh girl" that no man had "tasted" for a price of ten thousand rupees ($225), but I told her I did not want a virgin. She offered Urmila.

After I returned downstairs from my brief conversation with Urmila, I walked directly to Silpa to speak with her. It was not easy to check my emotions, but I swallowed my anger and told Silpa that I was an American student doing research for my degree—I had not yet received a book deal from Columbia University Press—and asked if she was willing to speak to me. I expected a stern rebuff, but Silpa was happy to talk.

"You ask questions," she said, "I will answer if I want."

I first asked Silpa how she came to Kamathipura.

"I was given a marriage proposal when I was sixteen," she replied. "After we were married, my husband sent me with a man who brought me here."

Silpa explained that after working fourteen years in Kamathipura brothels, she was promoted to *gharwali* by the brothel owner, a man named MB, who owned several brothels in the area.

"I am kind with the girls," she told me. "I tell them it is better to follow the rules."

I asked Silpa if the police came to the brothel, and she said the police harassed her constantly. Not only did they require a one-hundred-rupee bribe per prostitute per month, but also she had to spend large amounts of bail money each time they conducted raids and took the minors to prison.

"They do these raids to make money," Silpa said. "The police are the most corrupt in India. More than politicians."

I asked Silpa if it concerned her that young Nepalese girls like Urmila were performing sex work in her brothel.

"These girls are safer here than their homes where their father will beat them and their uncle will make sex with them. Here, no harm can come to them unless they misbehave. You see, men are weak. We can take what we want if we give them the prize in our legs. This is the lesson I teach my girls."

"Are any of the girls in this brothel victims of trafficking?"

"What does this mean?"

"Are any girls brought here against their will?"

"My girls are here to earn money. They send this money to their homes, you see. The parents desire this."

I pushed Silpa further on the issue of forced prostitution, but she fenced any attempt to establish wrongdoing. When I asked her if I could meet MB, she refused. I assured her I would keep our conversation anonymous.

"This is not the issue," Silpa said, "MB cannot give his time."

It took a great deal of hustling and a one-thousand-rupee payment, but I eventually convinced Silpa to help me meet MB.

The meeting was set for Juhu Beach, in front of the JW Marriot hotel. The beach was much cleaner than I remembered during visits as a young boy, when it was strewn with used coconut shells, mounds of trash, camel droppings, and piles of ash from beach fires. As I waited for MB, I felt more nervous than I could ever remember feeling in my life. MB was most likely a member of the Mumbai underworld, a notoriously ruthless bunch that enjoyed three square meals a day of extortion, drug running, and murder. He could easily see me as a threat and squash me like an annoying summer mosquito. Was it worth the risk? After several years of research, I was determined to conduct at least one interview with a brothel owner, and this was the closest I had gotten.

Twenty minutes after our designated meeting time of 10:00 a.m., MB arrived with two mercenary-looking colleagues. He was tall and pot-bellied, and spat constantly while we spoke. I tried to put on a brave face, but I knew he could smell the fear on me. I assured him that I would hold our conversation completely confidential, but MB did not care.

"I have no secrets!" he announced in English, eager to pontificate about his exploits.

As we walked in the sand under the blazing sun, MB told me that he operated four brothels in Mumbai, each with approximately four hundred women. He told me that his agents bought prostitutes from various places. Sometimes *dalals* brought batches of them to Kamathipura and auctioned them; other times he frequented a market north of Mumbai where women were brought from Nepal, Bangladesh, and other regions in India for sale.

"There is a premium on young girls," MB told me, "Under fourteen years of age. These girls have become very expensive. Sometimes sixty thousand rupees [$1,350]."

Like Silpa, MB complained about police payoffs.

"This is my biggest expense," he said.

MB told me that he rarely visited his brothels, as he spent the majority of his time in the Middle East pursuing business ventures. He claimed he also enjoyed investing in Bollywood films. MB wore several gold chains and had at least four gold teeth. A strict Hindu, he did not eat meat. He did not allow his brothel girls to eat meat either, though copious amounts of alcohol and hashish were allowed.

After twenty minutes, MB announced his departure. He turned to me and asked, "How many like me have you have spoken to?"

"Only you."

"You will write about me in this paper?"

"It is possible."

MB scrutinized me. I wondered whether he was having second thoughts about our conversation. I grew tense until he clapped me on the back and said, "When you finish, Siddharth Kara, you bring one copy to Silpa."

I nodded.

"Come to Kamathipura tonight, and Silpa can tell you more," MB said, "My driver can fetch you."

"That would be nice," I replied, and gave MB the name of a random hotel on the other side of town. MB clapped me on the back again and departed. I did not return to Kamathipura that night, but I did revisit Silpa several months later, at which point she helped me conduct the interviews used to construct the demand curves in chapter one.

Three Tiers, One Purpose

Brothel owners like MB profit from a local sex-service industry with a highly sophisticated economic structure. Mumbai has more prostitutes than any other city in India does, and I estimate that one out of seven are slaves. The main red-light areas in Mumbai are Falkland Road and Kamathipura. Of these two areas, Kamathipura is the oldest, established in the late seventeenth century to service British troops. It is a small rectangle of fourteen lanes, about three blocks wide, just a few minutes' walk from the bustling Grant Road train station. There are residential buildings, convenience stores, metal works, tea shops, and pharmacies interspersed among the *pinjara* and bungalow brothels. Kamathipura only comes to life as a red-light area at night, whereas sex can be purchased on Falkland Road in broad daylight. In the last five years, new red-light areas have sprung up in Navi Mumbai and Ghatkopar, each filled with trafficked slaves as well as local prostitutes. In New Delhi, the main red-light area is GB Road; in Calcutta, it is Sonagachhi; and in Varanasi, it is Shivdas Pur.

There are three tiers of economic model in Indian red-light areas: slavery and debt bondage, *adhiya,* and lodgers. Victims of sex trafficking are initially held in a slavery or debt-bondage system. I combine the two

Victim of forced prostitution outside her *pinjara* on Falkland Road

because even though the definitions of slavery and debt bondage differ, in Indian red-light areas, they function in the same way. Trafficked individuals are told they must work off a debt by sleeping with any client who selects them. They are held against their will and coerced to comply through torture, starvation, and drugs. Their debts are farcical. The *gharwalis* give the victims a number—say, one thousand dollars—onto which they pile interest of up to 100 percent per year. They also make deductions for food, medicine, and bad behavior. There are only a few ways that young women escape slavery. They may be sent home with nice clothes and a pocket full of rupees to recruit new victims; they may be evicted to the streets if they no longer entice a sufficient number of clients; or they may transition to the *adhiya* system after accepting a life of prostitution.

Each *adhiya* prostitute I met was a former slave, and each one of them wished she did not have to make a living through prostitution. In the *adhiya* (literally, "one-half") system, the individual remains in the brothel and splits half her earnings with the *malik*. *Adhiya* prostitutes decide whether or not they want to accept a client, but they cannot be too picky because the moment the *malik* judges that a prostitute is not generating sufficient revenue, he will replace her with a new slave. The economics of the *adhiya* system always disfavor the prostitute. Police bribes must be paid out of their pockets and the owners charge them for utilities, room maintenance, and other incidental costs. *Adhiya* workers often collaborate with *gharwalis* to acclimatize new slaves. They take a big-sister role, tending wounds and convincing new slaves that it is best to obey the *gharwali* so that they can be a "free" *adhiya* prostitute one day.

Lodgers are voluntary prostitutes or *adhiyas* who save up enough money to move out of the brothel but rent a room in the brothel where they accept clients. Rental rates are usually around 15 to 20 percent of revenues. Most lodger prostitutes leave the brothel when they find a boyfriend or husband. Lodgers are usually in their thirties and charge the least per sex act—fifty rupees, or around $1.10—because they are older than the other prostitutes and slaves.

Every large brothel I visited in India had some mix of the above three economic arrangements. *Adhiyas* and lodgers were usually in the front and lower floors and slaves were kept in the back or higher floors. *Maliks* make complex decisions about the ratios of slaves to *adhiyas* and lodgers. Slaves are the most profitable, but a certain number of *adhiyas* are required to assist with the transition of new slaves and to provide a clean front for the brothel to (noncorrupt) police and social workers. In all cases, *maliks* maximize income by providing as many slaves as possible, as they can be forced to have sex with any man who can pay for it. The average ratio of sex slaves to *maliks* I observed in Mumbai brothels was twenty to one, though there were some slave owners, like MB, who possessed many more.

A Big Mistake

On my third research trip to India, I planned a journey to retrace, in reverse, the most heavily trod sex trafficking route in the region: from rural Nepal to Mumbai via Varanasi. Before commencing that journey, I paid a quick visit to Falkland Road. The very first prostitute who solicited me spoke excellent English, something I found only twice before. She was dressed in a tight blouse, fully decorated with jewels and makeup, and bore an uncanny resemblance to a childhood friend.

In a flash, she clasped my arm hard and said:

"Hello. Two hundred rupees [$4.50] for fuck and suck."

"You speak English?" I asked.

"Yes. One hundred fifty rupees, I promise you will like."

"Where are you from?" I asked.

"Punjab."

"How long have you been here?"

"Six months . . . come, I will give you discount, first customer of the day. One hundred rupees."

"How did you learn English?" I asked.

"I went there, um, seventh standard."

"You went to school up to the seventh standard?"

"Yes."

"How old are you?"

"Seventeen . . . now come, one hundred rupees, I promise you will like."

She tugged hard on my sleeve, desperate to close a deal. I asked her how she came to Mumbai. She did not answer.

"Come sir, please," she implored.

From the corner of my eye I spied her *malik*, surveying me keenly. The opportunity to speak English was too good to pass up. I agreed to the price, and stepped into her cage.

The *pinjara* contained two soiled cots, pinups of bikini girls, a small, concrete sink, and a stainless-steel water jug. The girl asked for the money. I fumbled two hundred rupees from my money belt, which she swiftly tucked inside her blouse. When the young girl started to unclasp her skirt, I stopped her and said, "I only want to talk."

We spoke in whispers. She told me when her father removed her from school to earn money, a *dalal* offered a job as a seamstress in Mumbai. After she arrived, she was sold to a *malik*. She would not discuss her living conditions, and she did not answer when I asked if she wanted to return home. When I offered her information on a nearby shelter, she declined. At that point, I asked her something I had never before asked a sex slave: I asked to take a picture.

Not of her, but the *pinjara*. After entering countless sex establishments in numerous countries, I wanted to show people what the places actually looked like. In truth, I had planned the picture since the morning, because it was the only time I ever took a camera into a commercial sex establishment.

The young woman from Punjab was quick to decline. When I offered her more money, she stepped outside, and a second girl came in. The second girl made a fist and tapped it against her face.

"They will beat us," the Punjabi girl said.

The second girl returned outside and I immediately relented. I thanked the girl for speaking to me and was about to leave when the same *malik* who had eyed me earlier stepped into the *pinjara*. He was short and muscular, his hair tinted orange. Two *goondas* (thugs, strongmen) flanked him. I was blocked inside. "Camera! Camera!" the *malik* shouted, and angrily demanded my backpack. I refused to part with it. Three more *goondas* arrived. For the first time since I began my research, I was in real trouble.

The *malik* yanked at my backpack, which not only held my camera, but my plane tickets and passport. I tightened my posture and refused to hand over the backpack. The tough-guy response did not work. One of the *goondas* handed the *malik* a sharp-edged piece of metal. Another *goonda* shoved me hard. I weighed my options, pulled out my cell phone, and threatened to call the police. For a split second they balked, and in that moment, I bulldozed out of the *pinjara* and sprinted down Falkland Road. They chased, but I did not stop sprinting until I was halfway across Mumbai.

Later that evening, I cursed my arrogance. For so many years I had stepped into the fire pit and emerged unscathed. Of course these men would eradicate any attempt to expose them—they forced teenage slaves to have sex with twenty men a day! Of course the slave would signal to her *malik*; for all she knew, I was sent by him to test her loyalty. My past successes had made me cocky, and that cockiness was swiftly checked. Though I continued to research sex trafficking in other parts of India, I never returned to Falkland Road. I had no business there and I feared those young girls had received a fist to the face on my account. That night, I suffered violent food poisoning from mushrooms and vomited thirty-four times. Justice was swift. I accepted my punishment.

The Banks of Redemption

After two days of recovery, I started my journey north. The first stop was the holy city of Varanasi, followed by villages in the border state of Bihar, then across the border into Nepal and onward to the capital of Kathmandu. From Kathmandu I would journey to the remote region of Sindhupalchok, to understand why so many young women were trafficked from its isolated hills.

Nestled on the banks of the Ganges River in the northern state of Uttar Pradesh, Varanasi is one of the holiest cities in India. It is said that the river was formed during a previous cycle of time, when the mighty goddess Ganga threatened to drown the earth in a torrent of heavenly water that would wash the sin-ridden world away. The *sadhus* (saints) were terrified and made sacrifices to Shiva, beseeching his help. Because Ganga was the older sister of Shiva's wife, Parvati, he knew just how to foil her. When the time came, Ganga hurled herself toward the earth and Shiva appeared in a ravine of dry dirt directly below her. From a meditative position, he caught her violent descent in his matted hair. The knots in his tresses broke her fall, forcing her to stream gently down his face, over his lips, into a furrow in the earth that is now the Ganges River.

Because of the river's divine origins, Hindus believe that its waters can wash away negative karmic accumulation and advance individuals closer to release (*moksha*) from the imprisoning cycle of life and death (*samsara*) that torments the human condition. The best way to achieve permanent release is to sprinkle the ashes of the dead into the Ganges after cremation. Many philosophers and religious scholars have argued that because the Ganges River sprang from a god's affair with his wife's sister, every redemption is born in corruption. I learned just how much corruption teems under the surface of one of India's holiest cities when I visited Ranjana Gaur, director of the Social Action Research Center (SARC) in Varanasi.

The morning I arrived at her office, Ranjana was in a tizzy. She had just received word that parents in a nearby village had sold their daughter to a trafficker for five hundred rupees ($11). She immediately sent a field worker on a fact-finding mission and prayed it was not too late. While we waited, Ms. Gaur spent the day describing Varanasi's role in India's illicit sex trade. She confirmed Urmila's statement that trafficked Nepalese women regularly arrived in Varanasi, where they were passed to local *dalals* who distributed them to Mumbai, New Delhi, Kolkata, Chennai, and other major Indian cities. More recently, trafficking victims spent an initiation period in Shivdas Pur because Mumbai brothel owners expressed a preference for girls who had already been broken. *Dalals* could charge up to 20 percent more for such girls. The initiation period was thus a cold business decision. Break the girls first; enjoy greater profits later.

Shivdas Pur was not nearly as large as Falkland Road or Kamathipura. It consisted of *pinjara*-style brothels on a road no more than a quarter mile long. Typically, there might be around 2,000 prostitutes at Shivdas Pur, but the day before my arrival, they were thrown in jail by the local police for unknown reasons. Ms. Gaur informed me that during police raids in Varanasi, the brothel owners and customers were never arrested, only the prostitutes. After a few bribes, most prostitutes were returned to their owners. It was a regular racket.

Initially, I suspected that orthodox Varanasi society would offer better protection for women and children than would other areas in India. However, the orthodox Hindu culture seemed to facilitate greater abuse. Varanasi was infected with large- and small-scale slave traders who exploited countless women and children, both locals or those in transit from Bangladesh and Nepal. Rape, domestic violence, and pedophilia raged. I asked Ranjana why there was so much violence against women in Varanasi.

"Because men know women will not speak out," she said. Ranjana's mission was to change that fact, one victim at time. A child named Devika was among them. This is the story she shared:

> One day when I was thirteen, a man we knew named Raj harassed me on my way to school. He pulled my hand and said he will kill me if I cry for help. He took me to his house and raped me. He abused me every day and would bring other men to have sex with me. After one month and two days, my mother found me and came with the police. The next day Raj came to our home and said, "I have spoiled the life of your daughter, and I will spoil your other daughters as well." Raj said he would kill us if we made a case in the court. At that time, the SARC lawyers helped us take legal action. My case is still ongoing. I did not like having to testify in the court in front of so many people, but I want Raj to be punished so he cannot hurt other girls like me.

Because she was so young, Devika found it difficult to narrate her story. After a few minutes, she began to cry, so Ranjana excused her and filled in the details. She told me that when they first rescued Devika, she was pregnant, and no hospital would treat her because she was so young. Devika delivered the child after seven months, but the infant expired a few days after birth. Ranjana also explained that Devika was forced to have sex with over twenty men per day inside Raj's one-girl apartment brothel. Convincing the police to file a case against Raj was a nightmare. Initially, the police assumed that Devika willingly performed sex work. SARC pressured the police for a month before they filed a case against Raj in May 2005. When they brought him in for questioning, he claimed that Devika was his wife. He even touched the feet of Devika's mother, Shama, as his mother-in-law. The police told Shama, "You are a poor *dalit;*[4] you are getting a son-in-law. Don't complain." Because Devika had no birth certificate, there was no way to establish her age, which Raj claimed was sixteen, and thus by law, she was old enough to be married and have sexual relations.[5] SARC paid for a medical exam, which established that Devika was only thirteen. Despite the obstacles, SARC filed a case against Raj under Article 376, the Rape Law. Charges under the country's trafficking laws could not be established. At the time of my visit, Raj regularly threatened to kill Devika and her family. The police did not offer protection.

Seven other girls under Ranjana's protection shared similarly appalling stories with me. One young Bangladeshi girl named Manisha told me she was beaten every morning by her *malik* in Shivdas Pur with the buckle end of his leather belt. After the beating, she was forced to have sex with "the *malik,* his friends, the local shopkeepers, and young boys who brought the *malik* his tea and lunch in the afternoon." Manisha showed me the vermiculate welts on her back, permanent reminders of the tortures she endured before the age of fifteen. Another child named Aradhana was trafficked from Bihar and forced into sex slavery for three years in Varanasi, New Delhi, and Varanasi again, all before the age of seventeen.

Toward the end of the day, Ranjana and I were drinking tea when a disheveled and agitated woman approached. It was Shama, Devika's mother. She heard that someone from America was listening to stories and she desperately wanted to tell hers. She gesticulated wildly and pierced me with blazing eyes as she described an enormity of torment that only a mother could comprehend:

> I was going mad when Devika went missing! I searched every day. I begged the police for help. Come back tomorrow, they said. I was mad wondering what happened to my daughter! Only Ranjana Bibi helped me find my child. Now with our case, the police and judges take bribes. Who can we trust? No one is protecting our rights. No one in the government is protecting the rights of women.

Shama blasted the government, the police, and men in general for almost an hour. Ranjana asked if I wanted to curtail Shama's acerbic monologue, but I told her I would listen as long as Shama wanted to speak. She was not the only parent I met who shrieked at the wanton brutalization of a child. When she was finally exhausted, Shama calmly uttered three sentences I will never forget: "So many bad men are hurting young girls. How can we stop them? Is there any end to the suffering of women?"

At that very moment, Ranjana's field worker rushed into the office. After an entire day racing through villages trying to find the young girl, he learned the trafficker had already left for a city unknown. The child was lost.

Meeting a Trafficker

From Varanasi, my journey to Nepal continued with an overnight train ride into Bihar, the poorest state in India. My local colleagues

Supriya Awasti, Kanhiya Singh, and Deepak Kumar met me in the city of Khatiar. With their help, I traveled to the remote villages of Kamal Doha, Gorhiya, and others near the Nepalese border, where I learned that hundreds of Nepalese were trafficked each month through the region on their way to Indian urban centers. I also learned that traffickers heavily sourced these villages and others like them. One of those traffickers was the only such man I ever met, named Salim.

Like most areas in which traffickers recruit new victims, Bihar is wretchedly poor. Most Biharis live on approximately fifty cents a day, a depth of poverty that precipitates the worst crime levels in India. In Bihar, there is a murder every two hours, a rape every six hours, and one bank is looted each day. Since 1990, more than one thousand political officials have been murdered and there have been over thirty-three thousand kidnappings for ransoms. Only 17 percent of Bihari households have a toilet; only 10 percent have electricity. As the middle and upper classes in India have enjoyed rapid increases in living standards across the last two decades, clean drinking water, sufficient food, clothes, and basic medical care are luxuries most Biharis cannot attain. Amid the poverty and violence, traffickers have little problem recruiting new slaves with promises of wage-paying jobs in India and abroad.

Understandably, Biharis are highly distrustful of outsiders, especially in the Muslim villages near the Nepal border. When I first arrived in Kamal Doha, the village elder refused to allow me to meet with anyone because he took me for a government spy searching for rumored al-Qaeda activity in his village. It took Kanhiya over thirty minutes to gain his trust. Even then, the villagers were loath to discuss the possibility that their daughters were coerced into sex work. Such an event would bring great family shame. Nevertheless, I heard numerous tales of sex trafficking as I traveled from village to village. Men married teenagers and sold them to *dalals,* rickshaw drivers abducted young girls and trafficked them to Mumbai brothels, and former trafficking victims, such as Bibi Ahmadi, returned from brothels to recruit new girls. In private, Bibi Ahmadi told me that several parents had approached her about finding work for their daughters. When I asked the families about this claim, most parents denied it, but a small number confessed that they wanted to send a child for work under the dire hope of receiving sufficient income to feed their remaining offspring.

On the Nepal side of the border, the situation was the same. At a village called Amhai Baryati in the Marang district, a man told me, "So many young girls have gone from our village with *dalals* who promise jobs in India. We never hear from them again." Other men told me that women had been trafficked to the Middle East for domestic work; men had also been trafficked to the Middle East (mostly Dubai), Malaysia, and Singapore to work in construction. In every village, poverty and gender bias left women highly vulnerable to sex trafficking. "My daughter was raped when she was twelve," one father told me. "Because of this, she can never be married. We received a job offer for her to work in Kathmandu in a clothing factory. This was two years ago. We have not heard from our daughter since." Another father said, "My daughter was widowed at twenty-six years. She could not be allowed to work here. A man promised her a job in Punjab. She went with him to do housework for a family there. We have not heard from her since."

And then there was Salim. I had imagined for years what I might say if I ever met a trafficker. Would I demand to know how he could knowingly profit by sending women and children to be tortured? Would I throttle him, turn him over to the police, demand a list of victims and destinations so the slaves could be freed? When I met Salim on a sunny, crisp day in the remotest reaches of Bihar, my mind went blank. He was so ordinary - just a man, wearing simple village clothes. His aspect was common, his mustache trimmed, his hair neatly combed. He spoke without emotion of how he took male children for carpet weaving to the carpet-belt towns of Varanasi and Badoi[6] and female children for sex work in New Delhi and Mumbai.

"A man with money meets me in Varanasi," he explained. "I send the children with him. When I return, I use some of this money as payment to parents for the next children."

Salim told me that parents often asked for money in exchange for their children.

"I am paid usually five thousand rupees [$110] for a male child and seven or eight thousand rupees [$175] for females. From this I give one thousand [$22] to the parents. I am also paid one hundred sixty rupees' commission for each square meter of carpet made by the children I bring. I do not receive commission for female children."

As I listened to Salim, I felt like I was watching myself on a movie screen. With established metrics and deadpan candor, Salim explained how he made an impressive income through the slave-trading of local children. His business was simple and efficient, and he had no moral qualms because many parents approached him to send a child for work. I knew that there were thousands of Salims in the world, and for the first time, I realized they were not employed by the slave owners to whom they sold women and children, but by a far more malevolent criminal: poverty.

Before Salim left to eat lunch with his wife and three sons, I asked him how long he had been a *dalal*.

"I have been taking children to Varanasi for ten years," he replied. "Maybe three hundred children so far."

Trafficking and Bonded Labor

In addition to recruiting from their local villages, *dalals* like Salim have more recently begun recruiting individuals from bonded-labor sites in north India and trafficking them into forced-labor conditions throughout the country, be it for carpets, bricks, agriculture, or commercial sex. The pool of potential victims is vast—approximately six out of ten slaves in the world are bonded laborers in South Asia[7]—and because bonded laborers are already slaves, they present little or no behavioral complications for new slave owners. The primary tool utilized to secure these victims is the same that Salim uses with parents in his village: the purchase prices paid for children, in this case to help alleviate debts owed to the landowner or slave owner. Deceit is also a successful ploy, as any promise of a wage-paying job proves difficult to resist.

I met hundreds of bonded laborers in India, most of whom were *dalits*, and I quickly understood why so many ended up in the hands of slave traders. In a village called Mahi, over 2,500 *dalits* toiled as bonded laborers for two brothers who owned most of the land in the area.[8] These brothers were also the primary moneylenders, which was how they acquired bonded slaves. The Mahi villagers toiled in three industries: carpet weaving, agriculture, and bricks. Each of the Mahi villagers became a bonded laborer for one of two reasons: a major life ritual, such as a wedding or funeral, or a crisis, such as illness, environmental disaster, or injury.

From the day the Mahi villagers first borrowed money, they had little sense of the debits and credits of their accounts. If a debtor died, the debt was passed to the eldest son. Loans as small as forty dollars had

Child bonded laborer at a brick kiln

enslaved multiple generations of a family. The laborers worked year after year without ever generating enough income to climb out of debt. Almost all income, either through deductions or purchases of food, reverted to the moneylender-slave owner. Regular beatings ensured that bonded laborers worked fourteen-hour days. If they stepped foot outside the village perimeter, they might be tortured or penalized with more debt. Females and children were regularly exploited for sex by slave owners and their henchmen. At dawn, when the village women ventured into the fields to conduct their morning business, the slave owner often forced them to do so in his presence to humiliate them and reinforce his dominance. Meanwhile, the carpets, agricultural products, and bricks that Mahi villagers made were sold to wholesalers and distributors at tidy profits. Bricks were used to meet demand from India's high-paced construction boom and carpets woven in remote looms tucked inside dusty, cramped mud huts ended up in retail outlets in Singapore, London, and New York.

A skeletal man named Gurahu best summarized the living conditions of his fellow bonded laborers:

> I am so poor. I am dying here for bread and water. I have taken an advance of seven thousand rupees [$155] three years ago for my

> daughter's wedding. I cannot get enough work to repay this loan. If I repay the loan, we cannot eat. If we eat, I cannot repay the loan. The moneylender charges five rupees' interest on every hundred-rupee loan each month. When I earn fifty rupees, he takes twenty-five for my loan and twenty-five I keep for my wage. This way, my loan keeps growing. We are dying in this village. We can never repay our loans. We are dying.

Gurahu's wife added the following:

> Winter is here, and my children do not have proper clothes. How will they survive? I cannot buy clothes, and the moneylender charges us too much for food. One kilogram of potato costs ten or twelve rupees [$0.22–$0.27]. One kilogram of rice costs eight or ten rupees [$0.18–$0.22]. For wheat it costs nine rupees [$0.20]. How can we afford these prices? The entire village has taken a loan at some point. We are all in debt. None of us can survive.

Many couples I met in Mahi village became bonded laborers when they took a loan for their wedding. Others became bonded laborers when they took a loan for a funeral, and still others became bonded laborers when they had to borrow money due to a medical emergency, or to repair their huts after monsoon floods. Out of sheer desperation, several Mahi villagers told me they sold one or sometimes two children to *dalals* who promised wage-paying jobs. In an irony that left me utterly confounded, numerous men in several villages confessed that they sold their wives to a *dalal*, in order to repay the debt they incurred when they originally married that wife.

The lives of the bonded laborers in Mahi village were beyond desperate, and they provided the perfect trolling ground for shrewd slave traders. Payments for children or wives went directly to the moneylender-slave owner, who reasoned that from time to time a handful of cash was worth more than the slow and meticulous extraction of value from a bonded slave, whom he could easily replace anyway. I visited numerous villages in which bonded laborers were sold to *dalals*, and never heard from again. Such tales resonated across the fields of Uttar Pradesh, through Bihar, all the way up to the border with Nepal.

Crossing the Border

The border between India and Nepal stretches 1,850 kilometers through remote forests, plains, and hills. There are several formal border crossings and individuals with a Nepalese or Indian identity card can pass freely by virtue of the 1950 Open Border Agreement. No passports or visas are required. This agreement was designed to facilitate trade between the two countries, and it enables traffickers to transport victims with ease. Many anti-trafficking discussions therefore focus on how to stop trafficking at the border. Some argue that tighter border controls will make it more difficult for traffickers; others argue that awareness posters and social workers interviewing young female migrants before they cross are the best way to curtail the flow.

As I learned when I visited the border region, neither approach works. Tens of thousands of people pass through formal border points each day and tighter controls simply disrupt the livelihoods of millions of merchants and day laborers. In addition, traffickers can easily shift crossing points through the endless miles of unguardable forest and plains. Awareness campaigns and interviews achieved similarly poor results. The Nepalese saw them as nothing more than antimigration propaganda: As a man named Krishna said, "The Indians know we work harder and can take their jobs, so they send these social workers to prevent us from migrating." Even when people were aware of the risks of migrating with agents who promised jobs, they were so desperate that nothing could alter their decision to migrate.

Unlike Indians and Nepalese, other nationalities have a more difficult time crossing the border. At the bustling junction between Jogbani and Biratnagar, I spent over two hours at what must be the most tortured border crossing in South Asia. Supriya, Kanhiya, and Deepak crossed seamlessly thanks to their Indian identity cards, but the moment I pulled out my U.S. passport, all six border personnel dropped their lunches and vigorously debated how to process my passage. First, they spent twenty minutes searching for the box that held the necessary Indian government emigration forms. Dusty and unopened, the forms required another thirty minutes and three different drafts before the officials felt I had properly filled out the form. I then had to handwrite another three copies because they did not have a copy machine. Finally, there was another ten minutes of confusion because U.S. passports do not list the bearer's father's surname.

One immigration official was convinced that my passport was a forgery because my father's name was not listed. It took an arduous amount of explanation to convince him that, unlike Indian and Nepalese passports, U.S. passports did not define a citizen's identity by virtue of his or her father's name. Eventually, I completed the immigration process and proceeded to customs. The customs officials insisted on inspecting my luggage with painstaking thoroughness, making a list in a big black ledger of every item I was bringing into the country: five pants, five shirts, ten boxer shorts, ten pairs of socks, papers, files, one camera, one laptop, four batteries, one bag of potato crisps, and so on. When the saga was finally over, I repacked my belongings and passed into Nepal.

The very next day I crossed back into India in minutes, driving down Karsia Road in a large SUV through a scenic mix of potato and mustard fields. The border crossing was nothing more than a twenty-foot bridge over a shallow stream guarded by dust and cows. Kanhiya told me that *dalals* crossed the bridge often. If they needed to cross at formal border crossings—because they told the victim they would legally cross for a proper job in India—they simply paid bribes. Kanhiya and Deepak had gathered detailed statistics on bribes paid to police to ensure safe passage. A seasoned *dalal* paid two hundred fifty rupees ($5.50) for an older woman (not a teenager) and up to one thousand rupees ($22) for a younger one (teenager or early twenties). A neophyte *dalal* paid one thousand rupees ($22) for an older woman and up to two thousand rupees ($44) for a younger one. Trafficking was so common from Nepal to India that border bribes had normalized to 2 percent to 5 percent of the final price of a slave, depending on the experience of the slave trader.

Once the *dalals* crossed from border towns, such as Biratnagar, Bagdora, Kuchbihar, and Birganj, the victims were taken to Varanasi or Gorakpur, where they were often passed to local *dalals* who finished the journey. The only town for which there was not a pass-off was Kolkata, due to its proximity to Nepal. Most of the border towns had their own mini red-light districts, consisting of a few hotels that locals knew were populated with prostitutes. Indians and Nepalese were trafficked to either side of the border on a daily basis to work in the hotels. The exact routes were regularly changed to keep noncomplicit law enforcement off the traffickers' trails and avoid paying bribes. The *dalals* also took *chorbatos* (thief roads), secretive routes deep in the forest where it was impossible to patrol. I explored a few sex-service hotels in the border towns, but I had little luck finding anyone willing to speak to me. The hotels were among the most wretched and dreary sex-slave establishments I encountered. The halls were rank with urine and booze, and the rooms were infested with roaches and mosquitoes. Day after day, local day laborers and merchants feasted on the shifting supply of women and children inside these hotels. The local police did nothing, and there were no social services or shelters anywhere in the area. These border towns were slave-trading abysses.

Road to Perdition

Few Nepalese women trafficked to India ever escape, and few who escape ever return. A young woman named Sushila was one of those few. We met at a shelter for trafficking victims operated by Shakti Samuha ("Empowerment"), the first anti-trafficking organization in South Asia founded by sex trafficking survivors. With a flat voice and downturned eyes, she narrated the most detailed, unimaginable story of Nepalese sex trafficking I had yet heard:

> I was born in the Chitwan district of Nepal. When I was young, I helped my father work in a rice mill. The owners of the mill had a twenty-year-old son who came to my room every night and raped me. He threatened to kill me if I told anyone. I was only eleven years old, so the pain was terrible. My father did not believe me when I told him. Eventually I could not take it anymore, and I ran away.
>
> I came to Narayangadh by evening. I sat in front of a shop, and a woman approached me and said I could work in her hotel. A few days later, the couple took me on a bus and gave me ice cream. I fell asleep, and I do not remember anything after that. When I woke up, I was in another house of a Nepali woman married to an Indian. She took me to a bungalow in Mumbai. There were hundreds of girls in this bungalow. I did not want to go inside, but I was beaten and locked in a room. That evening the *gharwali* came to the room and said I was sold for forty thousand rupees [$890]. She said I had to do sex work to pay back this money. I told her I had already been raped, and that I could not bear to be with men.
>
> "I thought no one had touched you!" she shouted, "I paid the virgin price!"

She burned me with cigarettes and beat me with a wooden ladle. I was black and blue, and my entire back was bruised. I cried the entire night.

The next day, another prostitute told me if I wanted to eat I should start to work. I told her I would rather starve. After four days, another woman from the Mahato caste tried to convince me. I still refused. After one week, a Japanese man came. They made an arrangement for me with the Japanese man for sixty thousand rupees [$1,333]. They told him I was a virgin.

The Japanese man stayed with me for two weeks. I was forced to be with him, even though the pain was unbearable. Four days after the Japanese man left, another customer came. I was still bleeding, so the man went to the *gharwali* and shouted, "Why did you send me to a woman having a period?" The *gharwali* asked me if I was having my period, but I told her it was from the wounds in my vagina. The *malik* called the doctor, and he stitched my wounds. I was given rest for three days, then I was forced to be with customers. My stitches opened, and I started to bleed again. This process happened twelve times.

I do not know how many years I was in Kamathipura. I used to be with twenty-five customers a day. If we felt we would faint from pain, the *gharwali* gave us medicine. We had to keep making sex with customers no matter what.

When the Indian police conducted a raid in January 1996, I was locked inside my room, but I banged on the door, and they found me. After the rescue, I was kept in a shelter for seven months. The Nepalese government would not allow us to return. They said, "The prostitutes are a reservoir of AIDS from India who will spread the disease in Nepal."

With the help of NGOs, we were finally allowed to return to Nepal. They flew us back on two planes. The people in Nepal came to the airport and spat on us. They said they would contract AIDS just by touching us. I was lucky not to have AIDS, though I had other sexually transmitted diseases. I am still on medication. I wanted to take actions against the traffickers who sold me, but I could not trace them.

There is still a strong possibility that many illiterate, young girls can be trafficked from Nepal. Many girls are sold because of dowry practice. When a girl is engaged, her parents must offer twenty thousand rupees or as much as four lakhs[9] in cash to the groom's family. At the wedding, they must offer gifts that could be worth several years' income. For this reason, many parents sell their daughters rather than get them married.

Sushila's devastating tale left me speechless. I felt ashamed to be male. Across the next several days, many more young Nepalese women shared terribly similar tales.

A bony, bow-legged girl named Tara was given a false job offer in a carpet factory before spending two years on Falkland Road. Another young woman named Nidhi fled her abusive husband, but her parents would not shelter her because an unmarried daughter was a source of extreme shame. Nidhi was easily duped by a false marriage offer and trafficked to India. Sri Devi was sold by her stepfather before spending eight months in Kamathipura and Falkland Road. Gauri was abducted one night from her village and spent three years in New Delhi on GB Road. Aparna was removed from school at standard six and sold to a policeman-*dalal,* who trafficked her to India. Aparna told me that many Nepalese girls were removed from school at the sixth standard because that was when the schools begin charging tuition fees of sixty rupees ($0.80) per month, and parents typically removed daughters instead of sons.

Finally, a young girl named Priti from Sindhupalchok suffered a near carbon copy of Sushila's ordeal. She was drugged and trafficked to Mumbai by four men who sold her for fifty thousand rupees ($1,110). Her virginity was then sold to what Priti called an Arabian man for $1,333. After two weeks with the Arab, Priti spent the next three years at a brothel in Kamathipura, where clients and police had "violent and unnatural sex" with her. Priti saw two girls killed in the brothel for misbehavior, and one girl beaten so badly that her spine broke. When Priti finally returned to Nepal after the same raid that freed Sushila, her family disowned her. She was not even allowed to attend her mother's funeral because her presence would bring shame. The large raid in 1996 that freed Sushila and Priti remains the only one of its kind.

Massage Parlors and Dance Clubs

Not all trafficked sex slaves from Nepal go to India. Some are sent to China, where they are exploited in the red-light districts of Shanghai and other major urban centers. Some are sent to Pakistan and subsequently re-trafficked to the Middle East. And some are trafficked internally to Kathmandu, where they are exploited in hundreds of massage parlors and dance bars.

Kathmandu is Nepal's smoggy, bustling capital, situated in a beautiful valley with white-capped Himalayan peaks visible in the distance. The northern quadrant of the city includes the tourist area known as Thamel. Once the haven of hashish-smoking hippies, modern-day Thamel is filled with Internet cafés, restaurants that serve everything from Chinese stir fry to brick-oven pizza, and massage parlors at every turn. In addition, numerous dance clubs sell sex with young Nepalese girls. Many girls migrate from nearby areas, such as Katari, Gurung, Chitwan, and Nepalaganj, with hopes of dancing for money, only to be coerced into sex work.

I visited several clubs and parlors in Kathmandu and almost always found young, sleep-deprived, and drugged or drunk girls available for purchase. Massage parlors typically advertised Thai massage, Ayurvedic massage, or Nepalese "special massage." Some were legitimate parlors, but many were actually sex establishments, typically tucked away on the second or third floor of a residential building. There were usually small entry rooms in which proprietors arranged transactions. Behind the entry rooms were several numbered rooms with cots, upon which the massages were meant to occur. Similar to massage parlors in Thailand, asking for a massage in Kathmandu led to exchanges that would be comical in other circumstances. Prostitution is illegal in Nepal, so parlor owners do not explicitly solicit sex. It is up to the customer to do so, as I learned when I visited my first massage parlor. I walked up two flights of stairs to the reception area, where I was greeted by two women and two men.

"Hello, I would like a massage," I said.

"What kind of massage do you want?" one of the woman asked.

"Foot massage."

"We do not have foot massage," one of the men said.

"But your sign says you offer foot massages."

They mumbled in Nepalese.

"What kind of massage do you have?" I asked.

"What kind of massage do you want?" a woman asked.

"Foot massage."

More chatter in Nepalese.

"Okay," one of the men said, "Four hundred rupees for one hour."

"What about half an hour?"

"Two hundred rupees."

I agreed.

The woman behind the counter took my money and beckoned me through a curtain. I entered a small room with five young girls sitting in chairs. They were teenagers, wearing jeans and blouses. Some smiled; others made nervous eye contact.

"Which one do you like?" the woman asked.

"Do they speak English?" I asked.

"Maybe little."

I pointed to one of the girls who had not smiled.

"What is her name?" I asked.

"Resma," the woman replied.

I followed Resma up the stairs to a room that contained a twin bed wrapped in a filth-stained fitted sheet with a crumpled blue sheet on top. After we entered, I asked Resma where she was from. She shrugged as if she did not understand what I was saying. A moment later, the electricity went out. Resma said something in Nepalese and headed down the stairs. After a few minutes, she returned with candles, followed by the main woman from behind the counter. The woman took out the blue sheet and placed a fresh one atop it.

"This is for a foot massage?" I asked.

Lobby of Resma's massage parlor in Kathmandu

One of the men approached from the shadows. “No foot massage,” he said. “No hot water.”

“What kind of massage is there?” I asked.

“You can show this girl what you want.”

“I can get any massage I want?” I asked.

“Yes. You can show the girl.”

“Must I pay more money?”

The man grew exasperated. “You want hand job, fuck job, no problem,” he snipped, “You want something else, you pay more.”

It was then clear that Resma was not a masseuse. If she spoke English or Hindi, I might have been able to confirm my suspicion, but I chose instead to find a way out of the situation.

“I only want foot massage,” I told the man.

“No foot massage. No hot water.”

I shrugged my shoulders and walked down the stairs.

Other parlors were the same as Resma's. In each one, I found teenage girls who looked physically abused, and in each one, I was invited to choose a girl who would offer me a massage before later confirming that I was actually paying for sex. It would not take the Nepalese police more than a few minutes to investigate any of these massage parlors and discover the illicit sex operations, but as was the case in most countries I visited, police bribes were a customary part of the operation. Experts at Shakti Samuha told me that many of the girls were trained in Kathmandu before being sent to India, similar to the breaking-in process in Varanasi.

In addition to massage parlors, Kathmandu had around four hundred dance bars, each employing approximately twenty girls. The bars usually opened around eight o'clock in the evening, when the music was turned on and the girls started dancing. Each club had its own style: some played American music, some played Bollywood tunes, some were more aggressive in soliciting sex, some were less. Each had stages with dance poles and long horizontal sitting areas filled with tables. The girls sang and danced in skimpy outfits until around ten or eleven o'clock at night. When the club was full, the dancers sat with men at the tables and negotiated for sex. Bouncers patrolled to ensure that the girls closed good deals and were paid before leaving. Once the solicitation began, dancers came to my table in succession, and if I did not purchase sex within the first few visits, a bouncer asked me to vacate the table. In clubs where I saw sex for sale, there was always an attached massage parlor, the rooms of which were used for the transaction.

Many Nepalese girls were trafficked to these clubs, but many others initially came willingly. One girl from Janajati told me, "In my village we hear it is easy to make money for dancing. Once I came, we were pressured to have sex with clients. Now I am ashamed to go home." I cannot say for sure what proportion of young women in these dance clubs were coerced prostitutes, but the staff of Shakti Samuha told me that they had worked with numerous trafficking victims from the clubs and many more from the massage parlors. Neither the clubs nor the parlors appeared to be as violent as the brothels in India, though they were often the first step in a journey to those more savage places.

Sindhupalchok

Women have been exported from the remote hills of Sindhupalchok to India for sexual exploitation for almost sixty years. When the Rana dynasty came to power in Nepal in 1846, Jung Bahadur took young girls from the Helambu region of Sindhupalchok, called Helambu girls, for his personal gratification. Subsequent Ranas continued the practice until a 1951 revolt from which the Ranas fled to India. From exile in Delhi, the Ranas arranged for the transport of girls from Sindhupalchok for their continued pleasure. Such, I was told, was the beginning of the trafficking of Sindhupalchok females to India for sexual exploitation. The question was why the sex trade persisted decades later.

Sindhupalchok is strikingly remote. About a three-hour jeep ride northeast of Kathmandu, Sindhupalchok covers 2,542 square kilometers—about twice the size of greater Los Angeles—with a total population of a little over 335,000. The area consists of eighty-one districts spread across rugged mountains that reach as high as eight thousand feet. The inhabitants dwell in small villages that can only be reached by foot, usually several hours' hike up one hill and down another. The winding Dolalghat River is the primary source of water.

I spent two days and one very frigid night on a mat in a hut in three districts of Sindhupalchok: Pangretam, Thulopakhar, and Jethal. I also journeyed to the desolate Kodari border crossing with Tibet, one of the few passable routes into China for migrants and slave traders alike. In Sindhupalchok, entry into each district required extensive negotiations with the police at heavily guarded control stations, thanks to the Maoist insurgency, one of the primary drivers of human trafficking from Nepal.[10]

I was allowed into the deeper recesses of the region only because of local guides' assurances that I was a researcher with no subversive intentions. When I tried to visit Makwanpur, second only to Sindhupalchok as an origin of Nepalese sex trafficking victims, I was abruptly turned back not one hour from Kathmandu as a result of a guerilla attack on a police outpost the previous day.

In Sindhupalchok, I wanted to track down repatriated trafficking victims and their families to understand exactly why so many women and children were trafficked from its forbidding hills. A local NGO called Gramin Mahila Srijansil Pariwar (Community Women Awareness Family) assisted my search. Unfortunately, in my very first day at a village called Lamu Sanghu, I learned that it was virtually impossible to find repatriated trafficking victims in Sindhupalchok. Sushila's and Priti's anecdotes explained why: Young women trafficked for sex slavery were seen as a source of extreme shame. Mass ignorance about HIV/AIDS resulted in the misconception that the disease could be spread by touch, sneeze, or even the stare of an infected person. Virtually no trafficking victims from Sindhupalchok ever returned. A small number found their way to Kathmandu, but the majority remained in sex work for the rest of their lives.

Even though I did not meet sex trafficking victims in Sindhupalchok, I learned exactly why so many women were trafficked from this region. More than poverty, military conflict, or other social disasters, what drove rural women into the clutches of sex traffickers was a primary factor everywhere I investigated sex trafficking: Millions of women lived in a world that overwhelmingly disdained them.

In Sindhupalchok, females were systematically beaten, raped, denied basic rights, and brutally exploited by men. Desperation to escape this tyranny delivered them to slave traders. I encountered similar dynamics in every developing country I visited, but in the isolated villages of Sindhupalchok, the injustices against females transcended imagination. Women, children, and distraught parents from numerous villages traveled by foot for up to five hours when they heard that an American researcher was visiting to hear their stories. The victims I met ranged from ages seven to fifty-seven.

Puffy-eyed and distressed, a young woman named Uma told me that her husband had recently accused her of being a witch. As punishment, he and every man in the village gang-raped her. A few days later, her husband married a younger woman. Uma had no rights, no education, and no way to support herself without a husband. As a witch, not even her parents would accept her.

A fifty-three-year-old man named K. Khatri introduced me to Rupala, his somber, ten-year-old daughter. When Rupala was six, a seventy-year old man raped her.

"We have suffered great stigma since that time," K. Khatri told me. "The villagers shun my family because of what this man did."

Despite the stigma, K. Khatri stood up for his daughter. Rupala was the youngest of five children, of which he could afford to educate only one. He asked his eldest son to make the sacrifice of leaving school so that Rupala could be educated.

"Because of this rape, no man will marry my daughter, and no one will give her work," K. Khatri said. "I told my children if I do not educate her, she can never survive."

Family after family, woman after woman, child after child: The stories of violence fell upon me in waves. Countless children were raped by grown men. Countless husbands tortured their wives. Countless crimes passed without investigation. A woman named Laxmi told me that after her seven-year-old daughter Eka was raped, the police at the nearest checkpoint (two hours by foot) refused to travel to her village to investigate

Hut shared by K. Khatri's family and two other families in Sindhupalchok

because they felt it was too dangerous given the Maoist insurgency. A mother named Sonali told me that after she filed a complaint against the thirty-year-old man who raped her eight-year-old daughter four times in one night, the judge dismissed the case, citing insufficient evidence. The judge was the cousin of the rapist's father.

After two days of such tales, it was not difficult to see why Sindhupalchok was a breeding ground for sex slaves. When women were not being raped or abused, they were unable to survive due to a lack of education, job opportunities, and basic rights. Who could blame them for fleeing? If you were a beaten, starving woman in Sindhupalchok and an agent offered a job in a carpet factory or marriage to a fine Indian businessman, you would take the first bus out of town. No amount of border control or awareness-raising could stop you. Nothing could possibly be worse than the life you were already living.

When I asked the women of Sindhupalchok why the men treated them as they did, I invariably received the same two answers:

"This is our culture."

"Men want women as slaves."

Insufficient Resources and Unenforced Laws

Despite the suffering of hundreds of thousands of sex slaves throughout South Asia, the chief nations in which this suffering occurs do very little to address the problem.

India

The Suppression of Immoral Trafficking Act of 1956, renamed the Immoral Trafficking and Prevention Act (ITPA) in 1986, is India's most current anti-trafficking legislation. The act criminalizes pimping and running a brothel, yet pimps and brothels are everywhere. Even when the law is enforced, the penalties are minor: Brothel owners receive no more than three years' imprisonment and a maximum fine of forty-four dollars, pimps receive half this penalty, and there is no incremental fine for sex trafficking or for "detaining a person in the premises where prostitution is carried on."[11]

In addition to relatively anemic penalties, the number of prosecutions under the trafficking laws has been minimal. A few dozens criminals are convicted each year, but these numbers are deeply inadequate relative to the over two hundred thousand sex slaves in India. It is difficult to comprehend the absence of proactive measures (such as the raid in 1996) to liberate the country's sex slaves when it is so easy to walk into brothels in Kamathipura and Falkland Road and find them. Amid India's skyrocketing wealth and newfound global prominence, the country has all but forgotten the words uttered by Jawaharlal Nehru, its first prime minister, on the eve of independence:

> The future beckons to us . . . to bring freedom and opportunity to the common man, to the peasants and workers of India; to fight and end poverty and ignorance and disease . . . and to create social, economic and political institutions which will ensure justice and fullness of life to every man and woman.

Nepal

The Human Trafficking Control and Punishment Act of 2043 (2043 is equivalent to 1986 in the West) first criminalized the act of human trafficking in Nepal.[12] In 1999, the act received a more comprehensive update, including stipulations that it was a crime to enslave a person, to separate a minor or insane person from a guardian, or to force a woman or minor to perform sex work. Stiffer penalties included up to twenty years in prison for trafficking or purchasing a woman or minor, up to fifteen years in prison for sexually exploiting a woman or minor, and fines of up to two hundred thousand rupees ($2,666) for the aforementioned crimes.

Stipulations were also added to allocate money and assets collected from convicted offenders to compensate victims. However, top trafficking attorney Bhola Dhungana told me during a meeting in Kathmandu that in the few cases in which fines were collected and assets seized, the government did not distribute monies to the victims, citing the need to recoup the costs of prosecuting the case. Similar to India, prosecution of trafficking crimes in Nepal add up to no more than a handful each year,[13] even though the country has a special police unit for crimes against women. Sushila Singh, the deputy superintendent of this police cell, explained that her unit had only thirty officers who were supposed to investigate all crimes against women and children, including abuse, rape, abortion,[14] and trafficking. Superintendent Singh further said that her unit was heavily constrained because it received no funding from the Nepalese government other than minimal salary for her thirty officers. I asked Ms. Singh how many officers were in the drug-trafficking section of the police department. "Hundreds," she said. The drug-trafficking unit was fully funded by the Nepalese government, with top-of-the-line gear, vehicles, computers, and ample training and facilities. Ms. Singh was at a loss to explain why her country's war on drugs received so much more support than its war on slavery.

Mount Kailash

Two days after I met with Ms. Singh, I was supposed to fly from Nepal to Thailand, but on the morning of my departure I could not find my passport. I always kept it in a zipped pouch, buried in a zipped pocket in the bottom of a backpack, but when I checked for my passport before leaving my hotel, it was gone.

After a fruitless search in my luggage, hotel room, and the nearby money-exchange bureau, I raced to the U.S. embassy to apply for a replacement. At the embassy, I was told I had to go to the Yak and Yeti Hotel, where new passport applications were processed. At the hotel, I was greeted by a young lady who told me that new passports took two to three days to process, except for emergency cases of death or serious illness. Two to three days was not desirable, as I had several meetings scheduled in Bangkok the next day. The official said policy was policy and asked for my identification to begin the process. When she looked at my driver's license, she noticed that I lived in Santa Monica. As it turned out, she grew up not far from my apartment.

"Let me see what I can do," she said.

The official spoke with the consul and when she returned, she told me I could have a new passport by the end of the day. If I could get a new visa from Nepal immigration transferred to the new passport, which required a police report of the lost or stolen old passport, I might be able to leave the next day.

The first step was to procure new passport photos. I ran half a mile down the road to the closest photo shop, took the required photos, and ran back to the embassy, but the pictures were the wrong size. They were for a Nepal passport, not a U.S. passport. I ran back, got the properly sized photos, and gave them to the embassy. Next, I took a cab to the Thai Airways office and asked to be booked on a flight the next day. There were no seats available for three days, but the sales agent told me I could return the next morning in the event of last-minute cancellations. Disheartened but not dissuaded, I took a cab to the opposite side of town to the Interpol police office, where I needed to procure the police report that was required for my new visa. The Interpol police told me they had to conduct an investigation before they could issue a report. The investigation would take two to three days. I explained my situation, but the officer was unfazed. As he typed the investigation form, he said, "You are not American; you look Indian." I told him my parents were from India, though I was born in the United States. The officer said, "Let me see what can be done." He took me upstairs to his superior, who agreed to issue me a report without an investigation.

Report in hand, I rushed back to the U.S. embassy. My passport had been processed. I asked for the name of someone who could help me at Nepal immigration and raced to the office with five minutes to spare before closing. When I found my contact, she asked if I had a photocopy of my old thirty-day visa to transfer to the new passport. I showed her the photocopy and everything seemed in order until a debate among the immigration officials erupted as to how long I had been in the country. As it turned out, the officials at Jogbani had not properly processed my entry into Nepal, despite taking two hours to do so! They failed to date-stamp my immigration form, so there was no way to confirm if I had outstayed my original visa. The officials hinted that a bribe was the only way to proceed, but I did not offer one. Eventually, I received the new visa, and I went to find something to eat.

I treated myself to Mexican food and counted my blessings that everything had worked out. After finishing a vegetable burrito, I was wandering back to my hotel and noticed a few travel agencies open late. I entered one and inquired about tickets. The agent told me that the Thai Airways seats were cleared every night at nine, and that even though the sales office was closed, he could access the system for the seats that might be available before the morning rush. Two seats had opened up. I booked one.

As I continued to my hotel, I passed by a blaring dance club. A young girl, maybe eight years old, popped out of an alley and said, "Hello!"

"Hello," I replied.

She reached between her legs and patted herself.

"You want?" she asked.

My heart sank.

"Come, come," she said, and waved at me to follow.

I peered down the alley and saw a collection of closet-sized dwellings brimming with Tibetan refugees. Did this young girl even know what she was doing? Was she soliciting herself, her sister, her mother? I was too depleted to investigate further.

I dropped my head and trudged down the road. My thoughts turned to Shiva's thwarted meditation. Mount Kailash, where he was fabled to reside, was only a few hundred miles northeast of Kathmandu. Surely he was saddened. The world had indeed degraded into a plague of lust, greed, deceit, and violence. Untamed desire ran amok, governing the descent of man. I felt Shiva's solitude atop the icy peak and wished I could join him there.

After a sleepless night, I boarded a plane to Thailand.

3 Italy and Western Europe

All hope abandon, ye who enter here! —*Dante,* The Divine Comedy

Children of the Night

November brought a chill to the Roman air, but Julia wore only white panties and a matching bra. She shivered on the sidewalk as cars sped by on the busy Salaria. I asked if she felt cold. With tired azure eyes, she replied, "If I cover myself, I do not work."

Julia was seventeen and pregnant. She had arrived in Rome from Romania at the age of fourteen. Standing next to her, Alyssia was the same age and born in the same town. They had traveled together with the help of a man who had promised work in a restaurant. Instead, they spent the last three years as street prostitutes in Rome. Their "protector" (pimp) was never far away. He kept them locked in an apartment during the day and brought them to the streets at night. If his girls did not secure twenty clients per night, he would not let them eat. Such "protection" dumbfounded me. No one could say where the term came from, but calling a pimp a protector was akin to calling a man who purchased sex from teenage girls a guardian.

Street prostitution is legal in Italy, and in many major Italian cities, there are specific streets where prostitutes wait for men to drive by and purchase sex. In Rome, the three primary streets are the Salaria, Littoriania, and Via

Appia. In addition to street prostitution, there are countless massage parlors, nightclubs, apartment brothels, and house brothels that illegally sell sex behind closed doors. Many street prostitutes are victims of sex trafficking, but the majority of trafficking victims in Italy are exploited in closed-door establishments.

The night I met Julia, I met thirty other street prostitutes, twenty-seven of whom admitted that they were under the age of eighteen and thus working illegally as prostitutes. None were from Italy; they were from Romania, Russia, Moldova, Albania, Poland, the Ukraine, Belarus, Latvia, and Bulgaria. Meeting teenagers who had sex with twenty men per night was not easy. Despite their vocation, they appeared to be normal young girls. Even as they stood before me, half-naked children stripped down to bras and panties, my mind could not help but imagine those same children frolicking innocently at a sleepover party. I met these street prostitutes with the help of an NGO called Parsec, which the municipality of Rome permitted to send street units into prostitution areas to promote health and safety, including free condoms and abortions. The protectors typically allowed interaction with the street units; they encouraged the girls to go for the free abortions, thereby avoiding the expense themselves.

Morena, Nayla, and Shpresa were my guides in the street unit. We drove up and down the Salaria for hours in a van filled with information pamphlets, lubrication jelly, and condoms. Along the roadside, the girls huddled in groups of two or four. Small side roads branched off the Salaria, almost like the *gallis* off Falkland Road in India. The side roads were wooded and unlit. When men purchased girls, they took them to these alleys, where they completed the transaction in a car or in the bushes. The pace of purchase was rapid. More than once as we were conversing with a group of young women, multiple cars pulled up behind us and honked, as if any delay in purchase might make them late for dinner. On the side roads, I watched grown men take teenage girls into the bushes and emerge ten or fifteen minutes later. Old men, young men, filthy men on motorbikes, polished men in BMWs—each took the hands of children and defiled them. Gabriella, from Russia, told me that she had worked the streets since arriving two months ago and that almost every man refused to wear a condom. When we approached Angela, from Romania, she shrieked that we would get her killed. Anna from Poland asked me in perfect English with a spot-on American accent, "What is your name?"

"Siddharth," I told her.

She was twenty-five and had studied English in school until the age of seventeen. A man promised her work as a photo model, so she accompanied him to Rome. That same man sold her to the protector who had controlled her for the past seven years. Utterly relaxed, she asked me about my work, my family, and where I was from.

"I live in Los Angeles," I said.

"America!" she replied, "I have always wanted to go to America. How is life there? It must be great."

Later that night, I asked the street unit team, "Is it not illegal for minors to engage in prostitution, even if they say they choose to?"

"Yes," they replied.

"Then why don't the police assist them? Why don't they prosecute the protectors for pimping the minors?"

"The police are the main clients," I was told. "We see them here, time to time."

In a shelter in the north of Italy, I received several testimonials from victims of sex trafficking who were also forced to work as street prostitutes. One woman's saga began after Ukrainian independence, when the former Soviet central bank transferred all deposits from Kiev to Russia's central bank, thereby wiping out the life savings of hundreds of thousands of Ukrainians. In a desperate bid to earn income for her bankrupt family, she accepted what she thought was a job as a waitress in Italy. Another woman was trafficked from Bulgaria to Italy via Turkey after the promise of work as a nanny in Istanbul. Perhaps the most harrowing tale I heard was from a young Ukrainian named Bridgitte. Bridgitte was well educated with a nurse's degree, but her "pay slip" of thirty-five dollars per month was not nearly enough for her to make ends meet. She and her friends saw advertisements in newspapers for work in Italy, promising a monthly salary of four thousand dollars.

"We were stupid," Bridgitte told me, "We dream to find a rich and handsome husband to marry us, and love us, and cover us with gifts of diamonds. We were stupid."

Bridgitte was one of the innumerable East Europeans who were seduced by romantic illusions of a rich, fast-paced lifestyle in Western Europe, particularly after the fall of communism. Slave traders easily exploited dreams of a better life and the naiveté of youth. In Bridgitte's case, she was first trafficked to Serbia, where she was coerced into sex work in a nightclub. After a few months, she was re-trafficked to southern Italy via Albania and a speedboat across the Adriatic Sea. Agents met her at the coast and drove her and several other girls to northern Italy, where she was sold to a protector. Just like life on the Salaria, life on the streets near Venice and Mestre was a bleak sentence.

"The street is hell," Bridgitte explained. "The street completely destroyed me. I was always drunk, always not well covered in winter. The protector beat me constantly. The clients also beat me. I hated myself on the street."

The protector took most of Bridgitte's money, but he sent small amounts to her family in Ukraine. In this way, Bridgitte spent several years in sex slavery because her parents insisted she continue sending money. Bridgitte is the one who told me she felt like a "slot machine" to her family.

After several years of street prostitution, volunteers from an NGO called TAMPEP found Bridgitte passed out in an alley, bloodied and completely naked. She had several STDs and suffered critical psychological damage. Months later when she narrated her story, her dreams were as lucid as a child's.

"They only thing I want is to be normal," she said. "I dream for a husband, children, and a small house."

By Land, Air, and Sea

The complexity of the movement of slave labor from Eastern to Western Europe transcends comparison. An eighteen-year old girl named Tatyana exemplified the sophistication of the movement of victims across Europe more than any victim I met. Tatyana escaped sex slavery only two months before our meeting, after twenty-six months as a slave. Sunken, jittery, and morose, she explained that her journey began when she could not find work in her village near Chisinau, Moldova, to support herself and her single mother.

"My father died from cancer when I was ten, and my mother had weak bones, so she could not work," she said.

One day Tatyana responded to an advertisement in a newspaper called *Makler* for work as a housemaid in Italy.

"When I left home with the agents, they raped me and they did not feed me for days. They forced me to urinate in my clothes."

Like Bridgitte, Tatyana's first stop was Serbia, where she was forced to strip naked in front of potential buyers as they inspected her genitals for sexually transmitted diseases, her body for deformities, and her mouth to ensure she had all her teeth. Like a well-bred animal, she was a prized purchase for her Albanian traffickers, who compounded the humiliation of the inspection by testing her value as a sex slave. From Serbia, Tatyana's buyers drove to Albania, where she was sold a second time. In Albania, new buyers drove her to Greece, where they boarded a ferry for southern Italy. In southern Italy, Albanian men put her in the trunk of their car and drove straight to Milan, where she was sold to a man who owned a nightclub. Tatyana lived in the back of the club with several girls, all of whom shared one room and one toilet.

"They started the music at eight," Tatyana told me. "Every night there were men. I was with too many men."

The owner of the nightclub told Tatyana that she owed him four thousand euros for the cost of buying her and he would return her to Moldova after she slept with four hundred men. She slept with the required four hundred men in under two months, netting approximately twelve thousand euros for her owner and nothing for herself. The owner did not free Tatyana. Instead, he sold her to a protector who forced her to work on the streets. A few days later, she tried to escape, but with no money, no passport, and no ability to speak Italian, the protector's men tracked her down and locked her in an apartment, where they tortured her for several days.

Tatyana went back to work and did not try to escape. Like most sex slaves, she was kept in an alcohol- and drug-induced daze. "When I did not want to drink, the protector injected me with tranquilizers for animals," she told me. Eventually, Tatyana learned basic Italian and heard about a shelter from another prostitute. She had syphilis and two fractured fingers when she arrived there. Her uterus was severely damaged, rendering her unable to bear children. She also suffered nightmares, hallucinations, and memory loss. The Italian government provided her with a residency permit as well as psychological counseling and health care, but only if she signed a contract stipulating that she would testify against her protector and the nightclub owner; the former had not yet been found and charges were not yet filed against the latter.

"I do not want to testify in these trials," Tatyana told me, "The protector said he would kill me. He knows my village in Moldova. I am afraid for my mother. I want to go home."

Because Italy is one of the closest West European countries to the poorer countries of Central and Eastern Europe, and because it has an extensive coastline that facilitates clandestine entry by sea, it is one of the top destinations of sex trafficking victims in Western Europe. There are several common trafficking routes. The Italian-Austrian border is an open border with no controls, used for entry from Austria to Udine along Highway A23 by Central and East European traffickers. Highway A23 joins Highway A4, which passes through major the destination cities of Venice, Milan, and Turin. At the Italian-Slovenian border, traffickers cross the heavily wooded areas near Trieste on foot. Cars, buses, and vans have also been used in conjunction with border bribes to cross the border on Highway A4. The Italian-French border is a key route utilized by Nigerian traffickers, who take individuals on an arduous land journey from Nigeria to the North African coast of the Mediterranean Sea, then a boat to Spain or France, and finally a flight or train from Madrid or Paris directly to Rome, Milan, or Turin. The Apulian Coast is an entry point for speedboats from Albania and Greece, and to a lesser extent, for ships from Turkey that bring victims from the Middle East and South Asia. The Sicilian Coast is an entry point for boats from North Africa that can include victims from Africa as well as the Middle East; more recently, South Asians also have been trafficked through the Middle East by this route. Finally, all nationalities are trafficked through the Rome, Turin, and Milan airports, though Nigerians are flown more frequently than are other nationalities.

Estimates of the number of sex trafficking victims in Italy vary, but the purchase prices of these slaves are well established. Tabulating them is almost like writing a menu, as table 3.1 shows.

TABLE 3.1
Sex Slave Purchase Prices: Italy (euros)

Origin Country	Purchase Price	Price of Sex Act
Brazil	5,000	40
China	5,000	40
Russia	3,500	30
Moldova	3,500	30
Bulgaria	3,500	30
Poland	3,500	30
Albania	3,000	25
Ukraine	3,000	25
Hungary	3,000	25
Latvia	3,000	25
Romania	2,000	20
Nigeria	—	20

As in India and Nepal, the price of a sex act in Italy has substantially decreased across the last decade. At a café in Rome, Italian trafficking expert Paola Monzini explained that prices for sex have dropped as much as 50 percent in Italy, a direct result of the massive influx of low-priced East European and Nigerian sex slaves. Because of this drop in market price, Monzini told me, "it has become more and more a part of Italian culture to frequent prostitutes."

From Italy, victims are re-trafficked to almost every country in Western Europe. In addition to sex trafficking, East Europeans are heavily trafficked for construction throughout Europe, and children are trafficked for begging, petty theft, domestic work, and sweat shops. A more recent trend, according to Daniela Mannu, an expert who taught me more than anyone else about trafficking in Italy, is the trafficking of minors from Bulgaria, Romania, and Moldova for organ harvesting. Little is known about this practice other than the fact that, to some extent, Italian hospitals are complicit in the crimes, in which children are killed and their internal organs removed, to be transplanted later into ailing Italians.

Edo and Juju

"She good makin' suck, mistah man. She good, twenty euros."

Such is the pidgin-English dialect of the Nigerian street prostitutes on Corso Massimo D'Azeglio in Turin, near the verdant Parco del Valentino that hugs the River Po. There are more Nigerian sex slaves in Italy than any other nationality. In Turin, the Nigerians own the Corso Massimo D'Azeglio in the same way that East European street prostitutes own the nearby Via Ormea. Organized crime groups operating in Turin have made these geographic arrangements to avoid direct competition, ensure sufficient working space for their prostitutes, and enable clients to know exactly where to find what they want. In addition to these streets, the northern end of Corso Regina Margherita and the industrial areas in the north and south of Turin are populated with street prostitutes of various nationalities.

The dynamics of Nigerian sex trafficking are the most unique of any nationality I encountered. According to Rosanna Paradiso, director of TAMPEP in Turin, the trafficking of Nigerians to Italy was originally facilitated by commercial ties forged between the two countries in the 1970s, when Italian oil companies descended on Nigeria to grab their piece of the bounty. Civil war raged during this period, resulting in the deaths of over one million Nigerians and the displacement of millions more. Today, Nigeria is one of the poorest countries in the world, with a per capita income of $1,154, runaway inflation, and a massive debt load to the IMF that drains government coffers at the expense of social services. Over 90 percent of Nigerians eke out a destitute existence on fewer than two dollars per day. Famine, war, and HIV condemn the average Nigerian to a life lasting only forty-three years, among the lowest life expectancies in the world (see appendix C). As a result, trafficking in Nigerian women is a thriving business. Little or no subterfuge is involved and victims are sold in Italy to local madams who manage up to twenty sex slaves each. Up to 80 percent of Nigerian sex trafficking victims in Italy belong to a single ethnic group, the Edo, who live in the mid-southern region of Nigeria where interethnic conflict over oil towns continues to rage. Paradoxically, the Edo are one of the most conservative groups in Nigeria. Prostitution is strictly forbidden and if a married woman is even touched by a man who is not her husband, she is duty-bound to report this affront to her husband, and he obliged to ensure that she undergoes special purification rights to cleanse her.

An Edo woman's journey to Italy is lengthy and dangerous, involving rituals that employ levels of control far more powerful than the typical tactics that slave owners use. The journey begins with a trolley, a recruiter in Nigeria who usually knows the woman's family. The trolley paints a rosy picture of life in Italy and promises a high income. If the woman signs up, she is sent to a trafficker, who arranges an arduous land journey to Morocco through Niger and Algeria. From Morocco, boats are taken across the Strait of Gibraltar into Spain. From Spain, trains or planes are taken to Italy. Some Nigerians travel to Tunisia and take a boat directly to Sicily. A small number are flown directly from Lagos.

Before this grueling journey begins, the woman must first undergo specific juju rites, in which the woman's pubic hair, nails, and menstrual blood are collected and placed before a traditional shrine. During the ritual, the woman is made to swear an oath to repay her debt, never to report to the police, and never to discuss the nature of her trip with anyone. Failure to uphold this oath results in grave misfortune for the woman and her family. These rituals create a powerful hold over the victim, so much so that almost no Nigerian trafficking victims ever attempt to escape sex slavery before repaying their debts. Unlike the East European street prostitutes I saw in Rome, no protectors kept a watchful eye on the Nigerians. When

Nigerian victims are rescued and asked to discuss their ordeals, some enter into trances or suffer fits. Testifying in court is out of the question. Nigerian sex slaves live in constant fear, convinced that they and their families are in imminent danger due to the juju rites. As one Nigerian sex slave who suffered punishing beatings, starvation, and belt whips at the hands of her madam told me, "I can never be safe. My life is over."

Once the Nigerian women arrive in Italy, they are sold at slave auctions to the highest-bidding madam. The bid is not the same as a purchase price; rather, it is a bid for control. The winning madam receives the pouch filled with the woman's juju hair and blood, thereby conveying absolute control of the victim to her. After the madam takes possession of the new slave, she informs her that she will house and feed her, and in exchange, the slave must perform sex work until she has paid back a debt of up to fifty thousand euros. This sum is up to ten times the debts imposed on sex slaves of other nationalities. At twenty euros per sex act, minus deductions for housing, food, clothing, and so-called street corner rental of up to five hundred euros per month, it takes several thousand sex acts for a Nigerian slave to be freed. Just like Bridgitte's protector and the *dalals* in Mumbai, the madams send money to families in Nigeria to entice other families to send their women.

As Nigerian prostitutes work off their debts, the madams subject them to harsh living conditions, starvation, and other forms of abuse. If a woman becomes pregnant, the madam administers a back-alley abortion without anesthetic. Pregnancy is common, as Nigerian madams insist that their prostitutes perform sex without condoms in order to raise the prices of sex acts. Eventually, if a Nigerian sex slave is freed from her debt, she might continue working to save enough money to buy her own slaves. In Kamathipura, Silpa (see chapter 2) underwent a similar transformation from slave to slave manager. My efforts to interview working Nigerian sex slaves proved unsuccessful. None were willing to speak to me about anything other than the price of sex, except for one woman who offered me a short statement on a street corner in Turin. Her words were translated from pidgin English by the staff of a local NGO who knew her well because she had spent three weeks in their shelter before returning to the streets:

> I worked for my madam eight months. She was not painful. The men are painful. I went to the shelter, but when I spoke to my mother she said my uncle was sick and my daughter was sick. I

knew the madam did this. Now she hurts me. She cuts me here, on my leg, every night before I sleep.

Very Organized Crime

More than South Asia, East Asia, Africa, or anywhere else in the world, the slave trading industry throughout Eastern and Western Europe is operated by organized crime. Italy in particular is a hub in the female sex trade for numerous international mafia groups. I learned how these criminal organizations traffic people in and out of Italy from a special detective on trafficking in minors named Michael (a pseudonym). I met Michael in Turin at a coffee shop near a restaurant called the Stars and Roses. He had been working several years to thwart the trafficking of minors into Italy, and he agreed to speak to me on condition of absolute anonymity. Michael was a man with intense eyes, a taut face, and genuine anguish. He had witnessed horrendous suffering by countless children and he harbored acerbic disdain for the criminals who inflicted it upon them.

"There are five main organized crime groups that traffic women and children into Italy," Michael told me. "Albanian, Romanian, Russian, Nigerian, Chinese." Michael explained that each group operated in three tiers: high, middle, and low. The high-level operators were big bosses with big money. They managed the overall transport of individuals from origin to destination as well as contacts with political, diplomatic, and law-enforcement officials to ensure safe passage and arrival. They also organized the sale of victims to brothel owners and pimps in the destination countries. The mid-level operators oversaw specific territories, usually along the borders of the destination countries. They knew the borders well and facilitated transport across them. They also provided false documents, interacted with corrupt police, and chose the exact routes to be taken on any given day. The low-level operators worked in destination cities and delivered victims to the final point of exploitation. They might be taxi drivers or grunt men who took a small commission from the sale price and passed the remainder back to the mid-level operators, who took their cut and sent the bulk of the money to the bosses at the top. These high-level bosses typically reinvested trafficking profits into other illicit businesses—drugs, firearms—as well as legitimate businesses, such as travel or job agencies, that facilitated slave-trading operations. Not every organized crime group operated in this neat, tiered fashion, but according to Michael, most of them did, most of the time.

Once victims were transported to Italy, each crime group demarcated its territory in each city. In cities south of Florence, they did so in coordination with Italian mafias. North of Florence, the Italian mafias did not control territories for prostitution (only for drugs). As a result, more victims were trafficked for sexual exploitation to northern Italy than southern, thereby avoiding mafia pay-offs. In the south, there were four main Italian mafias: Camorra in Campana, Sacra Corona Unita in Puglia, Ndrangheta in Calabria, and the Cosa Nostra in Sicily (of *The Godfather* fame). These four mafias generated annual revenues in excess of one hundred billion dollars, much of it from drug smuggling, money laundering, extortion, and of course, human trafficking. If an Albanian or Romanian organized-crime group wanted to operate a nightclub as a cover for prostitution in any of these regions, they first had to obtain permission from the relevant Italian mafia and pay around 5 percent of revenues to that mafia. Beyond Italy, each crime group possessed extensive networks in almost every country throughout Western Europe.

"Italy is the starting point," Michael told me. "These victims are bought and sold in three, four, maybe five EU countries before they are discarded."

According to Michael, each foreign organized-crime group also had its distinctive habits and practices. The Chinese were the most secretive, and most Chinese slave trading was for forced labor near Milan in textile mills and sweatshops. Some victims also worked as prostitutes in massage parlors. Michael told me that the Romanian crime groups were the best at electronic crime, including credit-card fraud and using the Internet to solicit customers for child pornography and prostitution. Increasingly, the Romanians arranged for the sale of trafficked minors electronically, through emails and web pages. The Romanians were also the first to start a rental market for sex slaves in Italy. Rather than sell women outright, the Romanians began leasing them to protectors or brothel owners for six to twelve months at a time. In this scheme, the brothel owner paid 100 percent of revenues generated by the slave to the lessee (the crime group) for the first three months, then one-half of revenues after the third month. The arrangement sounded remarkably similar to the system controlling many sex slaves in India, wherein the slave owner first retained all revenues from the sale of sex for a period of time, then provided the slave the option to transition to an *adhiya* system and share 50 percent of revenues with the owner. In the Italian rental system, the brothel owner could return the slave to the lessee at any time in exchange for a new slave. In that way, the brothel owner avoided large up-front acquisition costs and could provide a greater variety of slaves to the consumer. For its part, the crime group enjoyed multiple, ongoing revenue streams from a single slave, as opposed to one lump sum up front.

Finally, Michael told me that of all the foreign crime groups, the Albanians were the most frequent "triple-play" traffickers, involving females, firearms, and drugs in a single shipment, usually across the Adriatic Sea. He also told me they were the most ruthless.

"I do not mean the others are like saints," he said.

> They are all violent. I can tell you that in 1990, the number of foreign women murdered in Italy was 5 percent of all murders, and last year [2004] it was 25 percent. This is because the crime groups kill trafficked women in Italy when they escape or try to testify. The Albanians murder the most. When we find Albanian trafficking victims, they beg us not to arrest them because they fear death for their families. This is how the Albanians keep the women from testifying. If a victim is arrested, her family is killed. If she does not have a family, her friends are killed. If she does not have friends, her neighbors are killed. It does not matter, they find someone to kill.

Michael ended our conversation by narrating an incident involving an Albanian minor that continued to haunt him:

> We conducted one raid about four months ago after a tip that minors were working as prostitutes in one apartment. When we raided this apartment, we found six girls, one from Albania. They were children. They were not yet fourteen years. Five girls came quietly with us, but the Albanian girl begged me not to take her. She begged me to leave her behind. "They will kill my mother!" she shouted. She was hysterical. It was against the law for me to do this, but I left her in the apartment. I left her to be a slave, so her family would not be killed.

Broken Heart, Find a Friend

In Italy, street prostitutes of myriad nationalities were easy to find. Finding closed-door sex slaves such as the child Michael described took more work. Closed-door venues included apartment brothels, club brothels, massage parlors, and house brothels. As with every country I visited, I endeavored to see firsthand the closed-door venues in which sex slaves were exploited. My efforts to uncover closed-door sex slavery in Italy proved challenging. I could not identify any club brothels, but I did find apartment brothels, massage-parlor brothels, and house brothels. My search began in northern Italy, with the help of the newspaper and my friend, Daniella Mannu, who informed me that the "Broken Heart" or "Find a Friend" sections of any major newspaper were the best ways to find sex slaves. Ms. Mannu and her colleagues had performed extensive research on these ads, calling the numbers and uncovering dozens of apartments, clubs, and massage parlors in which sex slaves were held captive. In ads like "Suzy, beautiful, 20 yrs, just arrived, sweet and sexy," Daniella showed me the key words: "Just arrived" almost always meant a trafficking victim, and "all day, no stop" meant there were several girls in an apartment brothel. Numerous massage parlors were also advertised—Japanese, Chinese, East European. Daniela told me most of these were covers for brothels.

After dinner at the Mestre train station, I started dialing numbers. The first four numbers went nowhere as the women who answered could not speak English. On the fifth try, I dialed an ad for "Marisa," who was "young, fine, beautiful, and nice" and "received everyday."

"Pronto!" a female voice answered, with the traditional Italian greeting.

"Do you speak English?" I asked.

"Yes."

"I am calling for Marisa."

"Marisa is not here, but we have others."

"Can I see them?"

I was told to go to the corner of Via Lussingrande and Via Giuseppe Calucci and call again for directions. I went to the designated corner and rang. I was asked what I was interested in, and I responded, "Italian girls, like Marisa." The woman told me to walk to an apartment building a few blocks from where I was standing, ring the buzzer for "Isabella Laggio," and climb the stairs to apartment 2C. I rang the buzzer and entered. The building was dark, quiet, and empty. I contemplated turning around, but when I arrived at the apartment, I steadied my nerves and knocked on the door. A woman in her forties opened it. She had big, black hair and smelled like bathroom freshener. "I am here for a girl," I said as gallantly as I could. She nodded me inside. I stepped into the sitting room of a smoky, dark apartment. There was a small kitchenette to my right with several empty beer bottles on the counter. To my left, two men sat on a black couch drinking beer as they watched football (soccer) on television. One wore an orange and gray long-sleeve rugby shirt. The other had shaved his head bald, but a shadow of black seedlings darkened his scalp. There was no sign of prostitutes, but a sliver of light slipped through the bottom of a hallway door and I suspected it led to a bedroom, maybe two.

The moment I stepped into the apartment, I wanted to leave. Bungalow brothels in India were one thing—there were people around, and I felt safe in the crowd. This apartment was empty, and I did not want to take one step further inside. The sophistication of a slave owner's mental screening process was not to be underestimated. Though I had successfully posed as a buyer many times before, I had never done so in a tiny apartment. One false step, and my research could take an undesirable turn. I started to think of a way out, and fortunately the hostess of the apartment offered one. She told me they did not have Italian girls, only East European. I told her I was not interested in East Europeans. She said I would not be disappointed: "The girls are young and fresh." I maintained my preference for Italian girls and headed out the door and down the stairs. Once I was a few blocks from the apartment, I quickened my pace until I found a taxi and returned to the train station. I never saw for certain if there were East European sex slaves in that apartment, but if I had to bet, I would wager there were.

After a night in Venice, I returned to Mestre and sought out a massage parlor. The newspaper was again my guide. Most listings advertised Japanese or Oriental massage. I had no doubt that the majority of these massage parlors contained sex slaves. One of the largest massage chains in Italy, Viva Line, was raided by police in 2003, freeing dozens of sex slaves. On the third phone call, I found a woman who spoke English. I took directions for a Japanese massage parlor not far south of the Mestre train station. The parlor announced itself with bright red neon lights: "Japanese Massage." Inside I saw several young girls sitting on chairs and an older woman at a desk. The conversation that followed was as ridiculous as any I had in Nepalese and Thai massage parlors. No massages were actually available, at least none that did not end in a sex act. Even more absurd, none of the girls were Japanese; they were Chinese. They looked older than the girls I typically saw in massage parlors. I was supposed to select one of these individuals and spend up to thirty minutes in a back room. The price tag was forty euros.

The previous day, Claudio Donadel, director of a government-run trafficking shelter in Mestre, had informed me that the trafficking of Chinese women to Italy was escalating and that victims exploited for commercial sex were primarily located in massage parlors. I wondered how it could be such common knowledge that Chinese sex slaves were masquerading as masseuses, Japanese or otherwise, and yet the police did nothing, just as they did nothing for the minors on the Salaria in Rome. It was possible that these young Chinese women had willingly traveled to Italy to work as prostitutes, but how possible? None of them spoke a word of English and I did not have any shelter pamphlets written in Chinese, so I left the parlor and caught a train to Turin, where I hoped to find the most elusive Italian prison of sex slavery: a house brothel.

I had received tips that there were house brothels in between Turin and Milan and that a taxi driver would be my best bet for finding one. I queried a few taxi drivers near the Puerto Nuovo train station in Turin without any luck. Because of their limited English, I had to communicate with words like "sex" and "villa," but to no avail. I walked ten minutes east to Via Ormea and found three East European street prostitutes. I asked them where I could find a brothel, but they insisted that I solicit one of them instead. Within a few minutes, a heavily bearded protector joined the conversation. Though he likewise insisted I purchase one of his prostitutes, he eventually arranged for a taxi to take me to a villa about thirty minutes east of Turin, wait for an hour, and return to the train station.

I was not terribly inclined to take a trip out of the city alone with a taxi driver that the protector recommended, but I could see no other way to confirm that house brothels actually existed. My taxi driver was a jovial fellow named Enzo, possibly one of the low-level operatives that Michael had described. Enzo was quite enchanted by the fact that I was an American. As we drove to the house brothel, he repeatedly said, "America, oh yes!" His spontaneous cheer helped ease my nerves.

Enzo pulled into a wooded street not far from the outskirts of Turin and parked in front of a two-story villa. The villa was surrounded by a short stone wall with a steel gate. Enzo followed me in. A bouncer stood at the front door smoking. He checked my backpack and found only my money belt and day calendar. I could not tell if Enzo knew the bouncer, but I suspected he had brought several men here before. Inside, the villa opened to a large parlor with couches, a bar area, a staircase, and several girls lounging in tawdry dresses. I took a seat at the bar and Enzo sat next to me. He ordered a Peroni and asked if I wanted one. I declined. Enzo egged me to take a girl as he chatted with the narrow-faced bartender. I thought the prostitutes might approach me and push for sex, but they did not. Some read magazines and some played cards. Some chatted amiably; others stared blankly. I listened intently, but I could not hear anyone speaking English. The women were entirely East European and most looked very young. On a few occasions, women came down the stairs with men, and other men entered the villa and walked upstairs with other women. The pace of purchase was not fast. About ten men smoked in the bar area. At most I counted sixteen females in the villa. European club music played from a boom-box stereo.

After Enzo finished his beer, he asked, "No girl?" I knew there was little chance any of the women spoke English, but I also knew there was at least one task I could accomplish. I pointed to the individual closest to me. She was a teenage brunette. Enzo indicated to the bartender that I wanted to make a purchase. The price was sixty euros, twice the price of an East European street prostitute. I figured I was getting the noninsider price—the price they would give to someone who did not regularly frequent the establishment—but I chose not to haggle, even though I did not want to contribute to the brothel's profits any more than necessary. I paid the money and walked upstairs.

Inside the young girl's room, I felt anxious. If anything went wrong, I could not speak Italian and I was far away from urban safety. I immediately asked the young girl if she spoke English. She stared blankly. I pulled out my folded, day-calendar map of the world and showed it to her. I pointed to myself, then to the United States. Next, I pointed to her and showed her the map. She offered a quizzical look. I repeated the sign-language query. She looked at the map and pointed to Lithuania. I figured a teenager from Lithuania had not traveled willingly to an Italian brothel to work as a prostitute, so I offered her a TAMPEP pamphlet tucked inside an envelope inside my money belt. She declined. I thought she might be afraid the pamphlet was too large to conceal, so I tore off the portion on which the phone number was listed, placed it in her hand, and with the gesture of a telephone I said, "Appoggio. Liberta." Assistance. Freedom. It was the best I could do.

I took the young girl's hands and said, "God be with you."

On the drive back to Turin, Enzo chanted, "America, oh yes!"

Confusing Laws, Poorly Enforced

Despite the large number of sex slaves trafficked to Italy since the 1980s, there was no law that specifically addressed victims of human trafficking until August 11, 2003.[1] Italian Law 228, containing measures against trafficking in human beings, prescribed eight to twenty years' imprisonment for the crime of human trafficking, and a more severe sentence in cases with aggravating circumstances, such as trafficking in minors. Unfortunately, there are no financial penalties outlined in this law, and despite a large-scale trafficking crackdown in late 2006 called Operation Spartacus, the levels of prosecution and conviction in Italy remain ineffectively low. Cristina Bianconi, special prosecutor for trafficking cases at the Institute of Justice in Turin, explained that since the passage of Law 228, between one hundred and one hundred fifty cases per year have been filed in Italy under it, with only a handful of convictions. More than half the cases were for Nigerian trafficking victims. Unlike in developing countries, corruption in law enforcement and the judiciary is not the primary obstacle to effective prosecution in Italy. Rather, limited resources for investigation as well as a lack of government-level cooperation with neighboring countries constrict trafficking investigations.

A more prohibitive obstacle to prosecuting trafficking crimes effectively in Italy is the fact that prostitution is legal, and though brothels and pimping are not, the illegality of the latter is poorly enforced. Brothels were outlawed in Italy in 1958 by Law 75/1958, known as The Merlin Law after Legge Merlin, the woman who proposed it. This same law decriminalized prostitution. The initial logic of criminalizing brothels while decriminalizing prostitution appeared sound. Adult women were given the right to choose prostitution, but brothels were forbidden because they proved to be exploitative and dangerous. Lawmakers felt the Merlin Law would safeguard the interests of prostitutes by relocating control of a woman's body from the pimp to the female. Unfortunately, the reality proved to be different. Prostitutes suffered harassment by police and were still controlled by pimps. With the massive influx of East European trafficking victims during the 1990s, Italian society blamed foreign women—and not the men who purchased them—for the moral degradation of their culture. As a result, street prostitutes were pushed inside to apartments, massage parlors, nightclubs, and house brothels.

Once inside, trafficking victims were subject to greater exploitation. Calls to legalize brothels returned, under the logic that if prostitutes were going to work behind closed doors, they might as well do so with the government safeguarding their interests. Other voices called for the opposite, the total criminalization of all forms of prostitution, arguing that the slightest sliver of legality led to the sexual exploitation of women, particularly trafficking victims and minors.

The debate to legalize or criminalize prostitution is hotly contested, with cogent arguments on either side. While prostitution and sex trafficking are not the same, it is undeniable that wherever prostitution is found, there are trafficked slaves forced to provide sex services. Any debate on the legal status of prostitution directly affects anti-trafficking efforts. My examination of the question of legalization will thus be aimed at the best way to eradicate the practice of sex trafficking.

To Legalize or Not to Legalize

The argument that prostitution should be legalized primarily rests on the premise that women have a right to control their bodies. Legalization would mean that prostitutes could enjoy the same benefits that other occupations do: health care, retirement plans, and unionization, to name a few. Legalization would also allow for state monitoring to ensure that prostitutes were less subject to violence and exploitation. Finally, legalization would make it more difficult to traffic women and children for sexual exploitation because such victims would have rights under the law, whereas criminalizing prostitution leads to increased victimization of trafficking victims, who are often arrested for prostitution.

Opponents of legalizing prostitution argue that purchasing sex and operating sex establishments should be criminalized because prostitution can never be a choice and the "profession" is inherently based on a system of male sexual dominance, appropriating the female body for pleasure and reinforcing the subordination and sexual objectification of women. Further, legalization provides cover for brothel owners to purchase trafficking victims and inflict greater exploitation behind closed but legal doors. Only governments, organized crime, and pimps benefit from legalization; women and children suffer state-sanctioned rape and slavery.

Whereas Italy straddles the line between these two positions, two European countries have taken firm stands on either side of the debate: the Netherlands and Sweden. To determine what happens when a country legalizes all forms of prostitution, I went to the Netherlands to find out.

Amsterdam's red-light district (*de wallen*) is brimming with prostitutes—in windows, on the street, and in brothels and sex clubs. Outside of red-light districts, the country's *tipplezones* serve as designated areas for street prostitution. Now shut down, the *tipplezone* in Amsterdam was once on a street called Theemsweg, and when I visited it was teeming with minors from Albania, Romania, and Nigeria (though I did not manage a conversation with any of them). Window prostitutes in *de wallen* were the easiest to access. At the corner of Oudezids Voorburg Wal and Enge Kerkstreet, I found twenty of the city's four hundred window booths, addressed two to forty, by twos. This was a Nigerian section of the red-light area, and one Nigerian prostitute stood in each window booth. Red neon lights glowed along the perimeters of windows, signifying that sex was for sale. Each booth possessed a small bed with clean sheets, a sink, a dark curtain to be pulled across the window when a client was inside, and black lights that cast an incandescent glow on the prostitute's white lingerie. Some window booths also had a small bathroom. Few were larger than four feet wide by ten feet long. They struck me as much fancier and cleaner versions of the Indian *pinjaras*. Each of the Nigerian prostitutes smiled or tapped on the window as I walked by.

I had a few brief conversations with Nigerian window prostitutes, learning little more than that they were from Nigeria, usually in their twenties, and charged twenty euros for oral sex and fifty euros for full sex (prices in the *tipplezones* were as little as one-half this amount, and in the top end sex clubs they pushed three hundred euros). Each conversation I had was heavily monitored by a pimp, who would not allow dialogue to continue for more than a few minutes without a purchase. There was no way to know for certain whether these women were trafficked, but a local trafficking expert informed me that of the twenty-five thousand prostitutes in Amsterdam, 80 percent were foreigners and the majority of these were trafficking victims. The best circumstantial evidence I gathered that the Nigerians were sex trafficking victims was from their pimps' behavior. Shortly after a few conversations with the prostitutes, I walked to a bench near the corner of Oudezids Voorburg Wal and Enge Kerkstreet to write down the name of the intersection be-

Amsterdam's red-light district (*de wallen*)

cause the spellings were difficult to remember. Not five seconds after I opened my notebook, an African man dashed towards me and demanded, "You speak Dutch?"

"No," I replied.

He tried to inspect my writings, but I did not want him to see my notes, so I snatched the notebook back and said in a stern voice, "Excuse me. This is my private information."

"This is also private!" he grunted, as he gesticulated to the window girls on the street. "You cannot take anything from this private!"

I closed my notebook and wondered why the pimp was so nervous. Window prostitutes were legal in Amsterdam. They were supposed to be willing sex workers with papers and a union called the Rodedraad ("red thread") that protected their rights, so what was the problem? After the encounter, I went for a falafel dinner and returned to the same bench an hour later. I noticed that the bench afforded a lovely view of the adjacent canal, so I pulled out my camera to take a picture. Like a bolt of lightning, another pimp charged at me from fifty feet away. "No picture of girls!" he yelled. A second pimp followed, and they demanded to see my camera. I showed them on the camera's screen that I had not taken any pictures of their girls. They stammered off repeating, "No picture of girls!"

There are cogent reasons why a pimp would not want a tourist to take pictures of his legitimate prostitutes. Perhaps he did not want me to post pictures on the Internet and charge clients to see them. Perhaps he was afraid that I was a competitor and would take pictures of his operation so I could set up my own. Or perhaps his prostitutes had been trafficked and forced to perform commercial sex work. Perhaps he was afraid that I would take the pictures to the authorities and expose his illegal operations. Even if the Nigerians were legal immigrants who were willingly working as prostitutes, Nigeria is not one of the foreign nationalities that the Dutch government allows to engage in prostitution in the Netherlands while working for an employer.[2]

A few blocks south of the Nigerian prostitutes, at 90 Dolebegjnin Steed, I found a very narrow alleyway with barely enough room for two people to cross. Two pimps stood at either side of each entrance. The alley was lined with window prostitutes, all from Eastern Europe. I spoke to women from Russia, Ukraine, and Romania, and other than the fact that they looked like teenagers (though they did not admit it), I learned that they charged about ten to twenty euros more for sex than the Nigerians did. I also learned that while prostitutes in other countries were almost always willing to lower the price to close a transaction, the Amsterdam prostitutes stuck to their prices. This firmness was a result of working in a legal red-zone area, where the legality of prostitution allowed pimps to charge more for a sex act because customers had easy access to women and could not be prosecuted for the purchase. The combination of minimum labor costs through the exploitation of slave labor and maximum retail prices afforded by legality made Amsterdam a compelling venue for any sex trafficker.

Prostitution was historically legal in Amsterdam, but the ban on brothels was only lifted on October 1, 2000.[3] Local authorities license new brothels contingent on adherence to certain standards, including panic buttons in work areas, hot and cold running water, and free condoms. According to the Dutch government, the ban on brothels was lifted because "the legalization of brothels enables the government to exercise more control over the sex industry and counter abuses. The police conduct frequent controls of brothels and are thus in a position to pick up signs of human trafficking. This approach is in the interests of the prostitutes themselves, and it facilitates action against sexual violence and abuse and human trafficking."[4] The primary problem with the Dutch government's position is that it does not allow the police to register prostitutes and medical checkups are not compulsory. As a result, the government cannot truly know if a prostitute has been trafficked, if she is in the country illegally, or if she is being abused and tortured. The police are allowed to inspect brothels if they "pick up signs of human trafficking,"[5] but it is unclear how they pick up these signs—and even if they do, they can only conduct inspections with the consent of the mayor that licensed the brothel. Local experts informed me that inspections were rarely carried out, primarily because of bribes paid to the relevant mayor. The contradiction of legalizing brothels while erecting hurdles to law-enforcement access to prostitutes makes it astoundingly simple for a brothel owner to import sex slaves, lock them up, and exploit them. The only way someone might confirm that a prostitute was trafficked, lacked proper documentation, or was exploited by a pimp would be to take notes in a notebook or snap a few pictures.

The Dutch government confesses that the effect of legalization on sex trafficking is unclear: "A study was conducted two years after the ban on brothels had been lifted, but it was too soon to draw any conclusions about its impact."[6] Despite the lack of conclusive data, observations from local experts indicated that, if anything, sex trafficking in Amsterdam increased after brothels were legalized. Even a Kurdistani shopkeeper told me that since the ban on brothels was lifted, "there are more foreign prostitutes in Amsterdam, especially from East Europe." According to the Dutch national rapporteur on trafficking in human beings, between 2000 and 2004, sex trafficking victims hailed from over fifty countries.[7] Half the victims were under the age of twenty-three and almost half had been prostitutes in another country before arriving in Amsterdam,[8] demonstrating the high level of re-trafficking throughout Europe as well as the strong link between prostitution and sex slavery. Interestingly, the national rapporteur quantified the average financial benefit enjoyed by convicted traffickers. In 2002, the average was 115,384 euros. In 2003, it was 193,776 euros.[9] Despite this data, the fines imposed on convicted traffickers are rarely greater than a few thousand euros.

While I did not have the opportunity to travel to Sweden to explore the effect of its ban on the purchase of sex services, it is worth discussing the logic of the ban and the preliminary results related to sex trafficking. Sweden passed its law prohibiting the purchase of sexual services on January 1, 1999. This groundbreaking law became the first to focus on male demand to purchase sex, assuming that if the buyer risked punishment, demand would decrease. The purpose of the law was to "create a contemporary and democratic society where full gender equality is the norm" and to "reject the idea that women and children, mostly girls, are commodities that can be bought, sold, and sexually exploited by men."[10] Violations of the Swedish law can result in prison terms of up to one hundred fifty days as well as fines up to a few thousand euros. The Swedish National Criminal Investigation Department (NCID) stated in its 2004 annual report that these laws have had a "limiting effect" on the trafficking of women for prostitution in Sweden, but the government also admitted that there was no clear evidence that sex trafficking had increased or decreased, only indirect evidence that in Denmark—which does not have legislation prohibiting the purchase of sex—the number of prostitutes increased from two thousand in the early 1990s to somewhere between five and eight thousand in 2004.[11] One might conclude that the sex trafficking market shifted from Sweden to Denmark as a result of the former's no-tolerance policy, or that like so many other countries Denmark saw an increase in prostitutes throughout the 1990s due to the ascent of the global sex trafficking industry after the fall of the Berlin Wall. The U.S. government agrees with Sweden that prostitution should be criminalized, especially as it relates to combating sex trafficking. In the 2005 State Department trafficking report, the United States took a firm stand on the issue: "Where prostitution flourishes, so does an environment that fuels trafficking in persons."[12]

I am not yet completely convinced that criminalizing prostitution is the right answer to curtailing sex trafficking, as corruption can easily undermine such efforts. Even in countries where brothels are illegal today, they often operate in broad daylight by virtue of bribes. In addition, many Italians told me that they opposed criminalizing the purchase of sex because they found that a large number of trafficking victims were rescued by Salvatorre, the term for clients who empathized with a victim and helped her escape.

Nevertheless, if I had to choose a policy today, one predicated on curtailing the trafficking of women and children for sexual exploitation, I would choose the stance of the U.S. and Swedish governments: the criminalization of prostitution, including the purchase of sex acts and the owning, operating, or financing of sex establishments. Special care must be provided to avoid the further victimization of sex slaves, who would be vulnerable to prosecution under antiprostitution laws. A criminalization policy must also be supplemented with prudent enforcement, lest the prostitution industry be pushed further underground, where exploitation can be greater. Governments, police, and communities must remain vigilant for signs of prostitution, and such vigilance can be challenging. That said, criminalizing prostitution and the purchase of sex services has a better chance of curtailing demand for sex slaves. Brothel owners would then have no excuse when the (noncorrupt) police pay a visit, and the tangible risk of purchasing commercial sex would assuredly lessen the consumer demand that helps to drive the sex industry in the first place.

Hope at the Basilica

After several weeks of research in Italy and other West European countries, I returned to Rome for a few meetings before commencing a journey to the "origin" nations of Central and Eastern Europe. On my last day in Rome, I had a short spell of time between morning and evening engagements. I felt exhausted and contemplated a nap in my hotel room, but something egged me to push a little further. I had already seen St. Peter's Basilica during my first research trip to Italy, but for some reason, I decided to take a second look.

I boarded an express bus from Stazione Termini and exited at the stop nearest the cathedral. I approached it on foot, along Via de Conciliazone. The road inclined gently, so that from a distance the structure revealed itself in hints. As I neared, I saw a large crowd gathered within the arms of the grand semicircular colonnade that reaches forth from the basilica's shoulders. At the end of the road, I gasped. The cathedral stood before me, filling the horizon with its immense majesty.

The purpose of the gathering was immediately clear. Pope Benedict was offering a sermon. I did not understand the words he spoke and I did not know the purpose of his rare public appearance, but I considered myself fortunate to be in his presence. Amid the gargoyles and goblins of man, I often sought measures of spiritual solace. From the Ganges in Varanasi to Swayambhunath in Kathmandu to the seat of the Christian god, a small sip from the cup of goodness was the only tonic that kept me going. I thanked fate for sending me to the basilica, and I thanked the pope when he offered his blessing.

Not long after, I wandered into the heart of the cathedral. I peered at Michelangelo's Pieta, transfixed by the noble sadness with which the Virgin Mary looked down upon the carcass of the crucified Jesus. Few take note, but the master fashioned her as a goddess, twice the size of her savior son.

Later, I gazed upward at the ceiling of the Sistine Chapel. In the center of inspired murals nonpareil, God's hand beckoned forth with a father's hope, and bestowed the spark of life to man.

"Consider your origin;" the poet Dante wrote, "You were not born to live like brutes."

4 Moldova and the Former Soviet Union

What do I care for a hell for oppressors? What good can hell do, since those children have already been tortured?

—*Fyodor Dostoevsky,* The Brothers Karamazov

Makler

Driving north from Moldova's capital city of Chisinau, the countryside quickly morphs into bleakness. A palpable cloud of despair hangs over the tiny country. Fires burn, shacks crumble, and the scent of ash infects the air. The depth of poverty rivals South Asia.

The absence of youth outside the capital is striking. More than any other country, Moldova epitomizes the socioeconomic ruin that fell upon the former Soviet Union during the tenuous transition years just after independence. Amid the upheaval, hundreds of thousands of Moldovans fled the country in search of wage-paying jobs. Some left legally, some left illegally, and some were trafficked.

Halfway between Chisinau and the town of Balti, I spotted several young girls standing along the side of the road. They wore skirts, blouses, and makeup.

"Men in cars will pick them up," my translator, Lily, told me, "They will be taken to Chisinau where they think they will have jobs."

Because Moldova is the poorest country in Europe, desperation for income is the Moldovan trafficker's top recruitment tool. False job promises are utilized in eight of ten trafficking cases.[1] The remaining recruitment schemes include false travel agencies, false marriage offers, and abduction. A classifieds newspaper called *Makler* is the primary medium for posting false advertisements. Every month, the staff at the Chisinau office of La Strada, an anti-trafficking NGO, perform a detailed analysis of each advertisement in *Makler*, which is printed twice per week. The newspaper is filled with hundreds of postings for work abroad, study abroad, marriage proposals, au pair placements, and services for emigration, citizenship, and travel. Job advertisements appear most frequently. Agencies promise almost any type of employment in over forty international destinations. La Strada takes special note of suspicious claims.

One advertisement I saw promised the opportunity to study in the United States, United Kingdom, or Italy. It seemed innocent to me, but Alina Budeci of La Strada explained that the advertisement was from a travel agency, and travel agencies were not licensed for study-abroad programs. Study-abroad opportunities advertised by travel agencies were among the most common false advertisements Ms. Budeci found. The agencies were often owned by organized crime networks that used them as front organizations to procure new slaves. More recently, La Strada noticed an increase in advertisements for travel to the Middle East and North Africa, specifically the United Arab Emirates, Turkey, Saudi Arabia, and Tunisia. Several anti-trafficking agencies in Moldova told me that the Middle East was a top destination for trafficking victims due to an absence of anti-trafficking laws and the ease of re-trafficking to West Europe.

Agencies that placed false advertisements in *Makler* rarely did so for more than a month. As some agencies disappeared, new ones popped up. One agency Ms. Budeci showed me began offering jobs in summer 2005 for dancing in Japanese clubs at an attractive monthly salary of two thousand dollars, "all documents provided." According to La Strada, "all documents provided" or "documents provided in ten days" were red flags for false advertisements. It was impossible to procure legal passports and visas for Japan in such a short time frame. Such promises typically implied that false documents were used to facilitate travel as a prelude to coerced sex work. Numerous offers for work and study in Japan began appearing in *Makler* around the same time that local NGOs confirmed that *yakuza* crime groups had established slave-trading activities in Moldova.

Given the apparent ease of diagnosing false advertisements, I asked the staff whether such ploys were successful.

"Moldovans are desperate," Alina told me. "Even if they are suspicious, they will take the risk and think, 'bad things won't happen to me.'"

Unfortunately, bad things do happen. I met several victims—including Tatyana in Italy (see chapter 3)—who were duped by *Makler* advertisements. Some were victims of sex slavery, some were trafficked for forced construction in Russia, some were trafficked for forced begging in Greece. One was a forty-year-old woman named Belina who answered a job posting for a nanny in Ukraine only to spend the next nine years of her life working in a shoe factory near the Black Sea, without ever being paid.

I called *Malker* to ask why they did not screen advertisements or seek verification of authenticity before printing classifieds. No one was willing to speak to me. Alina told me that they tried several times to pressure *Makler* into taking responsibility for their advertisements, but to no avail. Thousands of Moldovans were desperate to leave the country; *Makler* gave them a chance.

From Moldova to the World

Everywhere I went, Moldovans wanted to leave their country. Even trafficked sex slaves who escaped and returned wanted to leave again. From the mid-1990s until around 2002, most Moldovans were trafficked directly to the Balkan region, Russia, or Italy. In the Balkans, the large peacekeeping force deployed after the signing of the Dayton Peace Accords created abundant demand for sex services, and hundreds of brothels popped up to meet that demand. Moldovans, Albanians, Romanians, Bulgarians, and Ukrainians were heavily trafficked to fill these brothels. Thousands of Moldovans were also trafficked to Russia across the open borders between the Transdniestr region, Ukraine, and Belarus. The ease of entering Italy by land and sea has already been noted in chapter 3.

After the turn of the millennium, sex trafficking to the Balkans decreased as the region stabilized and foreign troop levels decreased. Trafficking to Western Europe remained active, though the victims I interviewed who were trafficked after 2002 told me that they were first trafficked to Russia, Turkey, or United Arab Emirates, then re-trafficked to Western Europe after a period of exploitation in the former countries. In 2000, only 22 percent of Moldovan trafficking victims went to these three countries; in 2004, 97 percent did.[2]

In a village not far south of Chisinau, I met a young woman named Isabel, who was part of the new wave of trafficking victims from Moldova to Turkey. Liliana Rotaru, director of an NGO called Children, Communities, Families (CCF), made the introduction. Isabel entered the interview room cautiously, sat in her chair, and clung tightly to her purse. She asked, "Is there any video camera?" She was afraid that traffickers might see her face and harm her or her son, Peter. I assured Isabel that there was no video camera or tape recorder. It was the first time Isabel had shared her story with anyone, and she did so only because she thought an American researcher might be able to help. She struggled through tears as she narrated these words:

> When I was nineteen I was studying interior design in Chisinau. My father died, and there was no one to support me. I saw a posting in the university newspaper for a job in housecleaning. The agent for the posting, Angela, promised a salary of five hundred dollars per month.
>
> Angela paid for my passport and sent me on an autobus to Istanbul. Six other girls came with me. In Istanbul a man named Uri met us at the station. He took us to a hotel called Meke. I will never forget that hotel. Uri took our passports and said, "You must shower and get dressed. Tonight you will go on your first program." I thought he meant we will go for house cleaning, so I did as he said.
>
> That night, Uri sold us to a German man. He raped us in the hotel with five other men. They made us have sex with many men that night. The Germans made me work like this for sixteen months. I was kept locked in a hotel room with three other girls.
>
> One client who came was a lawyer. He was named Farooq, and he offered to buy me from the German. The German sold me for four thousand euros. Farooq kept me locked with chains in a room in his home, and he forced me to have sex with men who visited. If I complained, he would cut me with a knife. After two months, I told him I was pregnant. He unchained me and let me live more freely in the home. He said he would marry me.
>
> I did not want to marry Farooq, so I made up my mind to escape. I saw a program on television about Moldovans trafficked to Turkey and an organization that offered to help them return to Moldova. This organization was in Ankara, so when Farooq went to his office,

> I took an autobus and went to this organization. I did not have a passport, so they gave me a white passport[3] to return to Moldova. I returned on July 13, 2005. My son was born on October 3, 2005.

Isabel sobbed convulsively the moment she finished speaking. She trembled with fear that at any day, the traffickers might track her down and harm her or her son. The day I met Isabel was the first day in weeks she had even stepped outside her home. She was afraid to search for a job lest the traffickers spot her, and she survived day to day only with the assistance of neighbors and a local NGO for food and shelter. Isabel was free from sex slavery, but her life was still a prison.

I met two more women that day who had been trafficked from Moldova to Turkey and two more who had been trafficked from Moldova to the United Arab Emirates. Both women trafficked to the United Arab Emirates were arrested for violating antiprostitution laws and both spent over a year in detention cells awaiting deportation. Neither was deported the first time they were arrested because the original slave traders repurchased both from their jail cells.

Several victims also mentioned a market in Istanbul called Lelele, where Moldovans were bought and sold by Russians. The victims said there was an entire section of the market where everything was written in Russian, and in broad daylight, Russian slave traders bartered for humans hailing from numerous East European countries. One victim named Alana told me she was sold at Lelele, forced to work as a prostitute for two years in Turkey, then re-trafficked by truck to Russia—passing back through Moldova—where she was forced to beg for sixteen hours a day for eleven months before she managed to escape.

"We were given robes like nuns," she told me, "And we were forced to beg near a church that had the same name that was printed on our robes. If we did not collect a certain amount each day, we were raped."

Beyond the Middle East and Russia, I met Moldovan women trafficked to more than two dozen countries, including Afghanistan, Egypt, Israel, Japan, Pakistan, Tajikistan, the United Kingdom, France, Italy, Germany, the Netherlands, and the United States. Trafficking from Moldova is so prevalent that I could not help but notice a deeply ironic advertisement when I ate lunch at the only U.S. fast-food chain in Chisinau at the time. The advertisement was placed on placards on each table. It pictured three men carrying off a smiling young girl.

Advertisement placed on tables of a U.S. fast-food chain in Chisinau

As if the picture were not remarkable enough in a country that suffers among the highest rates of human trafficking in the world, when I asked a friend to translate the slogan, my jaw dropped. The words at the top of the card, "Baietii tot Baieti," mean "boys will be boys," and the words next to the meal deal being advertised, "Iti da putere," mean "it gives you power." In other words, if you are in the middle of carting off a Moldovan girl and you need a pick-me-up, this particular meal deal will give you the power you need to finish the job. I wondered if the marketing executives at the fast-food chain had any idea that such messaging was being deployed to advertise their burgers and fries.

Whither Moldova?

To truly understand Moldova's slave-trading crisis requires an understanding of the country's turbulent history. For centuries, Moldova battled foreign occupation, social upheaval, and other major calamities that prevented the country from putting a stable foot on the ladder of economic prosperity. The troubles that descended on Moldova after independence from the Soviet Union are only the tip of this tilting iceberg.

Beginning with the Roman occupation in the second century A.D., Moldova was almost always fending off invasion or suffering under foreign rule. The Romans, Huns, Bulgarians, and Mongols took turns controlling the area until the principality of Moldavia was created in 1349 as part of the Romanian empire. Hungarians, Poles, and Turks subsequently conquered pieces of Moldavia until 1792, when the Ottoman Empire ceded the region to the Russian Empire. After Russia's defeat in the Crimean War, the region was held by several powers and eventually incorporated into Romania. In 1924, the Soviet Union reincorporated Moldova into Ukraine, including Transdniestr. In 1941, Romanian and German troops attacked the Soviet Union and reannexed the Moldovan and Transdniestrian territories, but three years later the Soviets reoccupied the same territory. The Soviets then forced radical Sovietization upon the Moldovans, including imposing Russian as the official state language, forced use of the Russian Cyrillic alphabet, and renaming streets after Soviet heroes. Trafficking from Moldova began long before the 1990s, as Leonid Brezhnev oversaw the deportation of over 250,000 Moldovans in the early 1950s to Siberia and Kazakhstan for forced labor. Moldovans lived behind the iron curtain until August 1989, when the Moldovan Popular Front reintroduced the Moldovan language and the Latin alphabet to the country. This bold move was commemorated by changing the name of the longest street in Chisinau to August 1989 Street. Elections were held in 1990; in June of that year, the Moldovan Supreme Soviet declared sovereignty from the Soviet Union. Full independence was declared in August 1991. Moldova barely had a year to get itself on its feet when the entire Soviet bloc spiraled into socioeconomic chaos precipitated by the IMF–U.S. Treasury-imposed market economy reforms discussed in chapter 1. Anguish over what Moldovans perceive as the failures of democracy led Moldova to become the first former Soviet state to elect a communist as its president, in 2001. In his inaugural address, Vladimir Voronin compared Moldova to Cuba and, famously, stressed the need to protect the country from the "imperialist predators" in the West.

Poverty and instability have long been Moldova's bedfellows, driving a history of desperation to find subsistence abroad. Numerous Moldovans told me they did not even think of themselves as Moldovan, but rather Romanian or Ukrainian. Migration abroad felt more like leaving the house to go to work, rather than leaving the country in search of a livelihood. Modern slave traders prey on this sense of desperation and dislocation, and the Moldovan government inadvertently supports their cause. In 2006, the total sum of remittances to Moldova was over five hundred million dollars, equivalent to approximately 25 percent of the entire Moldovan economy. The high level of remittances mimics a worldwide trend that plays directly into the hands of slave traders, as money sent home by family members abroad has become increasingly critical to the survival of hundreds of millions of people in developing countries, where jobs are scarce and the value of local currencies is eroding due to high inflation. Global remittances have doubled in the last five years alone, surpassing three hundred billion dollars in 2006.[4] These remittances have also become crucial to the survival of the governments of developing nations, which tax up to 25 percent of the remittances—this after money-transfer organizations deduct 10 to 15 percent for processing fees.[5] Governments such as Moldova's encourage migration to secure remittance-based tax revenues, thereby inadvertently promoting the supply of potential trafficking victims from their populations. Even so, most Moldovans need little encouragement to seek employment abroad. Despite the country's recent economic recovery, approximately 80 percent of Moldovan households in 2006 remained unable to generate a subsistence-level income of $48 per month, or $1.60 per day—less than the price of a cup of coffee at your local coffee chain.

Katia's Curse

The enduring poverty and instability in Moldova have created one more casualty: the victim of re-trafficking. Because most trafficking victims return to the same conditions of poverty and lack of economic opportunity that promoted the trafficking to begin with, an increasing number of individuals are trafficked numerous times. I met several victims of re-trafficking in Moldova, the most disturbing of which was Katia. When we first met, Katia was reluctant to discus her ordeal, but after a lengthy casual conversation about me and my life in California, she told me she wanted to share her story. This is what she said:

> I am from the town of Costesti. I am twenty-three years old. My father died when I was young, and my mother and I were alone. Job agents came to our village one summer. I was fifteen at that time. One of the women was named Asli. She made arrangements for young people from our town to work in foreign countries. I told my mother I wanted to go for these jobs so I could send money. I cannot tell you who took me from Moldova, but they made me do sex

work in four countries. I did this work for three years, and I could not contact my mother or send money to her. In Amsterdam I was deported. When I came home, my mother was gone.

I went to Balti to find work, but I could not find wages, so I was living on the streets. One night, men forced me into a truck and beat me. They drove me to Turkey with four other girls. We were chained together, and they did not give us food. I was in Turkey for a long time, but not so long as the other countries. I lived in two apartments. Turkish men came to this place. Russian men also came. Sometimes the pimps took us shopping, and one day I escaped.

I returned to Moldova, but I could not find work. I tried to find work in Chisinau, but there is no work in this country. Near the university, I saw an advertisement for housework in the U.K. The agents asked for money to arrange documents, but I did not have money. They arranged my documents but told me I must repay them from my wages. I lived in the home of the agent for three days, and I remember I told myself, "See Katia, you will be lucky now." When the drivers came, they pushed me in the trunk of the car and drove me to a club in Moscow. It was so dark in that car. I cried so much. I thought I must be cursed. How can so many bad things happen to one person? When I came to that club they gave me alcohol, and I had to dance with no clothes. Everyday I was drunk. The men did what they wanted, and soon I was very sick. The pimps left me on the streets. I never wanted to come back to Moldova, but the police deported me.

Invisibility and Transdniestr

Katia was initially trafficked in 1997; I met her in 2005. While she was bribed across borders the first two times she was trafficked, the third time she was trafficked exemplified a worrisome trend emerging across Central and Eastern Europe: invisibility. Every victim I interviewed who was trafficked after 2002 told me that she traveled with legal documents. In most cases, the documents were forgeries purchased on the black market, but sometimes they were authentic documents procured from embassies with bribes. The strategy works well because several East European countries are members of the European Union and identity cards or passports from these countries allow a Moldovan to pass into other EU countries without a visa. Using legal documents makes the victim virtually invisible, and that invisibility renders protecting them almost impossible.

The trend toward invisibility has sparked an important immigration debate in Europe. Two countries that are high-frequency origin nations for trafficking, Bulgaria and Romania, joined the European Union in January 2007. Another country that is a top destination and transit nation, Turkey, is scheduled to join soon. Passports from any of these countries would allow an individual to move freely to any other EU nation. The effect on trafficking from Moldova has already been severe. Because Moldova shares miles of empty border with Romania, a black market for Romanian passports developed long before Romanian acceptance to the European Union. In the first six months after acceptance, more than 900,000 Moldovans—one-fourth of the entire country—applied for Romanian citizenship. Some number of these applications will no doubt be future trafficking victims. Turkish entry to the European Union would only increase levels of re-trafficking from Turkey, as criminals could use the country as a legal stepping-stone to Western Europe. Some policy analysts thus have argued that borders must be tightened, including more patrols, checkpoints, and stiffer requirements for visas from select member nations. Others have argued that migration must be made easier, so that Moldovans and their fellow non-EU East Europeans do not fall prey to slave traders who offer false promises of proper documents, travel arrangements, and job opportunities in the West. Unfortunately, slave traders can exploit the system no matter which stance is taken. Where borders are tightened or visa requirements stiffened, more victims will be invisible by virtue of black-market documents that slave traders procure. When borders are loosened or East European countries are added to the European Union, individuals who lack the financial resources to migrate through proper channels will fall prey to cheap offers of assistance from front organizations for slave trading networks.

To make matters worse, Moldovans are increasingly trafficked through the breakaway communist republic of Transdniestr, which shares a highly porous 420-kilometer border with Ukraine and has become a free-for-all distribution hub for trafficking in weapons, drugs, and humans. Weapons produced in old Soviet munitions factories are exported to African nations in exchange for diamonds. Diamonds are traded for drugs. Drugs and money are traded for people. Occupying one-tenth of Moldova's modest landmass, Transdniestr has been teetering on the edge of conflict with Moldova every since the bloody civil war that resulted in the region's declaration of independence on September 2, 1990. No country actually acknowledges the existence of Transdniestr, though it possesses its own currency, its own army, and its own independence day. Igor Smirnov, a reputed crime boss, has been the president since independence. Tensions remain high as each side antagonizes the other by closing borders, cutting phone service, imposing exorbitant tariffs, and making the lives of everyday Moldovans and Transdniestrians miserable. Given Transdniestr's central role in the contemporary trafficking of drugs, diamonds, weapons, and humans in Europe, I planned a trip to the capital of Tiraspol to investigate.

Two hours after I boarded a rickety bus at the manic bus station in Chisinau, I arrived at the town of Bendery, at the Moldova-Transdniestr border. In 1538, Suleiman the Magnificent of the Ottoman Empire made his first inroads into the region by conquering the town; its name means "belonging to the Turks." Most passengers exited at Bendery, leaving only five for Tiraspol. No one I met in Moldova had actually been to Tiraspol, but they warned me that the border was an unpleasant place for foreigners. Just a few months before my arrival, a French journalist was shot there for taking pictures. Also, an American woman was recently detained for five hours for unknown reasons before securing release through the U.S. embassy in Chisinau. I was also told that there were four checkpoints before entering Transdniestr and that I should keep my head down, my mouth shut, and my ego in Bendery, should a border guard give me a hard time.

I cannot confirm that the Ukraine-Transdniestr border is an open free-for-all for trafficking in humans, diamonds, drugs, and weapons, and I cannot confirm that there are actually four checkpoints at the Moldova-Transdniestr border, because at the very first border, two guards entered the bus, checked my passport, and asked me to exit. The guards took me to an office and instructed me to sit without a word for what felt like hours before they interrogated me. One guard with a giant mustache led the charge. He asked me who I was and why I wanted to enter Transdniestr.

"What do you do here? What do you do here?" he kept demanding.

He plunked his dented semiautomatic Uzi on his desk, the business end pointed directly at me, and began rifling through my backpack with fingers stained in motor oil. He discovered my camera, notebook, and laptop and accused me of being an American journalist spy. He tried to scrutinize the notes in my notebook, but reading English was not one of his strengths. I was afraid he might confiscate my belongings, so I tried to convince him that I was a tourist. I showed him pictures I had taken during my trip and insisted that my sole intent was to visit his country and sample the local culture. He smirked and said, "Don't you know, you cannot acknowledge my country exists because this is against your U.S. policy." I shrugged my shoulders and explained that I had no political agenda. The guard did not care. He instructed me to return to Chisinau. I was forced to stand in the drizzly sleet for forty minutes before a return bus stopped at the border and let me in. As I waited, I watched the guard chain-smoke a second pack of Marlboro cigarettes, having burned through the first during my interrogation. Hungry and cold, I could not help but feel a sense of teeming irritation that while my Americanness meant that I was most certainly a threat to the security of his country, chain-smoking American cigarettes was not a problem. Drugs, guns, diamonds, cash, and women ostensibly passed to and from Transdniestr without a hitch, but a single tourist did not stand a chance. Then again, he did his job well, because in a way, I was in fact an American journalist spy.

Turks and Sex Tourism

The success of trafficking East European women abroad for sexual exploitation soon inspired the facilitation of the reverse: sex tourists traveling to urban centers in Eastern Europe for the sexual enjoyment of local women. In Moldova, Turks are the largest group of sex tourists. Beginning in 2002, Turkish business groups cultivated the business of sex with heavy investments in hotels and clubs in Chisinau. Numerous NGO personnel mentioned a specific hotel, which I will call the D Hotel, that was well known as a haven for Turkish sex tourism. Contemporary to this investment in sex tourism, Turkish Airlines added more flights to Chisinau from Istanbul; currently two flights per day, which is more than any other airline from any particular city to Chisinau. The increase in sex tourism also fueled a drastic increase in the level of internal trafficking. Once an origin country, Moldova became a destination for its own women, even though prostitution is illegal. Trafficking to Chisinau quickly became the first leg in a journey that involved re-trafficking abroad. This trend mimics the pattern in Nepal, by which rural females are trafficked to Kathmandu for sexual exploitation as a first step toward re-trafficking to India, Pakistan, or the Middle East (see chapter 2). I actually found a restaurant in Chisinau named Kathmandu, a coincidence that ironically reinforced the slave trading mimicry.

I went to the D Hotel to investigate the NGOs' claims of sex tourism. Upon entering, I saw a few shops to the right, reception to the left, and in the back left corner, the entrance to what I will call A's Pub. I entered the pub and sat at the bar. Turkish men drank and smoked heavily. Some men sat with young, well-dressed Moldovan girls in their laps. I told the bartender that I was interested in entertainment. He asked if I was a guest at the hotel. I responded that I was not. He told me he could not help me, but I should try a restaurant a few blocks away, named after a famous American city.

The establishment was a cabaret, restaurant, nightclub, and bowling alley in one. The restaurant was filled with Turkish and European men carousing with dozens of young girls. The line between "willing" and coerced prostitutes was impossible to ascertain. Many of the young women appeared at ease with being purchased. The prices quoted for sex were five to eight hundred lei ($40–$64) for two hours. There were no hourly options. These were high-end prostitutes; chances were that few of them were slaves. Nevertheless, the culture of sex tourism bred slave-like exploitation. Almost every hotel and club in Chisinau that I visited sold sex, many at price points that could only be provided by slaves.

Not five minutes after I checked into my own hotel, which I will call the Hotel N, a young woman in heavy makeup rang the buzzer of my door and asked, "Do you want the program tonight?" I had not yet encountered the term and thought she was talking about something on the television. The dumbfounded expression on my face must have alerted the woman that I was confused, so she asked, "Do you want another girl?" Suddenly I understood. I was caught off guard by the speed with which the young woman arrived, so I politely declined. If I had been prepared, I would have invited her in to learn exactly who she was and how she knew to knock on my door within minutes of my checking in. It was a lost opportunity, I thought, until the very next night, when the phone in my room rang at 10:00 p.m. with the question, "Good evening, would you like sex massage this night?"

I asked if it was the same woman from the previous night, and she said it was. I invited her to my room. Hunched and sallow despite layers of makeup, Steliana told me she was from Balti and that she came to Chisinau a year ago.

"I knew it was sex work," she said. "I would rather find other work, but there are no jobs." I asked Steliana how she knew so quickly that I had checked in. She smirked. "Girls are waiting in the casino. When a group of men check in, we are sent to the rooms."

"How often do groups of men check in?" I asked.

"Many times each day."

"Does the hotel take any of the money clients pay you?"

"I don't know," Steliana replied. "But my pimp, yes, for sure."

I asked Steliana if she was forced to perform sex work, but she denied coercion. I told Steliana I did not want to purchase sex, but I gave her the three hundred lei ($24) she requested. The next evening when I returned from meetings, I had miraculously received a free upgrade to a nicer room, with a balcony and a bigger bed. For the remainder of my stay in Hotel N, I received one phone call each night asking if I wanted sex.

Along with hotels, sex was for sale at several nightclubs in Chisinau. I visited four and each was filled with prostitutes. Sex was typically transacted in rooms behind the club. In one club where I was told by a local colleague that "disgusting" things occurred, some of the patrons engaged in sexual conduct in the main room itself. The nondescript alleyway venue had special chairs that were large, round, and cushioned with a seat that leaned backward, allowing room for two people to occupy the chair at the same time. In this particular club, where I had to pay a hefty five hundred lei just to walk in the door, I saw numerous girls who appeared to be drugged or were otherwise unable to maintain their balance. Others had visible bruises that were poorly concealed with thick makeup. Worst of all, a large number were barely pubescent. Men smoked, drank, laughed, and did as they pleased with these young girls. I could not stomach the scene for long and left shortly after I entered. Images from that club continue to haunt me. It was a dungeon of human disgrace.

I did not find street prostitution in Moldova and I was unable to find apartment brothels, though I met victims who had been exploited in both. One victim, Ludmila, told me the address and apartment number in Chisinau in which she had been forced to have sex with men for nine months during 2004. She traveled from Balti to Chisinau with a woman who promised work as a waitress, but the night she arrived, she was taken to an apartment, where two men brutally tortured her. The very next night, she said,

Alleged location of Ludmila's apartment brothel in Chisinau

> Men came to this apartment one after another. The pimps kept me drunk all the time. They woke me in the morning and there was a man waiting for me. Sometimes there was a group of men late in the night. I was alone in this apartment, but I think there was one girl in the next apartment because sometimes I heard crying. The pimps beat me and punished me sexually. One day I was so sick I kept vomiting. I vomited on one of the men and he started to beat me. The pimp also beat me and pulled out my hair like this [*gestures with her fist*]. He locked me in the bathroom and said he would not come back. That night I thought I would die, so I used my elbow to break the glass in the window. I jumped to the street, and I broke my wrist when I fell.

Gagauzia

Ninety-two kilometers south of Chisinau, I arrived in Comrat, capital of the self-governing republic of Gagauzia. Unlike Transdniestr, the Gaugaz territory remains a part of greater Moldova even though it is autonomous in regional affairs. The Gaugazes were originally Muslims who fled from Turkey in the eighteenth century during war with Russia.

They were allowed to settle in the region if they converted to Christianity. They speak a dialect of Turkish, they wave a Turkish-inspired flag, and a few of them study at a university partly funded by the Turkish government. Many Moldovans told me that they did not consider the Gaugazes to be Moldovan, but rather Turks. The Gaugazes are poor, illiterate, disenfranchised from mainstream society, and are among the most heavily trafficked people in Moldova. Men are regularly trafficked for forced construction, children for forced begging, and women for forced prostitution at the hands of their fellow Turks in Turkey.

In Comrat, I met two young girls named Selin and Bahar. Selin told me:

> I was married at nineteen years. His name was Zafer. He beat me each night, and I wanted to run from him, but my parents would not let me. I had no place to go. An agent at the market said he could find work in Italy. He provided the documents, and one day I left my husband and traveled with this agent.

In Italy, Selin was forced to work in sex clubs in Turin and Milan before being sold to a protector to work on the streets. When she discovered she had HIV, the protector abandoned her to the streets, where she was arrested. She refused to testify against the protector for fear of shame against her and her family, and she was deported.

Bahar was also married when she was nineteen, and her husband also abused her. She similarly fled with a job agent, but this one took her to Istanbul:

> I lived in one apartment for more than two years. I counted the days in my head. There was one other girl in this apartment. She was from Bulgaria. The men came for us every day. It was so terrible. I hated those men. One man came to me every week. He told me he loved me, and he brought me chocolates and jewelry. He told the pimps he wanted to marry me, but they did not let him. One day he helped me escape. I ran to the police, and they sent me to a detention center. They contacted my family. It took four months to send the money to transport me home.

When I met Bahar, she was blind in one eye because she had suffered a detached retina during beatings in the apartment in Istanbul. She and Selin were two of the numerous Moldovan trafficking victims I interviewed who cried of rape, beatings, and psychological abuse at the hands of their husbands, uncles, or fathers. Seven out of ten sex trafficking victims that La Strada has assisted in Moldova since 2000 cited despair caused by domestic violence as the primary factor in their accepting proposals to travel abroad. Many Moldovan women accepted the violence as normal relations between the sexes, so much so that when I asked a woman in Balti what recourse she had against a husband who beat her regularly, she replied, "In America you call the police, in Moldova, we call it tradition."

When I asked Moldovan women why they thought men treated them so violently, the answers were remarkably similar to those offered by the women in Sindhupalchok (see chapter 2). Some pointed to culture, explaining that Moldova was an Orthodox Russian country, which meant that women were considered inferior to men and were not even allowed near the church altar because they were impure. Other women pointed to economic troubles after the collapse of the Soviet Union. They explained that when men lost jobs, they became angry, and because Moldova produces wine, they turn to alcohol, which unleashes their rage against women. Finally, some women said, "Men beat us because they know nothing will happen to them."

Dilapidated home in Balti, where I interviewed several former trafficking victims and abused women

These same women, however, were outraged that it took foreign NGOs to descend on Moldova to enlighten men regarding how to treat women respectfully.

"Why must foreigners come to our country and protect Moldovan women?" one woman asked. "Why won't the Moldovan government protect Moldovan women?"

The woman is right to ask, as the Moldovan government does very little to protect its women. There is only one article in the Moldovan penal code, 47/1, that stipulates a fine of two hundred to two hundred fifty lei ($16–$20) for a man who is judged to have physically harmed a female in his household. There are almost no prosecutions under this article because it does not provide shelter for a woman who wishes to make a claim. Violence against women remains one of the chief causes of sex trafficking throughout Eastern Europe, and once trafficked, the women suffer even greater abuse.

Corruption, Corruption, Corruption

The single largest hurdle in the fight against sex trafficking from East European countries is the endemic corruption of government, judicial, and law-enforcement entities. Under pressure from the West, Moldova passed anti-trafficking legislation in July 2003. Articles 165 (trafficking in persons), 206 (trafficking in children), and 220 (pimping) of the Moldovan Criminal Code provide detailed definitions of trafficking and slavery, as well as penalties ranging from seven to fifteen years for trafficking in adults or children and up to twenty-five years if the perpetrator is a member of an organized crime group. Articles 165 and 206 were updated in October 2003 to allow for fines of up to two thousand five hundred U.S. dollars[6] for "moral damages." For pimping convictions, fines are only a few hundred dollars. According to Holly Wiseman of the U.S. State Department in Chisinau, in 2004, Moldovan courts handed down sixteen convictions for trafficking in persons, seventy-five for pimping, and seven for trafficking in children. Of these ninety-five total cases, only sixteen involved prison time. None of the traffickers were fined. The average prison time per trafficking infraction was a little over two years, primarily due to an amnesty law that allows individuals convicted of certain crimes, including trafficking, to pay a fine after two years to reduce or eliminate the remainder of the sentence.

even when crime is exposed, men can get out of it w/ little or no harm done

Why were there so many pimping charges and so few for trafficking? In a word: corruption.

Peter (a pseudonym), a tall, polished trafficking attorney, shed light on the question in his offices in Chisinau, on condition that I did not reveal his identity lest it become impossible for him to prosecute cases. He began by explaining that more than half the trafficking cases since the passage of the new trafficking legislation were reduced to charges of pimping.

"The traffickers offer bribes to prosecutors and judges to requalify the charges," Peter told me. "The criminals pay the pimping fine, and they are released."

Judges and prosecutors were not the only ones taking bribes in Moldova. "The police and border guards also take bribes to allow trafficking to occur in the first place," Peter said.

Sometimes, corrupt police and judges work together. "There was a case of ex-police officers who trafficked tens of women to Dubai," Peter said. "When the case was brought before a judge, he dismissed it on the basis that the women chose to work as prostitutes and 'felt good' being there. The prosecutors tried to refile the case with a different judge, but most of the victims disappeared."

I asked the obvious question about witness protection, but Peter shook his head. "The international community asked us to make witness protection laws," he said. "But what does this mean in Moldova? Where is the money to relocate and protect these witnesses?"

Along with the lack of funds, there was a more fundamental obstacle to a functional witness-protection program in Moldova: There was no place to go.

"Moldova is a small country," Peter explained. "Where can witnesses hide?"

I asked Peter what the chief factor engendering law-enforcement and legal corruption was. "Wages," he replied. Like many East European governments, Moldova is broke, thanks in no small part to the fact that it spends over 70 percent of its budget on external debt repayments.[7] Wages for police officers, state prosecutors, and judges are barely above subsistence level. Peter informed me that the average border guard or police officer makes one hundred dollars per month; the average junior prosecutor makes one hundred twenty dollars per month; the average senior prosecutor makes two hundred dollars per month; and the average judge makes two hundred to two hundred fifty dollars per month. A bribe of a few hundred dollars from a slave trader or slave owner is little more than a minor cost of doing business, but an irresistible boost in income to a prosecutor or judge. Even when Peter convinces a witness to testify, and even when he is assigned a judge who refuses to take bribes, the traffickers still escape with ease because they "flee to Russia or Turkey, and nothing happens. We have no extradition with these countries, and the case is finished."

Disheartened by the immense hurdles he faced, Peter told me that he was doing everything he could to fight sex trafficking in his country, but every possible card was stacked against him. Since the day we met, the problems of corruption, disappearing witnesses, and untouchable slave traders have only worsened.

Stephan cel Mare

My quest to understand Moldova's trafficking phenomenon led me to one final, unforeseen piece of information. I met one of my translators, Lily, for dinner one night, to treat her for her considerable assistance during my stay. She chose her favorite restaurant, a local microbrewery that was popular among the well-to-do of Chisinau. A battalion of Mercedes-Benz cars was parked in front and attractive couples reveled inside. Lily and I had to wait forty-five minutes for a table.

Lily had been living in Chisinau for a little over one year, after moving from her small town in Laloveni County for studies. After university, Lily wanted to find a job with an intergovernmental organization, work in a foreign office, and see the world. It did not escape her that her dreams were similar to the countless Moldovans who ended up toiling in slave-like conditions abroad; she was simply blessed with better channels with which to find a good job.

After we finished eating, I enjoyed a glass of *dulce,* or sweet wine, and Lily took a second glass of *negru,* or red wine. I told Lily about my visit to the National History Museum that morning and the interesting facts I learned about Stefan cel Mare, or Stephen the Great, Moldova's most cherished son and inspiration for the name of the street on which the restaurant we were eating in was located. A medieval hero, Stefan cel Mare repelled invading armies from the Ottoman and Hungarian empires during the fifteenth century. After a decisive battle against the Turks, Pope Sixtus IV bestowed upon him the term *Athleta Christi,* or

Champion of Christ. Only two other men had received the title at that time, one of them the father of Albania, Gjergj Kastrioti.

As I happily parroted the facts I had learned about Stefan cel Mare, I noticed Lily's face tightening; she dug her teeth into her lower lip.

"Is something wrong?" I asked.

"You will not understand," Lily responded.

I told her I would try.

Lily peered at me and whispered, "Moldova is cursed because of Stefan cel Mare."

I put down my *dulce*.

Lily explained that Stefan was the cousin of Vlad III, also known as Vlad the Impaler, or Drăculea, son of Dracul. Legend had it that Vlad II chose Drac, or "dragon," as his symbol because he made a pact with the devil that he would be victorious in battle in exchange for his soul. His son, Vlad III, was thus the son of the dragon, or the son of the devil.

"Stefan cel Mare could not defeat the invaders on his own," Lily said, "He took the help of Drăculea to defeat the Turks. Drăculea was an evil man. Because Stefan cel Mare took his help, the curse of the devil fell upon Moldova. For centuries, we have suffered this curse."

Lily's story left me speechless. She was an educated woman who believed everything she told me. Given the misery Moldova had endured, it was hard to argue against the possibility of a devilish curse. Starvation, invasion, war, drought, trafficking, slavery—Moldova had suffered it all. The curse of Vlad the Impaler even persisted into modern times in the guise of "imperialist predators" who methodically sucked the blood out of a newborn country.

I asked Lily how long this curse was meant to last. I asked her if there was any way the curse could be lifted. Her eyes fell quietly to the table, and she gulped down the remainder of her blood-purple wine.

5 Albania and the Balkans

The blood of a woman is not equal to the blood of a man.
A woman is known as a sack, made to endure. —*Kanun I Lekë Dukagjinit*

Sworn Virgins and Blood Vengeance

Part of being a "sack, made to endure" includes the provision that if a man "beats his wife bloody," he has only to explain his reasons to her family, and the incident passes without punishment.[1] A wife's duties to her husband are numerous, including to "submit to his domination" and "to fulfill her conjugal duties," whereas a husband's only duties to his wife are to "provide clothing and shoes" and to preserve her honor.[2] If a man wishes to divorce his wife, then "having cut off her hair and stripped her nude, the husband expels her from the house in the presence of relatives and drives her with a whip through the entire village."[3]

These are some of the prescriptions for marital relations that can be found in the Kanun I Lekë Dukagjinit, the Code of Lekë Dukagjini, a series of thirteen books that have functioned as the common-law bible of rural Albania since they were set down on paper by Lekë Dukagjini, a feudal lord, in the fifteenth century. Though the Kanun lost influence during five decades of communist rule, after the fall of communism in 1992 and subsequent socioeconomic strife that engulfed the country, many rural Albanians returned to the Kanun as a trusted guide to their daily lives. The Kanun's aggressive subordination of women and strict laws of personal honor and blood feuds are two of the top contributors to Albania's slave-trading crisis.

Being female under Kanun tradition can be so oppressive that there are actually prescriptions that allow a woman to liberate herself by becoming a man. An Albanian *virgjinesha* ("sworn virgin") transforms into a man by swearing virginity and renouncing all aspects of life related to femaleness. After taking the virgin oath, the *virgjinesha* adopts the male equivalent of her name, cuts her hair short and dresses like a man, works like a man, smokes, drinks, and recreates with other men, and governs her family with male authority. She is even referred to as "he." In exchange for the prestige associated with being male, the *virgjinesha* can never marry or have sex. Two conditions typically motivate the virgin oath: if a woman does not wish to marry the man to whom she has been prearranged to marry, or if a set of parents lacks male children. In the first case, Kanun law states, "The girl who is betrothed may not reject the young man, even if she does not like him. If the girl refuses to submit to her fate . . . she may never marry another man."[4] Without a husband, the virgin oath is the only way for a woman to survive in a community that does not allow women to live alone. In the second case, parents might encourage a daughter to take the virgin oath because "if the male line of a house dies out, even though there may be a hundred daughters, none of them have the right to any share in the inheritance of their parents."[5] Only a son over the age of fifteen can inherit a family's wealth and property.

The concept of *virgjineshas* provided an unequivocal sense of the bitter disadvantage associated with being female under the Kanun, but I wondered whether the real-world conditions were as oppressive as the tales of virgin oaths led one to believe. To answer this question, I planned a trip to Albania's rural north, where I surmised that if I could find a *virgjinesha,* I might be able to ascertain firsthand how and why the living conditions of rural Albanian women left so many vulnerable to trafficking and exploitation. My journey commenced with a two-hour ride on a *furgon* (minibus) from Tirana to the northern town of Shkodra. From Shkodra, I took another *furgon* heading northwest toward Han i Hotit. The corridor between these two cities was peppered with mushroom-like concrete and iron bunkers that were built during the repressive communist regime of Enver Hoxha (1950–1985). Hoxha ordered over seven hundred and fifty thousand such bunkers to be built across Albania, engineered to withstand the full assault of invading tanks. Today, Albanians do the best they can to decorate the eyesores with paintings and flowers, but the bunkers are a lingering testament to the paranoia that isolated Albania during its dreary communist times and motivated thousands to flee the country in search of a better life.

Thirty minutes south of the Han i Hotit border crossing with Serbia and Montenegro, I arrived in a muddy mountain town called Koplik. A city of no more than five thousand, Koplik is the capital of the Malesia e Madhe (Great Highlands) district of northwestern Albania. It is also the center of a region steeped in Kanun tradition. Few people in Albania study *virgjineshas* and no one knows exactly how many there are. I was told by NGO personnel in Tirana that Koplik would be my best bet at meeting a *virgjinesha,* but no one was willing to travel with me to translate an interview. After I disembarked from my *furgon,* I walked through the town and tried to ascertain the best way to track down a *virgjinesha.* Scores of men sat idle at run-down cafés and smoked innumerable cigarettes. I approached a handful of the groups and asked, "*virgjinesha?*" In response, I received dismissive waves or irritated grunts. I realized that I appeared foolish, perhaps even insulting, but I did not know how else to find a sworn virgin. I was not meeting with much luck, but I did manage to learn very quickly that Albanians had a curiously inverted (for Westerners) custom when they answered a question in the negative. Whenever I asked a local if he knew where I could find a *virgjinesha,* I received a verbal reply—"no"—accompanied by a nod of the head that, to me, signified "yes." Heartened at what I thought was a positive answer, I asked where I could find him, only to receive an irritable "no!" in reply, again with the head nodding "yes." I grew frustrated by the repeated confusion, but soon realized that Albanians nodded their heads up and down when they said "no," unlike most people who nodded their heads when they meant to answer in the affirmative.

I searched for several hours to find a *virgjinesha* in and around Koplik to no avail. I grew hungry and disheartened when fate shined favorably on me at an antique market that sold everything from one-hundred-year-old Swiss pocket watches to rusted pistols from before the communist era. A young boy named Dolar overheard me asking locals where I could find a sworn virgin, and with surprisingly facile English, he explained that his uncle was a *virgjinesha* who lived not far from the market. With newfound vigor, I explained that I was a researcher from the United States and asked Dolar if he would be willing to translate a conversation. Dolar led the way. Within minutes, we arrived at a dirt road with a series of small brick-cube houses along one side. His house was one of these cubes, with a few half-dead trees growing around it. Dolar asked me to wait on the road while he went inside to ask his uncle if he would be willing to be interviewed. A few minutes later he reemerged with a downcast face.

"My uncle will not meet you. He said I must not talk to you."

"I hope I did not cause you trouble," I said.

"No," Dolar replied. "but I cannot help you."

I shook Dolar's hand and thanked him for trying. I asked if he would return to the city center with me so I could treat him to a snack and soda, but he said he needed to remain home.

I returned to Tirana, disappointed that I had come so close but had not been able to meet a *virgjinesha*. Though my knowledge remained theoretical, it still seemed clear that the stringent gender prescriptions of the Kanun left Albanian women with only three life choices: marry, become destitute, or become a man. Not surprisingly, several NGOs informed me that over one-half of Albanian trafficking victims cited a false marriage offer as the reason they were trafficked. Whereas rural Moldovans were desperate for jobs, rural Albanian women were desperate to be married. One trafficking victim, Pira, told me exactly what happened to her:

> This man named Alban proposed marriage when I was seventeen. We had a wedding ceremony in my village. I remember dancing with my younger sister. After the wedding when I moved to my husband's home, he sold me for one hundred thousand leke [$1,000] to another man. That man took me by truck to Kosovo. We crossed the border by foot. I was forced for sex in a club one year before a police raid. When I returned to my home, I learned Alban married two other women and sold them also. The same priest conducted the ceremonies.

Just as the extreme disadvantage of being female in Albanian society promoted a high degree of vulnerability to slave traders, another set of Kanun laws rendered Albania a prime hunting ground for traffickers: the laws related to *gjakmarrja*, or blood vengeance. The guiding principle of the Kanun is honor, related to the individual, family, or hospitality. There are eleven ways in which a man's honor can be violated, among them: "if someone calls him a liar . . . if someone spits at him . . . if someone does not repay a debt . . . [and] if his wife runs off with someone."[6] If an offense against honor is committed, it "is not paid with property, but by spilling of blood."[7] Once blood vengeance commences, the cycle can continue for generations. According to the rules, only men and sworn virgins can participate in blood feuds, often leaving families without male members. Many families under threat of blood feuds do not leave their homes for fear of being killed. NGOs in Tirana estimate that over ten thousand such families are engaged in blood feuds across Albania, and whereas men were historically the sole targets, women and children have also become victims. As the blood feuds rage and families are left without men, women and children are vulnerable to slave traders who offer jobs, marriages, or payments for children with a promise of money from work abroad. Blood feuds under the Kanun have spread from northern Albania to central and southern cities, such as Durres, Berat, and Tirana. Beyond Albania, killings related to Kanun blood feuds have occurred in Italy, the United Kingdom, Canada, France, and the United States.

In light of the Kanun's pivotal role in promoting the trafficking of rural Albanian women and children, it would be easy to cast a solely negative light on its prescriptions. However, many thoughtful Albanians explained that the Kanun was not inherently unjust. Transcribed versions did not always reflect the subtlety and wisdom of its rich oral tradition. More broadly, the majority of the Kanun has nothing to do with a woman's place in society and it offers prudent guidelines for the peaceful functioning of civil networks. Women's rights are clearly repressed, but the Kanun also protects women from the lecherous intentions of men. Of this, I understood. My journeys had given me ample evidence that in the absence of negative consequence, a certain proportion of men abused women to bestial degrees. Just as the Albanian gestures for yes and no seemed to be reversed for me, perhaps the role of women in traditional Albanian culture only seemed oppressive due to my cultural perspective. Nonetheless, I could not help but think that, rather than locking the women behind cultural prison bars to keep them safe, perhaps the uncontrollable men should be locked up. Perhaps they should learn what it feels to live like a woman.

Vlora

Throughout the 1990s, Albania was the chief transit country for slave trading from Eastern Europe to Italy and from Italy to the remainder of Western Europe. Though several international organizations and the U.S. government have stated that this is no longer the case,[8] my experiences in a town called Vlora led me to conclude otherwise.

Getting to Vlora was not easy. The night before I was supposed to travel, I suffered an asthma attack. I had been struggling to breathe since I arrived in Albania due to the country's shockingly filthy air. During my plane's descent into Tirana, I saw a broad stream of mist flowing over sharply folded mountains, only to discern a few moments later that the mist was actually smoke rising from immense fires burning on a mountainside. Friends had warned me that Albania was a heavily polluted country; the warnings were an understatement. Tirana was blanketed in a brown haze that left me coughing and rubbing my eyes for my entire visit. Dust from construction, a high density of poorly maintained vehicles, and a lack of winter rain left Tirana choked with debris. The absence of rain had another negative effect: The country was almost out of electricity. Albania's energy resources were almost entirely hydroelectric, and as weeks passed without rainfall, rolling blackouts of up to ten hours were the norm in every city I visited. My taxi driver from Rinas Airport summed up the situation as only a local could. "Albania must have rains!" he said. "In Tirana, very dirty. In Tirana, no electricity. Electricity caput. Catastrophe!"

My first stop in Vlora was the Vatra Psycho-Social Center, the first shelter created for trafficking victims in Albania. The shelter was founded in 1998 by Vera Leskaj, a dedicated anti-trafficking crusader who had to flee Vlora more than once under threat from the Albanian mafia. Two of Vera's right-hand women, Donika Curraj and Brikena Puka, shared years of insight into the trafficking situation in Albania and the use of Vlora's harbor as a launch point for Western Europe. They told me that, from the early 1990s until a police crackdown called Operation Puna in 2002, Vlora was an oceanic superhighway of slave trading via speedboats into Italy. During this time, speedboats brimming with women and children raced in broad daylight across the sea to Italy several times a day, making the journey in as little as two hours. Up to two thousand people were trafficked each month. Drugs and illegal weapons were included in the shipments, which were controlled by the Albanian mafia. If the Italian coast guard approached the speedboats, "the traffickers would throw a girl overboard so the authorities must stop to help her, and the speedboat would escape," Ms. Curraj told me. She also said that Romanians, Moldovans, Russians, Bosnians, Montenegrans, and Ukrainians were heavily trafficked into Albania specifically to transport them from Vlora to Italy. Slave traders entered Albania with relative ease across its remote and mountainous land borders with Serbia and Montenegro, Kosovo, and Macedonia. Boats across Shkodra Lake, half of which is in Albania and the other half in Serbia, were also used for entry. For exit, the mountainous border between Albania and Greece was commonly used, as well as several hundred kilometers of blue border with the Adriatic Sea, from which Italy and the remainder of West Europe were accessible. Tens of thousands of women and children were trafficked from Eastern to Western Europe through Vlora, including thousands of Albanians. One such individual was a young woman named Ines, whom I met at the Vatra shelter. Ines shared a story with me that was one of the most disturbing tales of exploitation I heard in all three of my research trips. It began in September 1995, when she was only thirteen years old. With a meek voice and down-turned eyes, she told me the following story:

> I was walking to my aunt's house for ironing work when I was kidnapped by three men. They closed my eyes, gagged my mouth, and threw me in their car. They said if I try to escape, they will kill me.
>
> They drove one full day to Gjirokastra [a town in southern Albania], and we went to a hotel. One man stayed in the hotel with me. He raped me for two weeks. After two weeks, we went to Greece in a taxi. He paid money at the border and the guard let us through. From a village in Greece, we took a bus to Corinth.
>
> In Corinth, this man told me, "We have found a job for you." He took me to a bar where I saw women in sex work. I tried to protest, but the men in the bar took me to the bathroom and raped me one after the other until I went unconscious. I worked in that bar for four months. Most of the men were very cruel. They shouted at me and would beat me if I did not please them. Whatever they wanted to do, I could not say no, or the pimp would torture me. If I was sick or bleeding or in too much pain, I still had to work. One Albanian man was nice. He told me he loved me, and we became friends. When the pimp saw this, he moved me to another club. I stayed in this club for two years. We slept in small rooms above the club where the clients came for sex. I hated this work. I thought, God cannot keep me here forever, and one day I will be free.
>
> After two years, the pimp took us shopping. I saw a policeman and ran to him. I told him what happened to me and he took me to the police station. The police put me in a detention cell for seventeen

days. After this, they deported me to the Kakavija border point. I did not have money, and I told a border guard what happened and asked him to call my father. The border guard took pity on me, and the next night my father came for me.

When I arrived home, my father did not believe me. He said I chose this work and he denounced me. I had to leave my home. I felt so sad I cried for days, and I wanted to take my life. I slept on the streets one week, when a man in our village that I had known from my childhood promised to help me find work. I was very cold and hungry, so I went with this man. He took me to Vlora, and very late at night he sent me with other girls on a speedboat to Italy. He promised me these men would help me find work.

When we came to Italy, the men drove us to Torino. They told us we will work in a hotel as cleaning ladies, but in Torino they took me to an apartment and raped me. They made me take clients in that apartment, then a second apartment. After this second apartment, they took me to Belgium for three months, then they took me back to Italy to Firenze. In Firenze they left me with a very bad pimp who beat me every day. This is how I got the scar on my forehead [*points to a long gash across her forehead*] and also under my hair. Sometimes he would beat me until I fainted. I thought this man might kill me, so I tried to escape, but he caught me on the streets and pulled out one of my teeth for punishment [*points to the missing tooth*].

After Firenze, they sent me to Amsterdam. In Amsterdam I worked in a closed brothel for eight months. One day there was a police raid, and they seized the girls because we had false documents. The police put me in detention for two months. When they let me go, the same Albanian men who took me from Vlora to Italy were waiting outside the police station. I tried to run back to the police, but they forced me to go with these men.

The Albanian men took me to Utrecht and made me work in another closed brothel. At this time, I became pregnant. One of the Albanian pimps said I would have this baby for him, and he would send me back to the brothel.

I did not want to give this man my baby, so I ran away to nuns who have a shelter for abused women. I stayed in this shelter until my son was born, and the nuns helped me get documents. I returned to Albania on January 22, 2003. I went back to my family home and showed them my son, but my father shunned me again.

Every day I try to forget what I have suffered, but the faces of these men come in my sleep. I am afraid to leave this shelter in case I see them on the streets. I am afraid if they find me they will send me for sex again. I hate these men. I do not want to sleep with all these men. I do not want these men to kill me.

A Stakeout

As a result of Operation Puna, trafficking from Vlora harbor as well as the seaside town of Durres, about one hundred kilometers to the north, was supposed to be shut down. At the time of my visit, tales persisted that one or two boats each week continued to make the trip, and that the price for transporting an individual across the Adriatic had risen from five hundred euros to two thousand. I wanted to investigate Vlora harbor further, so I rented a room at the southernmost hotel along the Vlora waterfront, closest to the harbor. Aptly, the hotel had an Italian name: Hotel Bologna.

Vlora harbor consisted of two piers, each around one hundred yards long, at the end of which up to two or three small ships could dock. During the day, the harbor was packed with eighteen-wheelers into which goods were loaded and unloaded. There were always a few men fishing off the piers, and there were always men in suits standing next to Mercedes Benz sedans, chatting on cell phones. The pier was locked down each day at 6:00 p.m. and entry after that time was strictly prohibited.

I spent two nights in Vlora. On the first night I found a safe spot, elevated and behind a concrete wall, from which I could watch the harbor to see if there was any late-night activity. I drank two cups of coffee, wore three layers of clothes, took my camera, and huddled in my spot at 10:00 p.m. It was cold and damp, and there were no lights on either pier or in the harbor. The only sound came from a large electric generator that supplied electricity to the nearby hotels. As I sat in the darkness, I knew my mission was probably more foolish than my visit to Koplik, but as miniscule as the chances were that something might occur at the pier during one of the two nights of my visit, I had to give it a try.

Vlora harbor

At almost two in the morning, I watched two vehicles pull up to the northern pier of Vlora harbor, approximately thirty yards from me, even though the pier was supposed to be shut. The ink-black darkness prevented accurate vision, but I was able to ascertain that the vehicles were yellow pickup trucks. They idled for a few minutes; then the engines were turned off. I saw the shapes of people, but I could not hear anyone speaking because of the racket from the electricity generator. A few minutes later, the headlights of one of the trucks flipped on, the truck drove to the end of the pier, and the headlights flipped off again. After precisely fourteen minutes, the truck's headlights flipped on and it drove back down the pier. The second truck repeated the exact same procedure. After the second truck returned from the pier, both trucks left the harbor. In the pitch black of night, I snapped photos of both trucks as they drove down the pier and returned, though only the headlights appeared in the photos. I waited twenty minutes to ensure that a second round of trucks did not arrive. Then I returned to my hotel room.

There was no way to know for sure what transpired at Vlora harbor at two in the morning the night of my stakeout. Perhaps it was a brief, unauthorized fishing expedition off the end of the pier in the middle of the night, or perhaps last-minute cargo was unloaded from the trucks to be shipped early the next day, though I saw nothing on the pier the next morning. If anything was loaded onto a boat and shipped that night, one would assume it was probably not human, as there would be no need to drive to the end of the pier because people could walk—unless they were restrained or did not want to board the boat. Whatever happened on the pier, I can confirm that Vlora harbor is still being used in the middle of the night for some sort of activity. Claims that human trafficking operations from Vlora Harbor have been shut down may be premature, and it remains entirely possible that children like Ines are still trafficked to Italy from Vlora harbor to suffer similarly abominable fates.

Convergent Evolution

In addition to trafficking into Western Europe via Vlora and other seaside towns, such as Durres and Saranada, Albanian victims who were trafficked after 2003 revealed that they first crossed the border into Greece from towns such as Korce, Gjirokastra, and Kakavije; from Greece, they were trafficked via ferry or speedboat to Italy. Other victims mentioned the porous, 180-kilometer green border between Albania and Kosovo as a stepping-stone to Western Europe. An increasing number of victims were also trafficked through the Republic of Macedonia, which Albanians do not need a visa to enter. Most disturbing, organized-crime groups in Albania learned the exact same lesson as those in Moldova regarding the benefits of invisibility. Around 2003, Albanian traffickers began using passports, visas, and employment contracts to move victims from origin to destination, with high levels of success. A few well-placed officials, a few high-level bribes, a few complicit border guards, along with front organizations for travel, emigration, or study abroad, were all it took. On October 10, 2005, a travel agency called Go West was shut down by customs authorities and accused of forging visas, passports, and other documents for the purpose of human trafficking. Police employees at Rinas Airport, customs officers, and police at key land-border crossing points were also arrested for involvement in the network. During the raid, officials uncovered a laboratory with high-quality printing machines, scanners, machines for copyright seals, and printed passports from twenty-nine countries, including the United States, Italy, the United Kingdom, the Netherlands, Greece, Thailand, India, and China. The use of false passports and visas went far beyond Go West. As Bernadette Roberts of the U.S. embassy in Albania told me, "People show up with fake passports all the time. If the embassy confiscates the documents, they procure new birth certificates with matching false passports and try again." Roberts also told me that most recently, substantial numbers of Chinese and Indians were trafficked to Albania for forced labor in manufacturing, construction, and sex work. I did my utmost to track down Indian slaves in Albania, but I could not find any. I wondered if any of them had been re-trafficked from Kamathipura or Falkland Road. No one in India mentioned Albanian mafias as having commenced slave-trading operations from the country, but if they have, it would be an astonishing development in the sophistication and reach of the slave-trading networks of European mafias.

Similar to other origin nations, internal trafficking was also a new development in Albania. Several experts told me that they witnessed a shift beginning in 2002 toward a two-step process for Albanian trafficking. The first step was internal trafficking from rural regions to Tirana, where young women were forced to work as day prostitutes on the street or perform sex work in apartments, hotels, and clubs. Children were also trafficked for forced begging in Tirana before being trafficked abroad. As in Nepal and Moldova, the two-step process enhanced profits, lowered risks, and provided slave owners with ample time to make transnational trafficking decisions in a more systematic fashion, especially given the increased costs of making boat trips from Vlora or acquiring legal documents. Albanian mafias also used the internal breaking period to coordinate with affiliates abroad, ascertaining precise levels of demand for precise types of slaves in precise locations. Once a demand assessment was complete, slaves could be shipped accordingly. These complex marketing and distribution analytics demonstrated the highly developed nature of the business of the contemporary slave trade. The convergent evolution of the use of legal documentation and a two-step trafficking process in countries thousands of miles apart further demonstrates that good business is good business, anywhere in the world.

Despite my best efforts to track down prostitution in Albania, I was unable to do so. I met victims in shelters who confirmed that they were forced to perform sex work at small hotels, primarily outside Tirana. None of the victims I interviewed stated that they had worked as street prostitutes, and there were no well-known streets in major cities like Tirana, Shkodra, or Vlora where prostitutes were known to work. No taxi drivers I queried could take me to apartments or hotels where I might find sex services. If prostitution existed in Albania, it was deeper underground than in any country I visited.

Ancient Struggles and a Modern "Three Strikes"

An old Albanian farmer in the town of Fier told me, "We are Europe's forgotten child." He said this because Albania was the last European country to be freed of Ottoman rule, and it was the last European country to be freed of communist rule. Similar to that of Moldova, Albania's history includes centuries of foreign invasion, economic stagnation, and social instability. It is no coincidence that these analogous socioeconomic conditions rendered Albanians highly vulnerable to slave trading once the Berlin Wall fell. The country's unique geography also made it a slave trader's transit nation of choice.

Albania's history of foreign occupation dates back to the late fourteenth century, when the Ottomans defeated Serbia and overran much of the modern Balkan area. Similar to Stefan cel Mare in Moldova, a fearless child of Albania named George Kastrioti fought valiantly against the Turks, winning twenty-five battles against them. After Kastrioti died, Albania fell under complete Ottoman rule. Albanians fled to Italy en masse during the fifteenth and sixteenth centuries, across the same seas that so many are trafficked across today. Those who remained were forced to convert to Islam. For centuries, Albania languished under the Turks, falling further and further behind the economic advances of Western Europe. In 1912, a man named Ismail Qemali waged war against the flagging Ottoman Empire and declared independence at Vlora. Not three years later, with the outbreak of World War I, Albania was occupied by armies from Greece, Serbia, France, Italy, and Austria-Hungary in succession. Ahmet Zogu, the man who appeared on Albania's currency before communist rule, ruled from 1928 to 1939, the year that Mussolini invaded. In 1941, the Albanian communist party took control, led by Enver Hoxha, he of the aforementioned concrete-bunker fame. Under Hoxha, Albania's economy crumbled due to extreme isolationist policies. Hoxha allied the country with the Soviet Union, then China, but after the death of Mao Zedong in 1976, Albania was left without allies. When Hoxha died in 1985, the country was ready for change. Inspired by independence movements throughout Eastern Europe, student protests in the early 1990s called for democratic elections. In the midst of civil strife, Albania's economy deteriorated further. The first modern mass migration of Albanians to Italy occurred in March 1991, when twenty thousand Albanians fled from Vlora to Brindisi in search of a better life. To make matters worse, beginning in 1997, three catastrophes in three successive years left Albania in near ruins.

The first crisis was the spectacular collapse of several pyramid schemes in 1997, in which Albanians lost over one billion dollars, totaling the savings of over 70 percent of the country. Such schemes were rampant in postcommunist countries, where citizens had little experience with investing. In Romania, Russia, and Bulgaria, similar schemes resulted in the loss of billions of dollars from average citizens, exacerbating poverty levels and the desperation to migrate. Albania suffered the most destructive collapse, partially because almost every Albanian invested in the schemes on the word of then-president Sali Berisha, who famously said, "Albanian's money are [*sic*] the most dirt-free in the world." After the collapse, suspicions ran high that corrupt politicians and organized crime groups were responsible for the treachery. Across the country, Albanians looted, destroyed infrastructure, and eventually forced Berisha to resign.

In September 1998, Azem Hajdari, a close aid to Berisha, was assassinated. Riots followed, including the burning of several government ministries and the office of the prime minister. In Spring 1999, a third crisis struck Albania: refugees. Not long after Slobodan Milosevic and Serbians (Christians) initiated a genocidal ethnic-cleansing campaign against ethnic Albanians (Muslims) in Kosovo, the North Atlantic Treaty Organization (NATO) responded with an air campaign that contributed to the sudden influx of over six hundred thousand refugees into northern Albania, a sum equal to 20 percent of the entire Albanian population. Already reeling from economic decay, social upheaval, and political instability, the influx of frenzied Kosovars left Albania in utter chaos. Slave traders benefited mightily.

The Balkans

My only trip to the Balkans was in 1995, when I lived with Bosnian Muslim refugees at the camp in Slovenia. There, a bright young Bosnian girl named Alma told me a tale that culminated years later in the impetus to write this book. One afternoon, we sat on the grass under a cherry blossom tree and Alma told me how Serbian soldiers had attacked her village in 1992. They burned the cabins and shot the livestock. Then they separated the men from the women, children, and elderly, raped the women, and shot the men. They herded pubescent girls and young women into trucks. Alma and her grandmother were left behind, along with a fraction of the village's inhabitants. The survivors were told to leave Bosnia or they would be killed. They were also told that they would be killed if they buried the bodies of the men. Alma and her grandmother walked for three days before they arrived at the Croatian border, where UN personnel allocated them to a camp in Slovenia because the camps in Croatia were full. Alma later learned that her mother and sister were likely herded off to rape camps that the Serbs operated throughout Bosnia as part of their ethnic-cleansing campaign. The largest rape camp was at the Partizan Sports Complex in the town of Foca, where thousands of Bosnian women were systematically brutalized.

After the Dayton Peace Accords were signed on December 14, 1995, over twenty thousand troops from members and nonmembers of NATO were deployed to the region to ensure that peace was maintained. Part of this force included 1,411 police officers from fifty countries, called the International Police Task Force (IPTF). The IPTF's role was to monitor and advise local Bosnian police and to investigate claims of human trafficking and other human rights abuses. According to the Security Council resolution that created the IPTF, its forces could not be arrested or detained and were immune from criminal prosecution.

Shortly after the peace accords, the UN mission in Bosnia and Hercegovina stated that women were being trafficked from Bosnia and other Balkan nations, as well as Moldova, Romania, and Ukraine, for forced sex work in the over two hundred sex clubs that opened after the peacekeeping forces arrived. A UN mission called the Special Trafficking Operations Program (STOP) stated in a 2001 press conference that upward of 25 percent of the women in these clubs were sex trafficking victims.[9] STOP workers also discovered that most victims were promised jobs in Italy, most were raped and tortured en route, most were sold for the equivalent of two to four thousand dollars, and most were forced to perform sex work under threat of extreme violence. Interviewees spoke of military personnel, international workers, and Bosnian police as the primary clientele. Beginning in 2002, several NGOs noted shifts in sex trafficking to Bosnia, including the increased use of legal documents, re-trafficking of many victims who could not meet basic subsistence needs after escape, corruption of police who took bribes to offer warnings before law-enforcement raids, and the expanding role of organized crime in sex trafficking to and from the Balkan region.[10]

During the height of trafficking to Bosnia, the IPTF and U.S. military contractors from a company called DynCorp were accused of purchasing sex services from trafficked women, purchasing trafficked women and reselling them to brothels, and purchasing women for use as personal sex slaves. Even though the IPTF mandated a zero-tolerance policy toward frequenting sex establishments, most sex slaves cited IPTF personnel as regular patrons; patrons also included foreign military, contractors, NGO, and other international personnel. The clubs that DynCorp and IPTF employees most frequented included Crazy Horse I, Crazy Horse II, and the Apache Club, named after the U.S. helicopters of the same name held at a nearby military base. None of the cases in Bosnia that implicated DynCorp or IPTF personnel in sex trafficking or the frequenting of nightclubs with sex slaves resulted in criminal investigations or prosecutions.

In addition to frequenting sex clubs, several DynCorp employees were accused of purchasing sex slaves for personal use from established buyers' markets, such as the Arizona Market in Bosnia, so named for the prevalence of American buyers. Eight DynCorp employees confessed to purchasing sex slaves in 1999 and 2000. One employee encouraged the purchase of slaves because "it is good to have a sex slave at home."[11] Five of the eight DynCorp employees named were sent back to the United States, but no criminal charges were filed. Meanwhile, the whistleblower was also fired because he brought "discredit to the company and the U.S. Army."[12] No such label was attached to the employees who purchased female slaves.

When the Dayton Peace Accords were signed, little attention was paid to Kosovo despite pleas from the government for a peacekeeping force to protect ethnic Albanians from Serbian occupiers. Shortly after the accords were settled, Milosevic took control of Kosovo, extinguished political autonomy, and initiated a brutal repression of the country's Albanian population, roughly 90 percent of the inhabitants at the time. A small resistance force called the Kosovo Liberation Army (KLA) responded with a guerilla war against better-armed Serbian forces. Milosevic branded the KLA as terrorists and commenced a genocidal ethnic-cleansing campaign. When peace talks failed, NATO waged a thunderous air assault on Serbian targets from March 23 to June 10, 1999. Victory was decisive. In July 1999, UN Security Council Resolution 1244/99 authorized the deployment of forty thousand international peacekeeping troops to maintain security in Kosovo. Similar to the situation in Bosnia in the early 1990s, thousands of international staff from over two hundred NGOs accompanied the peacekeeping forces. The sudden influx of international personnel resulted in an analogous explosion of sex clubs filled with slaves. Having learned its lessons in Bosnia, the United Nations declared all such sites "off limits," but when local NGOs conducted interviews with escaped trafficking victims, they learned that over 80 percent of the clientele of these clubs were foreign personnel.[13] To combat the problem, a Police Trafficking and Prostitution Unit (TPIU) was created in November 2000 to gather evidence related to trafficking crimes. One of the TPIU's findings was that approximately 90 percent of the women working in the Kosovo sex industry were victims of sex trafficking.[14] This finding was startling, given that a few years earlier in Bosnia, only 25 percent of the prostitutes in brothels were estimated to be sex trafficking victims. The higher ratio revealed the extent to which organized crime networks had become more prevalent, more effective, and more focused on using slaves to meet demand for commercial sex.

Similar to Bosnia, allegations of UN police force and TPIU involvement in frequenting sex clubs quickly surfaced. There was greater international scrutiny the second time around, as well as a few investigations and criminal prosecutions, though very few punishments were meted out. Even though several laws have since been passed to prosecute international personnel who are involved in sex trafficking incidents while on deployments abroad, the participation of such personnel in sex trafficking continues to occur worldwide, with minimal investigation and prosecution.

The eruption of war and genocide in the Balkan region also was directly responsible for a category of exploitation even more insidious than the rampant trafficking of women into brothels for forced prostitution. That category is child trafficking. The influx to Albania of over six hundred thousand refugees from Kosovo meant that traffickers could easily procure new victims, many of whom were orphaned children. The acquisition and exploitation of thousands of child refugees in multiple slave industries across Europe remains one of the bleakest results of the Kosovo refugee crisis. The trafficking of children from Kosovo refugee camps was not, however, the only instance of child exploitation in Albania. At levels that rivaled those of South Asia, the children of poor minority communities in Albania have been trafficked for slave labor throughout Europe ever since the country was opened two decades ago. In fact, almost seven of ten trafficking victims in Albania were minors at the time they were trafficked, a ratio greater than any country I visited.

Innocence Lost

The streets of Tirana are filled with homeless children, many of whom are forced to beg in the trendy Blloku portion of town, where most international organizations and embassies have their offices. Most of the homeless children have darker skin, revealing their Roma ethnicity. Halfway between the offices of the Organization for Security and Cooperation in Europe (OSCE) and the U.S. embassy, I passed by a frightened young boy huddled on the sidewalk, crying for alms. At his feet, another boy lay on the filthy concrete, unconscious. A small pool of blood leaked from a gash in his head and crusted onto the sidewalk. He was barely alive. I approached the crying boy, but I was unable to communicate with him. I had seen countless similar scenes in India: children beaten or amputated to curry empathy from passersby. In Albania, the strategy did not appear to be working. Even though scores of people walked by, no one donated a single leke for the duration of the time I watched the children.

Thousands of Roma children have been trafficked to Tirana or abroad, where they are forced to beg or traffic drugs, or are sold for adoption, exploited for commercial sex, or sold for organ harvesting. I asked several NGOs for help in translating a conversation with the child on the sidewalk, but I was turned down. Most NGOs agreed that the boy was probably a forced beggar, but one after another, they said they could not help me because they were either resource constrained or had a policy of nonintervention unless a child approached a shelter, primarily because if a child were seen by his owner speaking to a translator the child would likely suffer punishment. Interviewing and assisting child victims of trafficking was a complicated exercise. While I was unable to speak to the children, I did offer them lamb *byreks* (a type of Albanian filo pastry snack), water, fruit, and a few of my wet wipes to clean the unconscious boy's gash. I did the same with as many other child beggars as I could.

In my search to learn more about the exploitation of Albania's children, a gentleman named Vincent Tournecuillert taught me more than anyone else. He was head of the Terre des Hommes mission to Tirana, a Swiss-based NGO dedicated to assisting abused, exploited, or trafficked children. In between deep puffs of French cigarettes, Mr. Tournecuillert informed me that most child trafficking victims from Albania were sent to Greece, where they were forced to beg on the streets of major towns, such as Athens, Thessalonica, Patras, and Ioannina. Entry into Greece

Roma child beggars in Tirana

typically involved a three-day hike over the border mountains, as a nine-year-old boy named Agim Guri explained:

> We walked through the mountains for days and we arrived at the Alexandria Bridge, very near Thessalonica. Then I started to beg and sell handkerchiefs at the seaside [in Paralia]. We slept on the bridge, all snuggled up together . . . Dritan [the trafficker] burned me with cigarettes because I did not earn enough money . . . he always beat me.[15]

Agim spent two years as a child slave in Greece until a car hit him at a crossroad while he was begging. He spent several months in a hospital before he was deported to Albania.

Even though forced begging is much less profitable to slave owners than forced prostitution is, the life of a child beggar can be just as horrific. Children interviewed by Terre des Hommes spoke of being forced to beg up to twenty hours a day; of being beaten, forced to drink shampoo to appear sick, or being starved to evoke sympathy; of being drugged to keep them docile; and of being brainwashed with new names and tales that their parents had abandoned them and the police would kill them. Albanian children even devised a name for themselves once they were trafficked to Greece: robots. In the town of Fier, a man named Ramiz, whose son Barim had been a slave in Greece, told me the children adopted this name because this is how they felt when they were forced to take drugs to beg day and night with no sleep.

Calculating the number of trafficked child beggars like Barim and Agim is not easy. Mr. Tournecuillert estimated that upward of three thousand children had been trafficked from Albania to Greece since the mid 1990s. Other estimates were three times as high. After 2000, the presence of child beggars in Greece slowly decreased because of the lower profitability of child begging related to increased awareness in the Greek population that such children were often slaves. Unlike trafficking for sexual exploitation, awareness campaigns related to trafficking for forced begging can have a measurable effect, as the decision to offer a donation to a beggar can be influenced by awareness of that child's enslavement, whereas awareness of the enslavement of a prostitute has little effect on the decision of a man who is already inclined to purchase a woman or child for sex. Put another way, a donation to a beggar is an act of moral kindness that can be influenced by a moral appeal. The purchase of sex is an act of self-indulgence or moral turpitude that a moral appeal is unlikely to influence. At present, Albanian children are more heavily trafficked to Kosovo, Italy, and other nations in Western Europe than to Greece. I saw numerous Roma children begging on the streets of Rome, including a mother and infant near the Vatican museums. The mother's face was covered in dirt, and the infant lay lifeless in her arms, baking in the afternoon sun. I wondered whether similar appeals not to support the exploitation of forced beggars had been made in Italy, because barely a handful of the hundreds of people I watched walk by the mother and child offered the mother a donation. For better or worse, I gave the mother all the change I had. It seemed the right thing to do, after just receiving a blessing from the pope on the other side of the Vatican walls.

Similar to the parents in Salim's region of Bihar, many parents in Albania sell their children to job agents even though they know the risks. When Mr. Tournecuillert discussed parents' roles in child trafficking, his voice grew somber and he pulled at his thick mustache repeatedly. He explained that the majority of children trafficked to Greece were sold or sent willingly by parents who knew they were trading a child's life for cash. The going rate for a child to an agent or trafficker at the time of my visit was one hundred to one hundred fifty euros. The going rate for the sale of a child to a slave owner by a trafficker was upward of one thousand euros. The children who were sold most often were Roma. Like the *dalits* in India, the *kamaya* in Nepal, and the Shan and Akha hill tribes discussed in chapter 6, the Roma are a poor and stigmatized underclass, the women and children of which are always at risk of exploitation. They live in rural areas or shantytowns like the Gaugazes in Moldova. They suffer deep stigma as being impoverished, illiterate, and dirty. Roma children are particularly vulnerable to trafficking because most are not registered at birth (there is a fee to do so), most are not in school, none are protected by social safety nets, and many families are unstable or broken due to socioeconomic hardship. Roma (and Albanian) children who live in orphanages are only allowed to stay until the age of fourteen, at which point they are sent to the streets, where slave traders await.

Rescuing trafficked children and reintegrating them into society is an extreme challenge. Working with trafficked children is also dangerous, especially children who have been trafficked for organ harvesting. When Mr. Tournecuillert first came to Albania to work on child trafficking, he received a warning from a judge on the International Criminal Court: "Work on child trafficking for sexual exploitation, begging, what have you. Work on child trafficking for organ harvesting, and you're dead." Including my own work, very little research has been committed to exposing the practice of procuring children to carve out their internal organs and sell them on the black market. Organs such as kidneys, livers, and hearts can be sold for thousands of dollars, making the traffic in child organs just as lucrative as sex trafficking is. Despite the risks, efforts to combat child organ harvesting must be escalated. There is no crime more disgraceful than murdering innocent children, profiting from the removal of their hearts, livers, kidneys, and eyes, and tossing out the remains like refuse.

A Solid Plan, Falling Short

Albania has stiffer penalties for trafficking crimes than do most countries I visited. The country's 2005–07 *National Strategy for Combating Trafficking in Human Beings* includes sanctions of up to fifteen years' imprisonment and a fine of fifty thousand dollars for trafficking, a minimum of fifteen years' imprisonment and a fine of up to eighty thousand dollars for "coerced exploitation," and even greater penalties for cases involving minors.[16] However, endemic corruption in Albanian law enforcement and legal institutions renders the above penalties relatively meaningless. Similar to the situation in Moldova, the salaries for police, state attorneys, and judges are low, which means that the level of bribery is high. Protections for victims who wish to press charges are virtually nonexistent due to a lack of funding to implement witness-protection programs. When victims seek habitation in a shelter, they are often turned down because there are only four shelters for trafficking victims in Albania, with an aggregate capacity of 165 persons. Since 2002, fewer than 10 percent of trafficking victims assisted in Albania filed charges against their traffickers; only 10 percent of those actually testified.[17] Despite government reports that indicate high numbers of traffickers prosecuted and convicted, Matthias Kalush of the OSCE mission to Albania told me, "no one in Albania really knows how many trafficking criminals have been convicted because the numbers at the end all disappear." These sentiments were echoed by members of the U.S. embassy in Tirana, who told me over coffee at the nearby American Café that the Albanian government provided "trumped up" statistics, and that few criminals were actually convicted due to corruption, dropped charges, or victim disappearance.

Heavens Unleashed

Protections for victims of sex trafficking in Albania only worsened a few days after I visited the Vatra center. I learned that a grant had been cut, and the shelter was almost out of funds. Without more money, Vatra would have to close its shelter for several months, putting Ines and the others who lived within its secure walls back on the streets. I did what I could to help with introductions to grantmaking organizations, but money is rarely donated to NGOs without extensive applications, audited financial reports, visits to or from the donor, and several other hurdles that drain the time and resources of overstretched trafficking shelters. It was difficult for me even to make phone calls or send emails from Albania during this critical time, due to the lingering absence of winter rains. Electricity resources were close to nil, and on the evening before my departure, the country remained shrouded in darkness. Everywhere I looked, people labored in the hazy gloom, praying for relief from the sky.

That prayer for relief was answered the night before I left. I was packing my bags for a flight the next day when I suddenly felt the wind quicken and the shutters of my window rattled vigorously. I looked north at the smoggy peak of Mount Dajti, and a legion of clouds swooped over the summit and raced toward the desiccated metropolis. In a flash, a fury of rain overwhelmed Tirana. Water spilled like ribbons across the body of the earth. Everywhere, people sprang to life. Old women flung open their windows and received the cool moisture across their faces; young children dashed to the streets and splashed innocently in countless puddles.

The air was clear, and the lights shined bright . . . but I feared for Ines, soon to be homeless in the cold and wintry rain.

6 Thailand and the Mekong Subregion

Lust is the bane of mankind. —*Buddha*

Nice Girl, Very Young

From sublime island sunsets to pristine mountain hikes, Thailand is a country blessed with natural beauty, warm hospitality, and serene images of the Buddha at every turn. Beneath the beauty, hospitality, and the Buddha's watchful eyes, however, a very unique ugliness resides. Children become slaves to the perversities of men, poor people flee from the hills into the hands of unscrupulous exploiters, and in no country that I visited was the line between willing and coerced more blurred. The word "trafficking" is sprinkled liberally in this steamy corner of the world, but rarely does it capture the evasive realities of the movement and exploitation of the region's mammoth number of slaves.

On both my trips to Thailand, the capital city of Bangkok was the port of entry. The official name of this hazy metropolis is Krungthep Mahanakhon Bowon Ratanakosin Mahintara Ayuthaya Mahadilok Popnopparat Rathathani Burirom Udomratchaniwet Mahasatha Amonpiman Avatansathit Sakkathatitya Wit Sanukamprasit, normally reduced to Krungthep, or City of Angels, like Los Angeles. The tourist sites are plentiful, but a few must-sees include the one-hundred–twenty-foot-long reclining golden Buddha at Wat Pho, centuries of royal artifacts on display at the sprawling Grand Palace, and the bustling sights and sounds of the tourist high street, Khao San Road. At Khao San, the visitor can enjoy Western-style restaurants and bars, street vendors selling everything from fresh papaya to roasted crickets, travel agencies, internet cafés, souvenir shops, tattoo parlors, and clothing outlets. Fifty-year-old white European men stroll hand in hand with teenage Thai girls, while other scantily clad teenagers solicit men for massage services. At either end of the pedestrian-only section of the road, *tuk-tuk* drivers wait for unaccompanied men, like me.

"Where do you go tonight?" they ask. "You want Thai girl? I have nice girl. Very young."

Surveying nine *tuk-tuk* drivers, I assembled the price list for services immediately available to a male tourist on Khao San Road, enumerated in table 6.1.

The prices for overnight or one-week purchases did not include feeding the individual, but a few extra dollars for wealthy tourists was not a problem. At numerous restaurants I saw dozens of couples—a thirty-, forty-, or fifty-year-old Western man with a teenage Thai girl eating dinner out on the town. Some of the girls giggled with their owners. Some stared blankly at the passersby while their date-owner chattered mindlessly. Others sat silent alongside an equally silent man, tacitly understanding what was in store once the meal was over.

Outside my hotel not far from Khao San Road, several taxi drivers awaited male guests. Each time I entered or exited, at least one of them approached and asked, "Where do you go tonight? You want Thai girl? I have nice girl. Very young." At hotels in the northern cities of Chiang Mai and Chiang Rai, the solicitations were equally pervasive, though prices were considerably lower. Sex was also for sale at dance clubs, Western-style bars, go-go clubs, massage parlors, karaoke clubs, brothels, and saunas. More than any country I visited, it was nearly impossible to avoid sex solicitation

TABLE 6.1
Sex Service Retail Prices: Khao San Road

Service	**Price (baht/U.S. dollar)**
Sex massage (30 minutes)	100–150/2.50–3.75
Full sex (1 hour)	200–400/5.00–10.00
Girl for one night	~1,000/25.00
Girl for one week	~5,000/125.00

in Thailand. At times, the country felt like a giant brothel, even though prostitution is illegal. Numerous cultural and socioeconomic factors have promoted Thailand's expansive sex industry, but there is also a much simpler reason for the plethora of sex for sale in Thailand, articulated to me by a twenty-year trafficking expert named Faye, who said: "Thai cultivate sex as business."

Most of the plainly visible sex for sale in Bangkok and other major Thai cities is tailored to foreigners. The center of the foreign sex market in Bangkok is an area called Patpong; neighboring Taniya Alley specializes solely in Japanese prostitutes. Tucked underneath an overpass of a superhighway, Patpong consists of three alleys filled with sex bars. Each alley also contains stalls spilling with trinkets, apparel, wood carvings, and other tourist items. Sex bars in the center of the three alleys are tailored to gays. Outside the Patpong sex bars, *touts* solicit the tourist crowd with small placards that picture the types of sexual acts that can be viewed on stage. The majority of females I saw in Patpong clubs were not slaves. They were a mix of Bangkok locals and young females from the rural north who chose sex work as a career. They received a share of money from drinks purchased while they performed and collected tips for lap dances. They also could negotiate sex on their own behalf with a

Young girls selling sex services on Khao San Road

client, for which they kept up to half the purchase price. Sex was almost always transacted off site. The girls were young, usually spoke English, and spent a great deal of money on clothes, makeup, and grooming. In the clubs I visited, most young women appeared to be healthy, though a few teetered with uneasy steps and droopy eyes. On stage, many of the females danced robotically, gazing into space as their bodies moved like automatons.

I had no doubt that a small proportion of the females in areas like Patpong were coerced, but many were also pressured by parents to make money for family subsistence. In Thai society, the duty of caring for parents belongs to the youngest unmarried daughter, and the allure of lucrative sex work pressures many rural teenagers into a lifestyle they might not otherwise choose. Several girls I interviewed explained the pressure they felt to be "good" daughters by working in sex bars. Once inside the bar, not performing and not transacting for sex were inadmissible. A dancer had to generate $800 to $1,000 per month for the club or she would be fired. Returning home to parents who expected financial support was out of the question, as there were few other jobs available for rural, uneducated Thai females. As long as the girls made money, the club owners treated them well. As long as they sent money home, their family duties were fulfilled. Many Patpong girls admitted that they entered sex work dreaming of the day when a rich foreigner would save them from a life of lap dances and seedy hotel rooms. They held these dreams for good reason: Foreign males often took Patpong dancers home as brides. There was even a marriage-license service less than four blocks down the road.

Several other cities in Thailand possessed similar high-end tourist sex areas, the most extensive of which was located in Chiang Mai. Surrounding a kickboxing arena near the main night bazaar, as well as a few blocks near the end of Loikhor Road, I found several bars where scantily clad Thai girls sat with drunk Western men and negotiated for sex. Like the lodger prostitutes in Mumbai, these girls paid a monthly fee to the bar owner as well as a one-half to two-thirds split of their profits from sex transactions they negotiated in the bar. The top end of the tourist sex industry in Chiang Mai included two high-end brothels not far from these bars. The brothels, like their bigger, more expensive analogues in Bangkok, catered to foreign sex tourists and businessmen, complete with plush bar areas, food service, and hotel-quality rooms for steam baths and other activities. In one of these brothels, over one hundred young females sat in an "aquarium," a large room in which they could be viewed behind a shield of glass, awaiting selection. Each wore the same yellow-green dress and sat on various levels of a tiered sitting area covered in green velvet. Some of the girls had a pin with the letter S fixed to their dresses. I asked one of the male managers what this pin meant.

"It means they are superstar," the manager said. "They have special sex talent." The price for these high-end superstars was two thousand baht ($50), ten times the price of a sex slave. Non-superstars started at one thousand baht.

As accessible as Patpong and other tourist sex areas were, they were not havens of sex slavery. These high-end establishments did, however, promote a culture of sexual exploitation that was more perniciously manifested in the country's countless sex-slave venues. Behind these corrosive walls, tens of thousands of female slaves were imprisoned at the lowest rungs of the Thai sex industry, where sex services were provided at bargain-basement prices. These lowest rungs were well hidden. To uncover them, I returned to the *tuk-tuk* drivers of Khao San Road, who were eager to take me into a world where human females could be purchased for only a few dollars.

A Girl Near Loikhor Road

In the Thai sex industry, the farther from the center I traveled, the more I found slaves. For a twenty- to thirty-baht commission from the establishment, Bangkok *tuk-tuk* drivers readily offered access to seedy sex clubs on dark side streets, massage parlors filled with teenage girls, and full-fledged basement brothels that stank of booze, cigarettes, and human filth. In every brothel, the clientele was almost entirely Thai men. Many girls were Thai, many others Burmese, and a small number Laotian. The price for an hour of unrestricted sex with a girl was equivalent to four or five dollars.

In addition to these closed-door sex slaves, I made a discovery during my second trip to Thailand that I could not believe: Nigerian street prostitutes. Though Bangkok was not known for street prostitution, I saw the Nigerians in the Sukhumvit area, where they had not been a few years earlier. Groups of two or three congregated every fifty meters on lanes (*soi*) eight, ten, thirteen, and fifteen, just off Sukhumvit Road on either side of the Ruamchitt Hotel and Plaza. In 2000, the only prostitutes I saw in this area were Thai, primarily servicing the numerous hotels that were originally built as rest-and-relaxation getaways for soldiers on leave from the Vietnam War. Almost six years after my first visit, those same Thai prostitutes were still in the same hotels and bars, but Nigerians had joined them. Some were no doubt trafficked directly from Nigeria. Others were probably re-trafficked from Western Europe. I knew the Nigerians spoke pidgin English, so I did my best to communicate with a few, but I gathered very little information other than the fact that a sex act with a Nigerian street prostitute was almost twice the price of the same with a Thai prostitute. In Western Europe, the Nigerians were at the bottom of the sex-services price list, but in Bangkok, they were priced as exotic.

Aside from Nigerians, the majority of trafficked sex slaves I found in Thailand were behind closed doors, in massage parlors and low-end brothels. I discovered several such establishments in Bangkok, but they were more common in the northern cities of Chiang Rai and Chiang Mai, closer to the hill tribe areas and borders with Burma and Laos. This lowest level of the Thai sex industry was not always a straightforward destination of sex slaves. Brothels, yes, but the massage parlors straddled the line. Some were populated with uncoerced prostitutes. Others were filled with teenagers who were visibly coerced. In Chiang Rai, there was no red-light area, but there were several massage parlors near the main night bazaar, three of which I visited. They offered foot reflexology massages on the ground floor and sex on the top floors with a selection of young hill tribe girls, who in one case were kept behind a padlocked door. When I asked the proprietor why the girls were locked inside, she said it was to protect them from drunken men who came in from the streets and caused trouble.

Chiang Mai's massage parlors were primarily located near the main night bazaar. Like the parlors in Chiang Rai, there was a facade of foot massage on the ground floor and sex with minors for sale on a second floor or in a back room. I visited eight parlors on two separate nights, and not once did I see anyone actually receiving a foot massage, though several men went up and down the stairs to purchase sex. Each parlor had a madam and several girls who sat in the front room and stared robotically at a television screen. On the second floor or in back rooms, so-called Thai massage was for sale, which included a steam bath with the girl of a client's choice. The price for two hours was two hundred baht ($5). On one occasion, I asked for a Thai massage and was invited by the madam to peruse a lineup of downcast teenage girls who disrobed to entice selection. The spectacle made me sick. As difficult as it was to contain my emotions, I politely indicated that none of the girls met my fancy. The

Massage parlor in Chiang Rai in which young girls disrobe to entice prospective clients

madam offered me her best hard sell: two girls for the price of one. I declined, and walked out the door.

Later that evening, a street-corner agent led the way to a dark, dusty brothel not far from Loikhor Road. It was a miniature version of the superstar brothel I had seen the previous day. Eleven Thai men smoked, drank, and guffawed at a bar. Eric Clapton music played in the background. More than twenty girls sat in a small aquarium, though here they called it a sitting room. The girls wore blue jeans and tee shirts, and stared obsessively at a television. A madam in a bright red *kameez* asked me which girl I wanted. For two hundred baht, a girl named Panadda was mine for an hour, provided I wore a condom. She was barely five feet tall, spoke rudimentary English, and met me in a tiny room with a chair, a dresser filled with her clothes, one mirror, one wall clock, posters of a female Thai pop singer, and a stain-covered bed. Used condoms in paper towels were piled in a wastebasket next to the bed; fresh condoms were in the top drawer of her dresser. Aside from the condoms, Panadda's room looked like the bedroom of any regular teenager, including a faded bunny rabbit print on her sheets.

After Panadda closed the door, she sprayed her mouth with mint breath freshener. She asked me what service I wanted, but I showed her my identity card instead and explained that I was a researcher from the United States. She was skeptical. I showed her notes from other interviews I had conducted, and she eventually agreed to speak to me when I promised I would not speak to any of the other girls. She said if word got out to the brothel owner, she would be punished. I told her not to worry; I had a policy of coming to a brothel only once.

Panadda was fifteen years old and a member of the Akha hill tribe. She was bright and had attended a government-funded school until the age of twelve, when her parents insisted that she help her father work in their small rice field. She said that most of the girls in the brothel were from Burma, a few from Cambodia, and the rest from the Akha and Shan hill tribes near Chiang Mai. Panadda also told me that she was given a contraceptive injection every week because even though the customers used condoms, the police did not. She was also given weight-loss pills to curb her appetite because she tended to gain weight from the large amount of alcohol she drank. Her customers were almost entirely Thai and Cambodian men, especially day laborers. The recent economic boom in Chiang Mai had fueled numerous construction projects, including new roads and highways, office and residential buildings, and four new high-rise luxury hotels. In much the same way that women were trafficked to Chiang Mai to service the sexual desires of day laborers, many of the day laborers were men trafficked from Burma, Laos, and Cambodia and forced to work grueling construction jobs for little to no wages. Minimal wages also meant that if they wanted to purchase sex, they could only afford slaves.

When I met Panadda, she had been in the brothel for slightly over a year. She contemplated suicide when she first arrived, but she did not because as long as she worked, the madam sent five hundred baht ($12.50) each month to her parents.

"Have you tried to escape?" I asked her. "There are shelters that can help you."

"I tried in the beginning," Panadda replied, "But the broker who brought me here found me in my village and told my parents I did not repay my debt. They said it was my duty to do this."

"How much do you owe?" I asked.

Panadda had no idea. The first broker bought her for eight thousand baht ($200), then sold her to another broker. The second broker sold her to the brothel in Chiang Mai, where she was told she had to pay back a debt of thirty-five thousand baht ($875) for the cost of purchasing her. Even though she was held against her will, she was charged monthly room and board of ten thousand baht ($250); she had to sleep with fifty men a month to repay it. It was only after the first fifty men each month that she began to make a dent in her debt, on which she was also charged random amounts of monthly interest. Money sent to her parents was also deducted.

Panadda bore her parents no ill will for selling her to the brothel or for sending her back when she escaped. It was her duty to care for them. With genuine pride, she showed me a necklace of small white beads fastened to a pendant of a lotus flower carved from teak wood that her grandmother made for her mother.

"One day I will give it for my daughter," Panadda said.

After an hour, Panadda pointed to the clock and said our time was over. There was so much more I wanted to ask, especially because it took me five visits to other brothels before I found such an articulate, brave young girl who could speak English. I could see that Panadda was nervous, so I thanked her for her courage and asked her if I could give her extra money.

"Give it to Siriporn [the madam]," she said. "She will take it anyway."

I offered Panadda the name and address of a nearby shelter that could help her. Before I left, I asked her how she felt talking to me.

"I feel grateful to tell someone my life," she said.

"With your permission, I would like to tell more people about your life."

Panadda folded her hands in front of her face, and bowed her head.

As I walked out of the brothel, the image of Panadda's bowed head felt like a spear in my chest. This gentle and grateful child was being devoured by beasts, and there was nothing I could do about it. As I talked to Panadda, the sounds of brutish grotesquery resonated from adjacent rooms. Knowing those sounds would soon be resonating from hers made my veins pulse with rage. I wanted the heads of those men on a platter. I wanted them to suffer tenfold the harm they caused to Panadda. If only I could tell you her real name, its meaning would break your heart.

That night I got drunk. I drowned my anger in beer after beer, unable to see goodness in the world. There was no justice. There were no "gentle"-men. Rather than protect children, these wretches feasted on them day and night. Three months into my third research trip, the relentless encounter with human ruin had taken its toll. I felt my spirit depleted, the path to justice far too complex. I yearned for a swift, decisive strike, not the rusted wheels of institutional redress laboring toward the mark. I stumbled to my hotel room and collapsed into bed. As slumber overwhelmed me, dreams of blood vengeance roused from the dark.

Fiat justitia pereat mundus.
Justice be done, though the world perish.

Ghosts in the Mekong

Like India, Thailand holds the dubious distinction of being the primary destination for its own trafficked slaves. Individuals trafficked within the Mekong Subregion are sometimes sent to Burma or Laos, but the majority are trafficked to Malaysia via Hat Yai or numerous sea entry points via the Indian Ocean or the Gulf of Thailand. In addition to its own internal victims, most trafficked slaves in Thailand arrive from neighboring Mekong Subregion countries. Like Albania, Thailand shares porous land borders with several war-torn nations (Burma, Laos, and Cambodia). China is only two hundred kilometers north along the Mekong River, and Vietnam is not more than a two-day bus ride away. The primary routes of entry from these neighboring countries are numerous. Between Burma and Thailand, there are land crossings at Mae Sot, Mae Hong Son, Mae Sai, and Ranong, and river crossings across the Mekong at Mae Sai, the Golden Triangle, and Chiang Sean. Between Laos and Thailand, there is a river crossing across the Mekong from Vientiane, directly across the border from the Thai towns of Si Chiangmai and Nong Khai, as well as river crossings across the Mekong at the Golden Triangle, Beung Kan, Nakhon Phanom, and Chong Mek. Land crossings are available west of Chiang Khan, after the Mekong River veers north. Between Cambodia and Thailand, there are land crossings at Aranya Prathet and Hat Lek, and Gulf of Thailand entry at Rayong, Pattaya, and Samut Sakhon. Between China and Thailand, there is river entry from Chiang Saen across the Mekong. Finally, Bangkok and Chiang Mai international airports are used to traffic Thai women to Europe, Australia,[1] and the United States.

Most Burmese trafficking victims enter from the rural north, somewhere inside the semicircle that begins west of Chiang Mai and traces to the Huay Kon–Nam Ngoen checkpoint with Laos. Countless Laotians are also trafficked into the north. From a base camp in Chiang Rai, I rented a car and spent two days exploring these densely wooded, mountainous borders to understand exactly how the movement of slaves throughout the Mekong Subregion was accomplished.

The roads in Thailand are as easy to traverse as any highway in the West, and just as scenic. Fields of tobacco, banana, pineapple, rice, tobacco, and poppy fill the countryside, and waves of verdant mountains crest skyward. About sixty-five kilometers north of Chiang Rai (five kilometers north of a giant Tesco–Kentucky Fried Chicken outlet), I arrived at the town of Mae Sai, the largest official crossing point between Thailand and Burma. There were numerous police checkpoints along the way, but I was not stopped at any of them. Slave traders knew well that the police rarely stopped cars, and when they did, a one-thousand-baht bribe ($25) per person was sufficient to pass.

Mae Sai was connected by the long Friendship Bridge over a narrow stretch of river to the Burmese town of Tachilek. Thousands of people crossed the bridge each day for the nominal fee of twenty baht ($0.50). Theoretically, they received a day-visa and were supposed to return, but no one ever checked. It was well known that many Burmese migrants met a local agent in Mae Sai who promised paid work in factories in Chiang Mai or Bangkok, but instead took them to brothels or sweatshops. As with India and Nepal, the open border between Thailand and Burma was critical to the livelihoods of countless laborers and merchants. Unfortunately, it was also an easy avenue for human trafficking. Even if the bridge were closed, the narrow river that separates Thailand from Burma near Mae Sai could be crossed with ease. I walked one kilometer along the river in either direction from the Friendship Bridge, and there were several junctures where the water was ankle deep and the width less than fifty feet. Beyond the river, the border ran through thick forest and rolling hills that would be impossible to guard. Several trafficking victims told me that they crossed from Burma near Mae Sai, through the forest, on foot.

Not far east of Mae Sai, I visited the Golden Triangle. Along the banks of the Mekong River, the countries of Burma, Thailand, and Laos meet. A resplendent, forty-foot, golden Buddha presides over this intersection of nations. I did not cross the river into Laos or Burma, but locals told me that slave traders did so all the time. Likewise, just southeast of the Golden Triangle at the town of Chiang Saen, large cargo ships from China docked to load and unload goods, including Chinese men and women trafficked in the ship's cargo hulls, with return shipments of Thai men and women to China. Several Chinese trafficked into Thailand through Chiang Saen told me that they traveled to Chiang Mai and Bangkok by bus, hidden in the luggage holds.

From Mae Sai, I drove south along Highway 110, then west on Highway 1234, where I arrived at hilly tea plantations near the town of Doi Maesalong, two kilometers from the Burma border. Not one person I had spoken to in Thailand mentioned this northwest corner as a route for human trafficking, but it seemed a logical place to check, particularly as there were fewer police checkpoints between Doi Maesalong and Chiang Mai than from Mae Sai. A few kilometers south of Doi Maesalong, I turned west and drove as far as I could down a dirt road until it ended. I spied a village at the base of a hill and walked to it. As I approached, children rushed down a muddy path and greeted me with giggles, waves, and repeated chants: "Goodbye! Hello! Goodbye! Hello!" I approached an elderly man smoking a pipe, pointed to the Union of Myanmar on my map, and asked if he would take me to the border. For one hundred baht ($2.50), he sent me with a teenage boy. I followed the boy up a hill through a dense thicket of forest for no more than twenty minutes, at which point we arrived at a small stream. A narrow bamboo bridge was the only crossing. The boy took my map, pointed to Myanmar, and pointed to the bridge.

I chose a spot in the trees a few meters from the bridge and sat for two hours to see if anyone crossed. In that short period of time, eight people crossed from Burma into Thailand, none the other way. The first group consisted of two men and four women who appeared much younger than the men. They walked right across the bridge and continued down the path toward the village. The second group was a couple, probably in their twenties.

When I returned to the village, the man who sent me with the teenage boy was speaking to the two men who had crossed the bridge. I did not see the four women who crossed with them. There was no way to know whether these women were weekend visitors, legal migrants, or being trafficked, but the fact that I watched eight people cross from Burma into Thailand in a span of two hours demonstrated the high frequency of movement at a random crossing point that no one talked about as a trafficking corridor. Even if the migrants crossed willingly but illegally, if they were Burmese citizens, they would be invisible and unprotected in Thailand and ripe for slave-like exploitation.

After two days at nine points along the Thailand-Burma-Laos borders, I arranged for a lanky guide named Ping to return with me to Doi Maesalong and take me by foot to villages on the Burma side. Ping and I trudged through dense rainforest for two days, chopping our way through the bush with giant machetes. We visited three Akha villages in Burma, including one sleepless night on the floor of a hut while dogs barked incessantly from dusk till dawn. Ping was familiar to local villagers as a hiking guide for tourists, and he translated several conversations with locals. With his help, I learned that Burmese people regularly crossed into Thailand in search of work. For a fee equivalent to five to ten dollars per person, an agent arranged for travel across the border and a connection with another agent in Chiang Mai who would facilitate job placements for tea harvesters, seamstresses, waitresses, factory workers, or construction workers, among others. Some of the villagers had spent years in Thailand before returning, not because they had been working wage-paying jobs, but because the job agents in Chiang Mai never met them, and in their search for work they were invariably exploited by criminals who forced them to toil in factories and brothels for months or years without pay. In other cases, the jobs that were promised turned out to be quite different than the workers expected. Wages were not paid, conditions were dangerous, and women were forced to work as prostitutes. Each and every Akha villager I met knew the risks of migrating to Thailand with the job agents, but they migrated anyway due to economic desperation. Very few migrated without an agent, and none said they knew of anyone who had been coerced across the border.

I was unable to explore the Thailand-Cambodia or Thailand-Malaysia borders on either of my trips to Thailand. However, with the help of Faye and the New Life Center, I met a stoic young lady who narrated a passage from Thailand to Malaysia that astonished me with a level of boldness and sophistication that rivaled Eastern Europe's most evolved organized-crime networks. The woman's name was Lisu, and her traf-

Akha village in Burma that I visited with Ping, close to the Thai border

fickers accomplished a bulk shipment of slaves with little more than a bus, a front organization, and a few bribes.

Lisu was twenty-two years old when we met at the New Life Center in Chiang Rai. Petite, with a scar on her head and black teeth in the front of her mouth, she bowed her head when I greeted her. As she narrated her story, she squeezed a small purple pillow until her knuckles turned white:

> I am from Palang Village, in Chiang Rai district. I belong to the Mien hill tribe. In June 2004, a woman came to our village. Her name was Daow, but she changed her name often, and later she was called Deun. She was well dressed and told me that "hill tribe people are stupid and need help to find work." She told me she could get me a job as a cleaning lady in Singapore, but I told her I would not go. She came back many times and said the job was not hard, and I would be paid a lot of money. She said, "Whatever you need for your home, you can buy it, a refrigerator, power generator, anything." Many other girls had gone from my village to work abroad. Those who returned said they had worked good jobs in restaurants and made good money. Eventually, I thought I would go for a few months and make a good salary.
>
> From Chiang Rai, I went with Daow on a bus to Bangkok. In Bangkok, we took a double-decker tour bus with thirty-five other girls to Haat Yai. There were two men on this bus; one was the owner of the tour, the other was the driver. The others were women, including Daow. Most were younger than me. Every few hours, the bus stopped and the men brought food for us. We did not talk much, but the girl next to me also said she was going for work as a cleaning lady.
>
> In Haat Yai we stopped for the night and slept in the bus. There was only one toilet and one shower in the bottom of the bus that we had to share. The next morning, we drove for two days to Singapore. At the border, the police stopped us, but the driver paid them one thousand baht [$25] for each girl on the bus, and we passed through the border.
>
> When we came to Singapore, we stopped at a bus station. Two vans were waiting for us. We went in these vans, and girls were dropped at hotels in the city. I was sent with five girls to one hotel and we were locked in two rooms. At this time, Daow gave us very short skirts and tops and told us we could not wear underwear. She

> said we would have to make sex with clients each night. I told her, "I will not do this kind of work. I came to work as a cleaning lady," but Daow said if we did not do this work, we would not eat.
>
> I told the other girls we should run away, but we were locked inside for two days without food. On the third night, a man said we could have food if we would work. We agreed.
>
> We were taken by a Thai man and woman five hundred meters from the hotel into the forest. There was no light, and we could barely see. The woman took down the man's pants and showed us how to put on a condom. She showed us how to make the man erect with our hand. She showed us six cubicles with brick walls. Each had a curtain in front, and no ceiling, and also a cot with a plastic sheet on top. She said we must stand at the front of these cubicles and the men will come from eight at night until two in the morning.
>
> The men came from the hotel to the forest every night. Each man paid twenty Singapore dollars for twenty minutes of sex. When they finished, there was a line of men waiting to be next. After each client, we had to put the used condom on the plastic sheet. We also had to clean the man's penis and clean ourselves for the next client. There was no water, so we used tissue, which we also threw onto the plastic. At the end of the night, the owners threw the plastic sheets in a dumpster.
>
> The clients were Malaysian men, Thai men, Chinese, Arabs, and a few Westerners. I do not know how long I was in that hotel. One day a client helped me escape.

At this point, Lisu began to tremble. She stood up and her eyes moistened. A few tears emerged, lost their grasp, and fell to the ground. She could not speak further. After composing herself over a cup of tea, she said:

> I wish I could make a television commercial telling everyone what happens to trafficking victims. I wish I could help poor people have a better life so they will not be treated this way.

A Good Cop

Not long after I met Lisu, I learned that there was one man in Thailand whose sole job was to prevent the victimization of women like her. It appeared to me that he was not doing a very good job of it, so I arranged a meeting. I brought a mood of indignation to our appointment, but I soon learned that this man was a dedicated and thoughtful officer with numerous insights to share.

Police Lieutenant Colonel Suchai Chindavanich was finishing a dumpling lunch when I entered his office. He was the first deputy superintendent of a trafficking police unit formed in July 2005 as a subset of the Crime Against Child, Juvenile, and Woman Suppression Division. When I visited Colonel Chindavanich, he proudly explained that the anti-trafficking police force had three hundred and forty officers. It was a small number for a country of sixty-two million, but he hoped that, with funding, it would grow. Even though the police force had been created by royal decree, it had not yet been funded, just like the trafficking police force in Nepal. As a result, the unit lacked computers, vehicles, and the surveillance equipment required to investigate trafficking crimes effectively.

The trafficking police force was created, Colonel Chindavanich said, because "most officers are not acquainted with trafficking, or they do not see these cases as a path to advancement, unlike homicide or drugs." I pressed Colonel Chindavanich on the statements of numerous sex slaves that police were among the primary customers, that they took bribes to allow brothels to operate, and that sometimes they returned escaped slaves back to the brothels.

"We do have some difficulty with this," Colonel Chindavanich admitted. "The salaries of police officers are not high enough, and they take bribes. I have also been apprised that some officers have become traffickers."

"Just to be clear," I continued. "Prostitution is illegal in Thailand?"

"Yes."

"But everywhere I go, I am solicited to buy sex."

"I would be lying if I say we do not have prostitution in Thailand," Colonel Chindavanich replied.

"If it is illegal, why don't the police crack down on the clubs and brothels?"

"We accept the fact that prostitution exists," Colonel Chindavanich said. "We do not want to override civil rights. The main concern of the government is that prostitution should not be a long-term occupation, because this leads to the spread of HIV and other crimes. In our country, the spread of HIV from prostitutes is a major problem."

"What about young girls who are forced to be prostitutes?"

"This should not happen. But I have known many victims who did not realize they were exploited, that the pimp took all the money, and they were grateful for what little they had left . . . this annoys me greatly."

"I met many prostitutes who were not trafficked, but they felt pressure from their parents to provide an income to the family."

"Yes, this also happens. Many hill tribe girls return from Bangkok with money and expensive clothes. The other parents see this, and they would like their daughters to make this kind of fortune."

During our two-hour conversation, Colonel Chindavanich confirmed that most of the trafficking in the Mekong Subregion was performed by individual agents, not organized crime groups. However, organized crime had become increasingly involved. The most prolific organized traffickers in Asia were the *yakuza* groups of Japan, which had been trafficking people from all six Mekong Subregion countries for at least twenty years. Other organized crime groups operating in Thailand included the Chinese, Russians, and Burmese. Colonel Chindavanich explained that Thai organized crime groups cooperated with foreign syndicates to traffic people into Thailand and traffic Thai people abroad. He said these syndicates maintained agents at all major entry points to the country, where they handed off victims to Thai agents who facilitated transit to their final destinations via prearranged safe houses. According to Colonel Chindavanich, there were hundreds of Russian and East European trafficking victims in the Thai sex industry, and even more Thai women exploited in Russia and Eastern Europe. He also mentioned that Nigerian mafias had become increasingly active, as I saw with my own eyes.

In addition to trafficking for forced prostitution, Colonel Chindavanich and his colleagues described several other forms of trafficking and slavery throughout East Asia. Children from several Mekong Subregion countries were trafficked to Cambodia and exploited in the bourgeoning pedophilia market in Phnom Penh, Cambodia's capital. Cambodian children also were trafficked to Thailand and forced to beg on the streets of Bangkok and Chiang Mai. Men, women, and children throughout the region were trafficked to Thailand and forced to work in sweatshops and factories that produced everything from curry spice to plastic toys. In Vietnam, hill tribe women were sold as brides in China for as little as one hundred fifty dollars. In Summer 2000, I witnessed these sales firsthand at Sapa, a bucolic mountain town in northwestern Vietnam. Every Saturday, the Black Hmong hill tribe people journeyed from the surrounding mountains and gathered in the city for *cho tinh* (the "love market"). Young

Hmong men propositioned girls for marriage, but if a girl was not chosen by the age of nineteen or twenty, she was considered too old for marriage. Rather than house a stigmatized single daughter, some parents sold them to agents at the market. The agents took the girls over the mountains into China, where they were sold into the Shanghai sex industry or promised as brides to Chinese men.[2] Vietnamese women were also trafficked to Taiwan and South Korea to be forced to wed local men.

The last form of human trafficking Colonel Chindavanich discussed was the one he considered the most atrocious. "The trafficking for forced labor in fishing is the most violent," he said.

> They are mostly Cambodian boys trafficked to the town of Aranya Prathet by bus. From there, a Thai agent takes them to the town of Samut Sakhon, on the coast south of Bangkok. The boys are taken to sea where they are forced to catch the fish twenty hours a day for many months. The ship captains force the boys to take amphetamines so they can work nonstop. Other ships come from the coast and transfer the fish, but the boys are kept on the ship.

I asked Colonel Chindavanich what happens to the fishing slaves at the end of the season. He said that many were shot and thrown into the sea. The phenomenon has become increasingly common throughout East Asia, South Asia, and even Eastern Europe and Africa. Ukrainian boys are trafficked for forced labor on Russian fishing boats in the Black Sea and young boys in Ghana are forced to work in the deadly fishing operations on Lake Volta. Countless lives are extinguished at the end of the fishing runs, so that profits for wholesalers remain high and prices for fish-hungry consumers remain low. Beyond the fishing runs, forced labor tactics are used throughout the supply chain, from processing to packaging of seafood for distribution throughout the West, most prevalently in the $1.5 billion shrimp markets of Bangladesh and Thailand.

The People in the Hills

Minority disenfranchisement in Thailand offers criminals a vast pool of potential slaves. Over one million hill tribe people, such as Lisu and Panadda, are poorer, less educated, and possess fewer rights than other Thai citizens do. Similar to the horizontal inequalities in Nepal that left millions in the western region of the country out of the mainstream and motivated the Maoist insurgency, Thailand suffers extensive "vertical inequality" (author's term), by which the rural north is much poorer than the central and southern business and tourist areas of the country. The north is primarily an agricultural center, populated by millions of poor farmers who eke out a living by harvesting rice, sugar, pineapple, cotton, jute, and soybean. The north is also home to the majority of the country's hill tribe people, more than half of whom are not Thai citizens. Similar to the situation of the Roma in Albania, this lack of citizenship disenfranchises the hill tribes from education, health care, and employment. They are not allowed to own property and have no right to vote. Most hill tribe people cannot earn a sufficient income on agriculture alone and descend on the major towns of Chiang Mai and Bangkok to beg, sell handicrafts, or send their children for work. Because they are not allowed by law to venture outside their home districts, they are constantly subject to arrest and harassment as they search for subsistence income.

The primary reason for the disenfranchisement of hill tribe people is that most are not originally from Thailand. They are refugees who fled from tyranny, military conflict, or economic degradation in Thailand's immediate neighbors. The main hill tribes, the regions they occupy in Thailand, and their countries of origin appear in table 6.2.

Of these groups, the Akha and Lahu are the poorest and most often exploited. I visited several Akha and Lahu villages in Thailand, and while they were certainly destitute, they were better off than their *dalit*, *kamaya*, Gaugauz, and Roma counterparts. Most villages had partial electricity and almost all had running water. Nonetheless, making even the most modest ends meet was difficult, so many families sent daughters to earn

TABLE 6.2
Thailand Hill Tribe Origin Nations

Tribe	Area Occupied	Origin Country
Akha, Lahu, Shan	Chiang Rai, Chiang Mai	Burma
Karen	Chiang Mai, Kanchanaburi	Burma
Lisu	Chiang Mai	Burma
Palong	Chiang Rai, Chiang Mai	Burma
Hmong	Chiang Rai, Chiang Mai, Nan	Laos, Vietnam
Mien	Chiang Rai, Chiang Mai, Nan	Laos

money in sex work. Some of the parents spoke candidly that their daughters worked in dancing or entertainment. Others regretted the need to send their children for sex work and decried a system that excluded them from basic citizenship. Most tribal people did not exist in the eyes of the Thai government; their children did not exist either, unless they were registered in the nearest government office—often dozens of miles away—within twenty-four hours of birth. In a controversial attempt to remedy the problem, the Thai government offered citizenship to any hill tribe person who could demonstrate that he or she had been living in Thailand since 1982. The only way to demonstrate this, however, was to have appeared on every government census since that time, which are conducted every three to five years. Very few hill tribe people qualified.

In addition to the Akha and Lahu, the Karen deserve special mention. Outside of a few tourist reservations in the north, the Karen live almost entirely in refugee camps near the Burma border. The Karen are a minority ethnic group from Burma, where they have been oppressed by the military regime of Senior General Than Shwe since 1989. Similar to the genocidal oppression of ethnic Albanians in Kosovo, General Shwe has led a bloody campaign to bring all ethnic groups in Burma under his control, especially the distinctive and seminomadic Karen, who lived in the southeast regions of Burma. When the Karen lobbied for democracy and self-governance in an independent territory, General Shwe responded with military attacks, mass arrests, forced relocation, and torture camps. Over one hundred fifty thousand Karen fled to Thailand, and today there are numerous refugee camps along the Thailand-Burma border, the largest of which are near Mae Sot in the central southwest of Thailand. Colleagues at the UNHCR in Bangkok informed me that Karen women and children were frequently trafficked from these camps. I took a bus from Chiang Mai to Mae Sot to investigate. There were several camps near Mae Sot, including the two I visited: Mae Ra and Mae Loke.

The Karen refugee camps were much more crowded, noisier, and more polluted than the Bosnian refugee camp I lived in during Summer 1995. Thousands of refugees were crammed into tiny bamboo huts. The camps were like small towns with no electricity or plumbing, though car batteries were used to generate power for everything from a few central lights to a makeshift cinema showing bootleg Hollywood films. Half-naked children played in the dirt and teenagers chain-smoked cigarettes while they patrolled the environs. With the help of American volunteers, many of those teenagers spoke English, and I was able to interview several, as well as their families. I met one man who had been in the camp for twelve years, with two children born during his stay.

"I am sad my children do not know their homeland," he told me. "But we can never go back. We would be killed. My father died in prison."

Because they are refugees, the Karen cannot work in Thailand. Many are eager to leave the camp and they know the only way to do so is to make enough money to subsist outside it.

"Agents promise jobs to us," one mother of three sons and one daughter told me. "Many people go and think they will make money. Sometimes this happens, but most do not come back."

For a slave trader, a vast pool of refugees eight hours from Chiang Mai and twelve hours from Bangkok is a perfect fishing pond. The dislocation and disenfranchisement of refugees make them highly susceptible to false job offers. Women leave to be dancers, children to work in noodle factories, and men to work construction. Refugees are rarely paid, and because they have no legal basis to work in Thailand, they have no recourse when they are mistreated. Like other trafficking victims, invisibility renders refugees easy to exploit. Despite the risks, most refugees felt they had no choice. As one refugee explained, "The UN officers say we must not take these offers, but what else can we do? My son is drunk on opium. We rot like milk in the sun. I sent my daughter to Bangkok two years ago. She sends money with an agent. With this money I buy schoolbooks and clothes for my other children."

The refugees in Mae Sot were not the only Burmese citizens exploited as slaves in Thailand. Burma is one of the poorest countries in the world, afflicted with among the world's highest inflation rates, worst public health systems, and of course, fiercest political oppression. As I learned during my trip with Ping, thousands of Burmese migrate to Thailand each year to secure remittances for relatives back home. Just like the tens of millions of poor people across the developing world who migrate to wealthier nations, the Burmese venture to Thailand in search of a better life, often finding slavery instead.

Thai Women, and Buddhism

"To have a daughter is like having a toilet in your front yard."
"A woman is only worthy when she has a husband."

"Women are buffaloes. Men are humans."

These three traditional Thai proverbs speak directly to the subordinated status of women in Thai society. Among other factors, this status is very much defined by strict interpretations of Buddhist doctrine. A great deal is written about the role of Buddhism and female inferiority in Thailand, so it is important to understand exactly how the former allegedly promotes the latter; also, my own affinity for Buddhist doctrine begs that I indulge the topic.

Of the two main sects of Buddhism—Theravada and Mahayana—Theravada ("Teaching of Elders") is the earlier, more orthodox school. The Mahayana school developed later in the Himalayan lands of Nepal, Tibet, China, and Mongolia. Ninety percent of Thai citizens are Theravada Buddhists, who limit their practice to those doctrines codified after the passing of the Buddha. The Mahayana school built upon these teachings, in an effort, it was said, to respond more appropriately to the needs of lay people, who could not ascribe to strict Theravada doctrines. In Mahayana Buddhism, it is possible for a lay person to achieve the ultimate spiritual goal of *nirvana* (*nibbana* in Thailand), whereas a Theravada Buddhist must first ascend to the level of monk before *nirvana* is possible.

The starting point of both traditions is the same—desire (*tanha*) leads to suffering (*dukkha*) due to the impermanence (*anicca*) of all things, including the human self (*anatman*). All objects, all feelings, all life is impermanent, thus all desires remain unfulfilled, which leads to human suffering. To extinguish (*nirvana*) suffering, the Theravada Buddhist must follow the Eightfold Path, as articulated by the Buddha after he achieved enlightenment. Theravada Buddhists live by very strict interpretations of these doctrines, and they do not believe it is possible to achieve *nirvana* in any individual lifetime. Rather, they endeavor to accrue karmic merit in the hopes that they will be reborn higher along the path to *nirvana*, which ultimately requires several lifetimes spent at the level of monk. The modes of achieving merit and the subordinated role of women in traditional Theravada society have been crucial factors in the evolution of the sexual exploitation of women, as a business, in Thailand.

For Theravada Buddhists, the world ascribes to a strict hierarchy, ranked by karma. Karma is the consequence of all actions and intentions. Positive or moral actions accrue positive karma, and negative or immoral actions accrue negative karma. At the end of life, the sum of these two results carries an imbalance. This karmic residue (*sesa*) dictates the nature of rebirth. Positive residue leads up the ontological hierarchy; negative residue leads down. Through cycles of rebirth, the ultimate goal is to eliminate the residue by extinguishing the self, so that rather than suffer rebirth, the spirit is released. *Nirvana* is this release, and it is achieved upon the individual's attainment of enlightened unattachment to the world—no more desire, no more suffering, no more actions that require karmic settlement.

Theravada Buddhists place great importance on the hierarchy of rebirth as a sign of spiritual advancement. On earth, the king resides at the top of the hierarchy, followed by the monastic, the wealthy, men, women, the crippled, the destitute, and animals. Manifestations of wealth and power are evidence of the accumulation of positive karmic merit in past lives, whereas manifestations of poverty, disease, female gender, or slavery are evidence of past negative deeds. In this way, Thai people reconcile themselves to inequality, and the only way for the downtrodden to be reborn into better shoes is to abide their position dutifully and to accrue positive karma, even if that position entails slavery.

The question of why females are lower on the hierarchy of rebirth than males is at the crux of Thailand's historic subordination of women. In certain passages in the original Pali texts, the Buddha states that women are equal to men.[3] Other passages can be interpreted to indicate that they are inferior.[4] For reasons far too complex to explore in this book, the Theravada tradition that took hold in Thailand maintained the inferiority of women. As a highly educated Thai woman who worked for a major IGO in Bangkok told me, "In Thailand, the best thing a man can do is become a monk, the best thing a woman can do is be reborn a man." The moment she uttered those words, I thought of the doctrine of sworn virgins under the Kanun in Albania (see chapter 5). It was astounding to me that in countries thousands of miles apart with completely different cultural and religious traditions, the optimal outcome for the female gender was nevertheless the same: become a male. While such beliefs are more entrenched in rural Thailand than in Bangkok, the culture of female inferiority nevertheless pervades the capital. Thailand remains one of the few countries that still has not signed the 1985 International Convention on Elimination of All Forms of Discrimination Against Women, in objection to various articles related to equal rights for women to education, employment, property, and inheritance. Women are spiritually and civically inferior in Thailand, and this subordination has been most keenly (and not accidentally) manifested through centuries of systematized sexual exploitation by men, within the country's longstanding and well-developed prostitution industry.

History of Prostitution

The Thai cultivate sex as a business, as Faye told me, and as in the Netherlands, this business provides the perfect veil behind which women and children can be exploited as slaves. The history of Thai women being held as male property dates back to the fifteenth century. As codified in law, men were allowed to beat wives without sanction (as under the Kanun) and they could sell wives as slaves if they grew tired of them. It was also generally accepted that men had a greater sex drive than women and that there was abundant prestige in having multiple wives. Three types of wives were classified: a major wife (*mia klang muang*), a minor wife (*mia klang nork*), and a slave wife (*mia klang tasi*). The major wife was arranged by parents. A minor wife was added for more children and prestige, and a slave wife could be purchased for sexual gratification and the performance of menial tasks. All housewives were conditioned to be submissive, obedient, and to bear children. They were also socialized to dampen their own sexual desires and properly satisfy the desires of their husbands. Using prostitutes to secure sexual gratification rapidly escalated after polygamy was declared illegal by royal decree in 1934, as the centuries of polygamy and male sexual entitlement provided the perfect underpinnings for an expansive prostitution industry. Rather than commit adultery, Thai society deemed it preferable for a man to purchase sex from prostitutes, many of whom would have been purchased as slave wives before the 1934 decree.

After the decree, the cultural superiority of men and the acceptance of prostitution as a means for men to express their supposedly greater sex drive converged with the Theravada precepts of karma, duty, and merit transfer to ensnare countless Thai women in a life spent gratifying male sexual desire. Recall that the best outcome for a woman in the Theravada tradition is to accrue sufficient positive karma to be reborn as a man who might one day become a monk and achieve *nibbana*. Thai children feel a deep sense of obligation (*bun khun*) that they must care for parents and show appreciation for being born on this ladder toward *nibbana*. Men show appreciation by working hard, having families, and temporarily ordaining as monks before marriage, an act that transfers abundant karmic merit to parents. Females cannot become monks and transfer religious merit to their parents, so the best they can do is to care for parents through financial contributions. Often uneducated and unable to find wage-paying jobs, poor Thai or hill tribe females turn to the country's prostitution industry as the primary vocation to fulfill parental obligations. "Good" daughters work as prostitutes for many years and send home money to elevate the status of the family, whereas "bad" daughters flee prostitution before their debts are repaid, or before they send enough money to provide for parents into old age.

Though the prostitution picture in Thailand was more complex than it was in any country I visited, two trends were clear: Both the number of prostitutes and the percentage of those prostitutes who were trafficked or exploited as slaves were rising. Estimates of the number of prostitutes in Thailand vary from one hundred and twenty thousand (Thai Ministry of Public Health) to two million (various NGOs). My best estimate stands at approximately five hundred thousand, with one in ten being the victims of directly coerced sex work. The growth in the industry has been catalyzed by swelling wealth in Thai society as well as swelling sex tourism to Thailand. Two out of three tourists to the country are unaccompanied men, and Thailand's reputation as a destination for inexpensive and exotic sex means that demand for female bodies will only rise. Domestically, 90 percent of Thai men have visited a prostitute at least once. Half had their first sexual encounter with one. With demand for prostitutes on the rise, the Thai sex industry remains hungry for bodies, and the poor daughters of Thailand and the Mekong Subregion are conscripted to meet that need. Despairing rural and hill tribe families migrate from near and far in search of any means of survival, and with elevated levels of efficiency and facility, criminals enslave them to service millions of sex-hungry men.

Commit

Though Asian nations often lag behind the West in efforts to address human rights issues, I discovered one anti-trafficking endeavor in East Asia that was head and shoulders above the rest. The Coordinated Mekong Ministerial Initiative Against Trafficking (COMMIT) achieved an unprecedented level of cooperation among Thailand, Cambodia, Burma, Laos, Vietnam, and China. Each nation signed a memorandum of understanding with specific commitments to addressing human trafficking, a shared definition of the problem, a shared approach to assisting victims, and multilateral migration agreements to help reduce the number of individuals who risked migration with slave traders. As I learned about COMMIT from local staff in Bangkok, I recalled the wish lists of every anti-trafficking advocate I met in Europe, which included a desire for multilateral, comprehensive agreements of exactly this kind. In Turin (see chapter 3), Cristina Bianconi blasted the lack of bilateral law-enforcement agreements that made it nearly impossible for her to gather the evidence she needed to prosecute a case. In Chisinau (see chapter 4), Peter shook his head at the large number of traffickers who escaped justice by skipping to Russia or Turkey, with which Moldova shared no extradition agreements for trafficking crimes. That the Mekong Subregion countries, consisting of governments as different as the United States and Cuba, could find common moral, legal, law-enforcement, and policy grounds regarding the way to best combat human trafficking should inspire similar efforts across the world.

Despite its commitments to COMMIT, Thailand's national efforts to address slave trading leave much to be desired. There are no fewer than ten laws relating to human trafficking and slavery,[5] yet government apathy and law enforcement indifference have rendered many of these laws ineffective. The average sentence for convicted traffickers has been about three years, with no fines. The country achieves no more than thirty or forty convictions per year out of thousands of annual trafficking victims and tens of thousands of migrants who toil as slaves. The paucity of will to eradicate these offenses is a disgrace.

Worms, Birds, and Jaguars

I suspect government officials in Thailand will bristle at my use of the word "disgrace" to describe the country's anti-trafficking efforts. To be fair, Thailand does not do much worse than most other Asian nations at combating slave trading and slavery. I may have spoken more harshly in this chapter in large part because it was the most difficult for me to write. The subject matter was not more harrowing, but the moment I put pen to paper, a recollection of the raw and depleted emotions that hounded me during my second trip to Thailand infected every word I wrote. This second visit to East Asia was toward the end of my third research trip, and months of encounters with brutalized sex slaves left me disheartened and disoriented. I felt helpless to make a difference. I could concoct a dozen solutions, but as long as a certain proportion of men preyed upon women and children, what effect could my insights possibly have?

This sense of profound hopelessness reached its peak during my time in Mae Sot. After a day of interviews with refugees, I felt bleary and exhausted. I ambled away from the crowds toward a gathering of mist-capped trees. My head pounded in spasms, and images from Slovenia arose from the cemetery of my mind. A refugee camp began my journey into sex trafficking, and more than ten years later, I was in another one, in which trafficking still reigned. I felt the purpose of my journey evaporate. All around me, I saw nothing but cruelty. Even in the forest, the nourishing rain that was falling unleashed a cycle of predation. The gentle drizzle moistened the dirt beneath my feet, which provided a home for the worms, who would eventually be devoured by birds, who would in turn be consumed by jaguars. Then the jaguar droppings would fertilize the soil so that the worms had nutrients to eat, and when they ate the nutrients derived from their devoured forefathers they would excrete nitrogen, which would help the trees grow tall. But one tree would be taller than the rest and block the sun so that the others could not grow as tall and strong at all, because if there were too many trees there would not be enough water in the dirt to keep it moist for the next generation of worms who must be devoured.

Wandering among those trees, I feared a terrible truth: Just as the totality of the forest required predation in order to survive, so too might the world of man. Perhaps slaves had to be meals to the jaguars of the world. Perhaps their suffering was just as necessary as rain to the forest trees.

7 The United States

The test of our progress is not whether we add more to the abundance of those who have much; it is whether we provide enough for those who have too little.
—Franklin D. Roosevelt, second inaugural address, 1937

So Close, Yet So Far

It was not easy to meet Sunee. She was one of only two women I met inside a place of business in the United States that I can say with confidence was a victim of sex trafficking. With limited resources, I narrowed my search for trafficking victims to New York (2000 and 2001), San Francisco (2000), Las Vegas (2003), and Los Angeles (2001, 2002, and 2006). In addition to these cities, cases of human trafficking have been documented in San Diego, San Jose, Fresno, Seattle, Reno, Chicago, Dallas, Minneapolis, Atlanta, Miami, Fort Myers, Jersey City, Newark, Boston, Philadelphia, and Washington, DC. The victims in these cases hailed from over thirty countries. The United States is not one of the three primary centers of sex trafficking that erupted during the 1990s, but individuals from every corner of the world are trafficked to the "land of the free, and the home of the brave," where they are treated no better than Africans who arrived on slave ships two centuries ago.

The Thai massage parlor in which I met Sunee was located in Los Angeles, not far from the intersection of Western and Hollywood Boulevard. Like many large cities, Los Angeles has Asian massage parlors that are often fronts for prostitution. Some of these parlors are populated with slaves. I stumbled upon Sunee's massage parlor after several days of searching in March 2006 with no indication in five such parlors—plus two go-go clubs in Koreatown and four nude dance clubs—that there were trafficking victims in the establishments. The parlor appeared to be more upscale than many others I visited, so I expected a minimal chance of encountering slaves. Inside, the scent of lemongrass filled the waiting room. Behind a curtain, there were private massage rooms where so-called traditional Thai massage took place. A short middle-aged Thai man greeted me. He showed me a price list and said he could offer fifteen dollars off the sixty-dollar price of a one-hour traditional Thai massage. I agreed.

The proprietor invited me to a back room and said, "Pick your girl, sir." He pointed to four Thai girls wearing black pants with ethnic-printed tops, reading magazines in a small sitting area. I asked if any of the young women spoke English, and with pride the proprietor replied, "My girls speak very good English!"

I chose Sunee, who looked the youngest. "Enjoy your massage, sir," the proprietor said. Sunee led me to a small, bare, but clean massage room. There was a mattress on the floor with fresh sheets. A sliding door offered privacy. Sunee gave me a pair of loose-fitting cotton pants and a shirt to wear. After I changed, she returned to the room with hot towels and a plastic carrier kit that contained lotion, oils, and Escape mint gum. She started to chew the gum and asked, "Is this your first massage?"

"No," I replied.

Sunee asked me to lie on my stomach and washed my feet with one of the hot towels.

In a soft voice, she asked, "You like special massage?"

I sat up and asked her what she meant.

"For tip we can make sex."

Sunee clinically laid out the prices of various supplementary activities, which ranged from an additional ten to forty dollars.

I showed Sunee my identity card and explained my research. I told her I could try to help her find a different job. Her face tightened.

"Don't be nervous," I told her. "I can leave if you like."

Sunee did not respond.

"Were you brought here from Thailand?" I asked.

She nodded.

"Are you from the north? Maybe near Chiang Mai?"

Here eyes lit up when I showed familiarity with her country.

"You know Thailand?" she asked.

I told her I had visited twice.

Barely above a whisper, Sunee told me she was born in Fang and lived in Chiang Rai. I knew exactly where Fang was, about an hour west of Chiang Rai, thirty minutes south of Doi Maesalong. The younger of two sisters, Sunee dropped out of school when she was fifteen after her father became ill and could not work. He needed expensive treatment. A man named Aran offered a job to Sunee as a waitress at a German restaurant in Chiang Mai. Aran told Sunee's parents he would arrange the job in exchange for a commission from Sunee's earnings. Her parents agreed.

"Was the restaurant on Loikhor Road?" I asked, recalling the numerous European-style restaurants and beer houses west of the night bazaar there. Sunee said she did not know. When she went with Aran in his pickup truck to Chiang Mai, he sent her with a woman named Sawat, who told Sunee the job at the restaurant had been taken. Sawat informed Sunee she could get her a better job in Los Angeles with a salary of two thousand dollars per month working at an American restaurant. Though Sunee had never left the country, her parents agreed. Her father needed the medicine.

"Sawat bought my plane ticket and passport. One other girl came with us. We flew from Bangkok to Los Angeles on Thai Airways. I was never on a plane before. When we landed, I felt very tired, but Sawat said I had to go straight to work. She sent us with a man who drove me to this place."

Once in the massage parlor, Sunee was told that she owed twenty thousand dollars to the owner, Chuvit, and that she would have to pay back the sum by performing massage and sex work, starting that night. Sunee refused. She was raped and whipped with a leather belt by several men. Ten months later, her daily routine consisted of receiving patrons from 10:00 a.m. to 10:00 p.m., seven days a week. She rarely had more than eight customers a day. Most were Thai men. The money from Sunee's "work" to date—easily seven thousand five hundred dollars per month—went to Chuvit, except for a small amount sent to her parents. As proof, Chuvit offered Sunee a receipt each month for one hundred dollars that he wired to Chiang Rai. Other than those payments, Sunee had no contact with her parents.

Before my sixty minutes expired, I asked Sunee if she would like me to contact her parents for her, or if she had any relatives with a phone or email address. She said no. I asked if I could call the police on her behalf, but she said that Chuvit had told her that the police would throw her in jail because she had stayed past her visa. Sunee refused to believe me when I told her that Chuvit was lying. I told her the United States had laws against forcing women to work under such conditions and that the police would protect her. I gave her the number of the U.S. trafficking hotline as well as the number for a nearby shelter that could help her find a proper job and make enough money to support her parents. Sunee did not want to take the risk.

"If I make trouble, Aran will harm my parents."

I did not know what to say.

As difficult as it was to meet trafficking victims in far-off countries, meeting a victim in Los Angeles was worse. I knew that the police would not take a bribe to return Sunee to the massage parlor and that a shelter just a few miles away could offer her a bed, counseling, legal support, medical care, and vocational training. Yet I could not offer her help. Just behind a concrete wall in the town in which I lived, Sunee was a slave.

I do not know if Sunee ever called the hotline, and there is no indication that she ever called the shelter. I live just fifteen miles from Sunee's massage parlor, and every day since we met, I have anguished over her fate. I debated calling the national trafficking hotline myself. Surely it was in Sunee's best interest, as well as the interests of the other girls in the massage parlor, even if Sunee did not see that at the time. Surely it was the right thing to do, to combat sex trafficking in the United States. I did not make the call for two reasons: Sunee needed the money for her family and there was the threat of violence against her parents. Still, I thought, perhaps her parents would tell her to come home because being a slave was not worth it. Perhaps the other girls in the massage parlor wanted to be free, but it was not my call to make. Even if there was no threat of violence, I knew the families needed the money to survive. A modest sum required for basic subsistence had shackled these young women to slavery, and while a phone call might save Sunee, it was not up to me to decide that Sunee's life was more important than her father's. I chose not to call the hotline. To this day, I do not know if I did the right thing.

In Search of Slaves

Almost one hundred fifty years after the Emancipation Proclamation, there are still slaves in the United States. However, despite what you might read in the papers and see on television or movie screens, trafficking for sexual exploitation is not a fast-growing epidemic within U.S. borders. The annual number of sex trafficking victims to North America is approximately 0.9 percent of the global total; the number of total human trafficking victims is approximately 1.1 percent. Several West European countries with one-fifth the population of the United States receive a greater number of annual victims. Embedded in these numbers is the fact that the majority of human trafficking to the United States is not for the purpose of commercial sexual exploitation. People are trafficked for forced labor in agriculture, domestic service, factory work, and street peddling. Of the seventy-five (as of 2006) human trafficking victims assisted by the Coalition to Abolish Slavery and Trafficking (CAST), an L.A.-based NGO with the only trafficking shelter in the United States, roughly one in eight were trafficked for forced prostitution. The others were trafficked for other forms of forced labor and the victims hailed from twenty-one countries: 35 percent were from Thailand, 17 percent from Mexico, and 12 percent from Indonesia.[1]

The lower per-capita rate of human trafficking to the United States can be directly attributed to a few key factors. First, the greater distance of the United States from origin countries, except Mexico, makes trafficking more difficult and expensive. A long-haul flight is required from Eastern Europe or East Asia, versus buses, trains, trucks, or short flights to reach Western Europe. Aside from illegally crossing the Mexican border into Texas, New Mexico, Arizona, or California, with the help of border-crossing experts called *coyotes,* passports and visas must be procured for entry at major airports. In addition to more challenging dynamics for movement, relatively less corrupt law-enforcement and judicial systems make it harder to exploit slaves in the United States. Finally, in 2000, the United States passed aggressive anti-trafficking legislation, the Trafficking Victim and Protection Act (TVPA), which sparked increased levels of prosecution and conviction of trafficking criminals.

The smaller ratio of sex trafficking to the United States versus other forms of human trafficking raises interesting questions. In most of Europe and Asia, sex trafficking represents 30 to 45 percent of the total amount of human trafficking in a country, but in the United States, it represents closer to 15 to 20 percent. There are a few possible explanations for this difference. The first is that, outside of thirteen counties in Nevada, prostitution is illegal in the United States. Thus, there is no legal veneer under which sex-slave exploitation can take place. Second, the illegality of prostitution is substantially enforced, unlike in many other countries. Third, law enforcement in the United States is relatively less corrupt than in many East European or Asian nations, hence; it is more difficult to find police officers to bribe to set up a brothel and avoid raids. Make no mistake, the United States is a vast country with its share of corruption, and sex slavery does exist within its borders, but it does so to a lesser degree per capita than every other country discussed in this book. A fourth reason for the smaller ratio of sex trafficking to other forms of human trafficking to the United States is my subjective assessment that there is less real demand for sex services among U.S. males than there is among males in other countries. I have no way to justify this assessment objectively, but having traveled throughout Europe, Asia, and Latin America, I can say from personal observation that market demand for prostitutes appeared greater in all of those areas than in the United States. This market demand is assuredly driven in large part by greater supply-side forces. There was more pornography for sale at street corners in Europe, more prostitution visible and easier to access in Asia, and of course, in several of these countries, prostitution is legal in some form or another. I am not suggesting that U.S. males desire sex services less than other males; only that, at a minimum, lower accessibility engenders less real demand.

Even though the per capita rate of sex trafficking is lower in the United States than in most countries, the United States still has thousands of sex slaves. Tracking them down, however, proved prohibitively difficult for me. Despite numerous attempts with solid leads, I failed to converse with sex trafficking victims in New York, San Francisco, and Las Vegas. I was only successful in Los Angeles. In 2000 and 2001 in New York, I searched Chinatown, Koreatown, and the Russian areas of Brooklyn. I searched hotels, clubs, saunas, massage parlors, and warehouse-brothels in the garment district, but I did not meet any sex slaves. The primary obstacle was that many of the localities were in ethnic areas, and the establishment did not allow individuals of a different ethnicity to enter. In Summer 2000, I also searched San Francisco, primarily in the Mission, Tenderloin, and Polk districts. Advertisements in newspapers for Asian escorts proved to be my best leads. I contacted one service that led to a brothel on the second floor of a Chinese restaurant, but none of the prostitutes spoke English and I could not say for sure if they were slaves. In an episode similar to that of Italy at Isabella Laggio's apartment (see chapter 3), another phone number led me to an apartment brothel, but I was first told to travel to a specific street corner and make a phone call from a pay phone to receive directions. When I made the call, I was told to get lost, in more profane terms. In Las Vegas in 2003, I was sure that if I dug deep enough, I would find sex slaves. Prostitution was everywhere, which suggested that somewhere off the beaten path someone might exploit slaves under the cover of legality. I visited numerous establishments, both near the Las Vegas strip as well as farther from the city center, but I could not identify anyone who appeared to be the victim of forced prostitution.

In 2001 and 2002, I conducted searches in Los Angeles, including strip clubs on the east and west sides of town (south of Olympic Boulevard), as well as massage parlors, karaoke clubs, and dance clubs in Chinatown and Koreatown. Most of the women were Hispanic or Asian, and none of them appeared to be slaves. The most probable case of sex slavery was an entertainment club in Koreatown, just off Vermont Avenue, where I saw a dozen girls huddled around the main dance stage and a handful of customers transacting with a proprietor before taking the females to the bar for drinks, or through a door that likely led to back rooms. I also found a Thai grocery store in Thai town that had a massage parlor in a back room, though the masseuse-prostitutes did not appear to be coerced into soliciting sex, which they did so regularly. As for interviews in the only trafficking shelter in the United States, CAST rightfully limits access to the individuals in its care. I was, however, able to discuss several cases with Sister Judy, who manages one of the two locations for CAST trafficking survivors. One of those cases involved a woman named Lucita.

Lucita was trafficked from Guerrero, Mexico to Pomona, California after a recruiter promised work in Los Angeles. Lucita was told that entertaining men would be involved, but the income was too good to pass up. She and two other girls went with the recruiter to Nogales, Mexico, just across the border from Arizona, seventy miles south of Tucson. There, Lucita met two *coyotes,* and early the next morning, they ran across the desert. On the other side, a woman met the girls and drove them to Phoenix, where they spent the night in a safe house. From Phoenix, they drove to Pomona, where Lucita and the girls were dropped at a house and forced to have sex with men:

> When the first customer chose me, I didn't know what to do. The other girls who I came with had some experience. One of them told me to take a shower with the man, to wash and massage him, and to give oral sex. I had never bathed naked with a man and I had never even heard about oral sex. However, I did the best I could.

> We worked twelve hours a day, from eleven in the morning to eleven at night. We never had a day off. We were given sponges to use during our menstruation. No matter if we were sick, we still had to work. We had to sleep in the same place where we worked.[2]

After one month, Lucita was moved to a second house. She was never allowed to make a phone call or even look outside the window. When the police raided the house on suspicion of prostitution, the girls hid because the slave owners had convinced them that the police would shoot them. Lucita was never paid a penny, though on occasion she was allowed to send small amounts of money to her parents. Her clients were almost entirely Asian men.

The Cadena Family

One of the cases prosecuted by U.S. district attorneys that best represents the dynamics of sex trafficking in the United States is the case against the Cadena family, from Veracruz, Mexico. The Cadenas trafficked over twenty Mexican females as young as fourteen through Texas, where they were deposited into trailers, driven to migrant workers' camps in Florida (Avon Park, Fort Myers, Oceche, Zolfo Springs), and forced to perform sex work for migrant workers inside the trailers as well as in a house-brothel. The women agreed to cross into the United States illegally on the promise of jobs as waitresses and landscapers. One victim, Maria, described the bait and switch:

> Once in Florida, Abel Cadena, one of the ringleaders, told me I would be working at a brothel as a prostitute. I told him he was mistaken and that I was going to be working in a restaurant, not a brothel. He then ordered me to work in a brothel. He said I owed him a smuggling debt of twenty-two hundred dollars and the sooner I paid it off, the sooner I could leave.[3]

Like most slave brothels, the conditions were violent and dehumanizing. The Cadena family forced the victims to sleep with customers by shooting at the ground near their feet, threatening their families, and raping them if they tried to escape. Maria testified that she was forced to sleep with up to thirty men per day. She was regularly tortured, starved, and forced to undergo painful abortions:

> We worked six days a week and twelve-hour days. We mostly had to serve thirty-two to thirty-five clients a day. Weekends were worse. Our bodies were utterly sore and swollen. The bosses did not care . . . we worked no matter what. This included during menstruation. Clients would become enraged if they found out. The bosses instructed us to place a piece of clothing over the lamps to darken the room. They did not protect us from client beatings. Also, at the end of the night, our work did not end. It was now the bosses' turn with us. If anyone became pregnant we were forced to have abortions.[4]

Another victim, Ignacia, was trafficked by the Cadena family when she was fifteen:

> I hated to be in the brothels. There were so many clients that came to the house. I was so scared. I would try to hide from them so they wouldn't pick me. The bosses told me I had to work and to stop behaving in this manner. Also, the bosses would rape some of the other girls. This scared me. I was afraid they might rape me or hurt me in some other way. I didn't know anyone. I was alone. I was very frightened.[5]

Violence, isolation, drugs, and alcohol were used to maintain complete control over the victims. Threats against families ensured compliance. In another high-profile trafficking case, a man named Mishulovich, who trafficked five Lativan girls and forced them to dance in strip clubs in Chicago, used similar tactics. At his trial, Misulovich testified, "I told them because of my organized-crime connections in Riga, I can always make a phone call and harm may come to their families."[6] One of the victims offered a more graphic account: "He would describe it in detail . . . like they would cut off her [family member's] ears, and then her nose, and then just kill her."[7]

The Cadenas were eventually brought to justice in Spring 1999. The ringleader, Rogeria Cadena and six other Cadena family members, were sentenced to lengthy prison terms and forced to pay restitution to their victims. In 2002, one of the fugitive Cadena family members was apprehended at the U.S.-Mexico border, and yet another member was convicted in Mexico with the help of the Mexican government. In 2005, another Cadena family member was arrested and is awaiting trial. Because U.S. anti-trafficking prosecutors have abundant resources at their disposal, they can pursue a case more completely. Had the Cadenas been operating in Eastern Europe or South Asia, the case probably would have fallen apart due to corruption, victim disappearance, or a lack of resources to maintain investigations.

For all its successes, the Cadena case was also remarkable for the manner in which it failed. On numerous occasions, law-enforcement officials did not identify the women as slaves, consigning them to extended exploitation. Three months after the first group of women was trafficked from Mexico to Florida, they found a telephone inside a closet in the brothel, of which the traffickers were not aware. One of the women had seen a television show in Mexico in which a Latino child in the United States dialed 911 to get help. When the Cadena victim dialed 911, ambulances, firefighters, and police rushed to the scene. Two Cadena guards kept the women inside the house while others spoke with the emergency responders. They claimed that the call was an accident and no one in the house was injured. The emergency responders did not investigate further. Remarkably, the women called 911 two more times, emergency services responded, and the Cadena guards sent them away. Not long after, one of the Cadena guards shot one of the slaves in the foot. A neighbor heard the screams and called the police. The police arrived, but the Cadena men claimed that the shot was a mistake and that the inhabitants of the house were happily married couples. The police registered the incident as a domestic dispute and did not investigate further. Only much later, after tips from locals that there was prostitution occurring inside the house, did police and FBI agents raid the home and free the slaves. Similar failures to identify slaves remain far too common, despite increased awareness and training for emergency responders. This is why, among the other measures listed in chapter 1, dedicated anti-slavery inspection forces and specially trained community vigilance committees can help ensure such failures to identify slaves are not repeated.

How Do They Get Here?

Trafficking to the United States is not nearly as extensive as it is in other regions. As mentioned before, there are only two modes of entry: flights from East Asia and Europe or crossing the U.S.-Mexico border.[8] A very small number also arrive in the cargo holds of tankers from China. When flights are required, victims travel to the United States with passports and visas to gain legal entry. The visas typically utilized are for study or work, or visa waivers from countries such as the United Kingdom are employed. In one case, a man named Lev Trakhtenberg secured work visas for several Russian women to perform as folk dancers, but upon arrival, he confiscated their documents and forced them to dance in strip clubs in the New York area. Most trafficking victims from Europe fly directly to the United States, though there have been reports of a small number of victims who first fly to Mexico with European mafias and then are subsequently trafficked across the border with the help of the same networks that traffic Mexicans into the United States. Mexico City and Tijuana are often cited as first ports of exploitation before U.S. entry—though when I investigated Tijuana and found several bars and street corners filled with Mexican prostitutes, there was not one European among them, East, Central or otherwise. At least a third of the Mexican prostitutes appeared to be minors. A few of them sat at tables drinking alcohol with American men who had purchased them for the night, just like the Thai teenagers purchased on Khao San Road (see chapter 6).

Most Mexicans who cross illegally into the United States are smuggled rather than trafficked. The difference is subtle but important. Smuggling involves an individual who chooses to cross the border illegally, alone or with the help of an expert. Whereas smuggled individuals are technically on their own once they cross the border, a trafficking victim's ordeal is just beginning, as the trafficker sells the victim to an exploiter or exploits the victim himself. Trafficking is thus smuggling with coercion or fraud at the beginning of the process and exploitation at the end. Because so many Mexicans enter the United States on their own, there is less need to traffic them to acquire free labor. One unique aspect of trafficking to the United States, which I saw replicated to a similar degree only in Thailand, is that many individuals who migrate illegally become trafficking victims after they cross the border. Up to one-third of trafficking victims in documented cases in the United States were "trafficked" once they were already in the United States—reinforcing the imprecision of the term "trafficking" as opposed to "slave trading" and "slavery." Shrewd operatives are well aware that large numbers of people migrate illegally each day, and rather than incur the expense and risk of moving slave labor into the country, they take positions in key border towns with promises of wage-paying jobs that become one-way tickets into slavery. A man named Tomas, in a case involving hundreds of Mexicans and Guatemalans coerced into forced agriculture work, described the process:

> When we crossed from Mexico to Arizona . . . we had to wait around for a few days. . . . And the *coyote* said he found a guy who says he'll take people to Florida. . . . So we met with the *raitero* [transporter] and he told us all . . . he could bring us to Florida to pick tomatoes and earn $150 a day. . . . So we discussed it . . . and we said, OK, let's go. . . . But we didn't get any of that money he described to us. We were stuck working for four months without being able to leave.[9]

Traffickers who cross the border from Mexico into the United States do so in a highly systematic fashion. Four U.S. states border Mexico, and each possesses vast stretches of desert and river that are impossible to guard. Trafficking into Texas involves crossing the Rio Grande at any of the numerous border towns—Rio Bravo, Nuevo Laredo, Guerrero, Ciudad Acuna, Ojinaga, Esperanza—or any of the isolated stretches of desert along the river, for which tubes, rafts, or swimming are employed. The same tactics are used for New Mexico. For Arizona, Nogales is the main city from which crossings are attempted, along with miles of remote desert. Mexicali, Tecate, and Tijuana are the primary cities from which traffickers cross into California from Baja California.

To secure victims, recruiters troll small towns in the Mexican interior in search of poor and uneducated Mexican women and girls. A bus journey is arranged to a greeter, who takes the victims to a hotel or residence near the border, where a crossing party is assembled, including *coyotes* and migrants. Before crossing, *coyotes* monitor the border and determine the best path. Crossing is almost always attempted in the dark. Once the border is crossed, *raiteros* on the other side receive the migrants and transport them to their respective points of exploitation. Safe houses are used for long journeys until the destination is reached. Each member of the chain is part of an organized system, and each member receives a fee for services. *Coyotes* receive the largest fees: up to one thousand five hundred dollars per person per crossing. Organized crime groups from Russia and China operate in a similar segmented fashion. Chinese smugglers ("snakeheads") have been known to smuggle scores of individuals in the cargo holds of major tankers that arrive in the ports of San Francisco, Los Angeles, and Long Beach. Chinese smuggling expert Peter Kwong described how the victims are

> starved, deprived of fresh air and sunlight, and beaten regularly. At times they are ordered to inflict pain on one another. Many are shackled and handcuffed to metal bed frames. Males are told that they could be killed; the females are threatened with work in a whorehouse.[10]

Because smuggling channels from Mexico into the United States are well established, the approach to human trafficking across the U.S. Mexico border is very much linked to the U.S. policy on illegal immigration. While I was writing this book, the streets of major U.S. cities were filled with hundreds of thousands of individuals protesting the further criminalization of the millions of illegal immigrants currently residing in the United States. Others blasted proposals by President George W. Bush that illegal immigrants receive guest-worker status. The roots of the debate are the same as those for trafficking: Businesses hire illegal aliens to take advantage of cheap or free labor. U.S. low and middle-income citizens are either pushed out of the job market because they cannot subsist on the low wages, or they suffer depressed wages because of the millions of illegal migrants who can. U.S. taxpayers absorb the financial burden of the public-education and health-care costs of the illegal immigrants. Caught in the middle, the immigrants are subjected to violence and exploitation because they do not exist in the eyes of the law. As with poor people across the globe, the motivation to migrate from Mexico to the United States is the opportunity for remittances. Mexican immigrants remit more money ($24.3 billion in 2006) than do the immigrants of any other nation except India ($24.5 billion in 2006),[11] and India's population is ten times that of Mexico's. The idea of building border walls to cease the flow of illegal migrants from Mexico is foolish at best. Desperate and poor people will always find a way to move. The more difficult governments make that movement, the more organized criminals step in to help in exchange for exploitation.[12]

The Carreto Family

The image of the United States as a beacon of hope and opportunity captivates many people who fall in with a slave trader who promises a dream. A young woman, Ms. Kim, who was trafficked from China to the Northern Mariana Islands (a U.S. commonwealth) and forced to perform sex work at a karaoke bar, captured these emotions:

> One day, I fell for their trap. I had a little dream of my own. It was to make some money and to buy my house. I arrived in [America] with such hopes and dreams. Who would have known what would be waiting there for me instead? Since the day I arrived, I had to live like an animal. [The karaoke bar] was a prison that was filled with nothing but curses, threats, and beatings.[13]

After false employment offers, the most prevalent form of recruitment for trafficking to the United States is seduction. Many U.S. slave traders employ long-term courtship, marriage, and pregnancy to convince women to migrate to a better life. Such courtship rituals are time-consuming, expensive, and fraught with false starts, as not every female for whom a trafficker buys chocolates becomes a wife or long-term girlfriend. One case that demonstrated the extent to which traffickers invested time and money to seduce women into forced prostitution involved the Carreto family of Mexico. A brief filed in New York City on March 15, 2005 described how,[14] from 1991 to 2004, the Carretos trafficked sex slaves from Mexico to Queens and Brooklyn, NY. The brief included the direct testimony of nine victims who were forced to have sex with twenty to thirty men per day, for twenty-five to thirty-five dollars each. The primary brothels were located in apartments at 104-56 41st Avenue and 37-71 104th Street in Queens. The Carretos recruited their victims from Tenancingo, Mexico through extensive courtship rituals that lasted months. They showered the teenage girls with gifts, professed undying love, and in some cases married the girls and fathered children. The Carretos used the relationships to gain control of the young women and convince them to travel to the United States, at which point they were forced to engage in prostitution. "If you love me, you will do this," was the oft-repeated refrain. Those who resisted met with torture and threats against the children that the men had fathered. To secure clients, the Carretos advertised in the community and enjoyed a steady flow of customers, generating hundreds of thousands of dollars across fourteen years. The victims were forced to abide by strict rules: no talking, no hiding money, no contacting family in Mexico, no looking outside the window. Disobedience resulted in rape, whippings with leather belts, or beer bottles smashed over the skull. Throughout the ordeal, some of the Carretos impregnated their wives or girlfriends several times and forced them to undergo painful abortions. The Carretos were eventually discovered when one of the victims escaped, leading to a police raid on the apartments on January 4, 2005. The three primary defendants entered guilty pleas on April 4, 2005. Sentencing was aggressive; the judge purposefully went beyond general guidelines due to extreme circumstances. Under condition of anonymity, one of the attorneys involved in the case told me that the Carretos perpetrated barbaric mistreatment of the victims in ways that were not released to the public.

"The things they did to the women were just gross," the attorney said.

The Carreto case demonstrated that sophisticated sex trafficking operations exist in the United States, but not on the scale that they exist in most countries. The Carretos exploited a relatively small number of victims across fourteen years. Brothels in Asia or Europe might victimize hundreds of individuals in the same period of time due to a much higher number of clients, especially repeat customers who demand a variety of women to choose from. The Carreto case also demonstrated that the coercion and fraud associated with trafficking to the United States can be a far more lengthy and expensive process than simply purchasing victims at well-established buyer's markets. Whereas the pool of victims in Europe and Asia is almost limitless, the number of victims who can make a land crossing into the United States is limited to Mexico and those who travel to Mexico from the Caribbean or Latin America. There is no known entity that integrates the recruitment, transport, and exploitation of victims from Mexico to the United States on a scale that allows individual brothel owners to contract for new victims or purchase them at established markets for female flesh. At least, not yet.

The Trafficking Victims Protection Act

The Trafficking Victims Protection Act (TVPA) was passed by the United States in October 2000 as the foundation of its efforts to combat human trafficking and forced labor. The legislation defines "severe forms of trafficking"[15] and stipulates protections for victims and penalties for those who exploit them. Two primary categories of trafficking victims are not included, and those individuals are not entitled to benefits. First, the act excludes cases of sex trafficking for which it is deemed that the acts were not induced by "force, fraud, or coercion." Demonstrating these qualities can be very subjective, and many cases of sex trafficking are judged not to be severe if the victims originally agreed to work as prostitutes, albeit under false promises of rosy conditions that turned out to be slavery. Second, the act excludes illegal immigrants who fall prey to exploitation once they cross the border. The individuals in these two categories represent up to one-third of all victims of slave-like exploitation in the United States.

The TVPA stipulates penalties for trafficking criminals, benefits for victims, and broad-based programs to combat human trafficking domestically and abroad. Assistance is offered to other nations to meet U.S. defined minimum standards to prevent human trafficking and the threat of halting non-humanitarian assistance can be levied against countries that do not comply with these minimum standards. Considerable prison terms and hefty fines are stipulated for various degrees of trafficking and forced labor violations.[16] The TVPA Reauthorization Acts of 2003 and 2005 sought to address holes in the original legislation, including stipulations that U.S. government employees or contractors who commit trafficking offenses while abroad (as in Bosnia) are prosecuted under U.S. trafficking laws; the reauthorization acts also put forth programs to combat child sex tourism. Implementation of the former provision has been shaky at best. During the current occupation of Iraq, several sources uncovered human trafficking operations under the umbrella of Halliburton and its two hundred subcontractors that provide logistical and service support to the U.S. military. According to the *Chicago Tribune*, Halliburton subcontractors recruited up to thirty-five thousand workers from several South Asian and Middle Eastern countries to work on U.S. military bases. Upon arrival, an unknown number had their passports confiscated and were forced to work in debt-bondage conditions. In June 2006, Robert Boyles, a U.S. air force colonel, testified to the U.S. Armed Services Committee that such behavior was "standard practice."[17]

The TVPA Reauthorization Acts' provisions against child sex tourism have been enforced more successfully. In 2003, the FBI launched Operation Innocence Lost to capture and prosecute U.S. citizens who traveled abroad to engage in sex acts with children, under new legislation called the PROTECT Act.[18] Since that time, there have been over five hundred arrests, almost entirely of males between the ages of thirty and eighty-five. Most of the men traveled to Cambodia, Thailand, and the Philippines to have sex with children. The first two men convicted under the new laws were John W. Selijan and Michael Clark,[19] aged eighty-five and seventy, respectively. Each traveled to East Asia to sexually abuse children, taking suitcases packed with condoms, pornographic materials, and several pounds of candy.

From 2001 to 2006, over one thousand trafficking victims were assisted in the United States, or roughly 1 percent of the total trafficking victims who entered the country during that period. The number of victims assisted is directly related to the number of investigations that lead to the discovery of slaves. They are also related to the number of good Samaritans who uncover slaves. Approximately one-third of trafficking victims in the United States are discovered by individual citizens, not the police. The Paoletti case contains one of the most remarkable examples of everyday citizens who facilitated the rescue of trafficked slaves. The chief traffickers, Jose Paoletti and his son Renato Paoletti, were deaf Mexicans who recruited other deaf Mexicans at a nearby school. The well-dressed Paolettis promised good jobs in the United States, showing pictures of cars, houses, and the wonderful lifestyle they could provide. Dozens of children were trafficked from Mexico to Los Angeles, then across the country to several cities on the east coast. The children were forced to sell trinkets on the street, in subway stations, and at airports. The traffickers kept the children locked in cramped apartments at night, but allowed them to roam freely during the day, believing that because they were deaf, they could not solicit help. One day, a deaf man at Newark Airport saw the children peddling trinkets and surmised that something was amiss. He communicated with the children through sign language and helped them write a note in English, which the man took to the police. Shortly thereafter, the FBI raided several sites where the children were being held. Eighteen members of the Mexican trafficking ring were arrested and convicted.

The unanimous criticism of the TVPA relates to T-visas, the special, three-year-residency visas provided to victims of severe forms of human trafficking, which entitle them to local and state benefits. T-visas are subject to several conditions, including cooperation with criminal investigations and legal proceedings against a trafficker. Cooperation is defined as "any reasonable request for assistance in the investigation or prosecution of acts of such trafficking."[20] This broad definition leaves many victims reluctant to sign the dotted line. While traffickers cannot be prosecuted without witness testimony, many victims are far too traumatized to participate in the jurisprudence process. They also fear threats made by traffickers against family members. To make matters worse, most applications take up to nine months to process, consigning victims to a state of residency limbo while they are required to participate with investigators and prosecutors. Data I gathered from the U.S. Citizenship and Immigration Services (USCIS) Vermont Service Center, where T-visas are processed, indicated that almost 50 percent of applications are denied, primarily because the individual is deemed not to be a victim of severe forms of trafficking.

Despite being the richest country in the world, the United States has spent an average of only sixty million dollars per year on anti-trafficking efforts since 2001. This sum is three hundred and thirty-three times less per year than the twenty billion dollars spent annually to fight the war on drugs. The annual U.S. anti-trafficking expenditure works out to approximately $22 per trafficked slave in the world. The over two hundred billion dollars spent each year in Iraq since 2003 to assist the country's twenty-six million citizens—fewer than the total number of slaves in the world—by deposing a dictator and instituting democracy (as the mission came to be stated) works out to $7,700 per Iraqi per year. This sum is $4,800 (66 percent) more than the average per capita income of Iraqi citizens ($2,900) and far greater than the per capita income of every developing nation explored in this book.[21] What values are demonstrated by this allocation of resources? Is democracy in Iraq worth three hundred and thirty-three times more per person than fighting slavery? If the U.S. government spent $7,700 per slave per year in resources, law enforcement, and prosecution of slave-related crimes, the end of those crimes would be far nearer to realization.

Taking Responsibility

The anemic financial resources deployed to combat contemporary slavery, the misdirected deployment of global influence, and the posture of programs such as T-visas as benefits instead of rights belies the most essential truth of contemporary slave crimes: The United States is more responsible than any other nation for the inimical accretion in human exploitation, trafficking, and slavery since the fall of the Berlin Wall.

Through the IMF and other institutions, the U.S. government rapidly imposed its particular brand of unfettered market economics upon the developing world, unleashing catastrophic increases in poverty, social upheaval, mass migration, and lawlessness. The United States is not responsible for the acute levels of gender bias and minority disenfranchisement that promote sex trafficking, but it should accept far more responsibility for the global exacerbation of the factors that ignited the ascent of contemporary slavery. At the beginning of the 1990s, the United States had every opportunity to support stable and steady transitions to democracy and market economics throughout Eastern Europe and East Asia. Instead, it chose to promote a corporate raider approach to newly opened economies, precipitating unprecedented imbalances in global wealth. Disdain for the harms caused by the policies of the United States and its economic allies pervades the developing world, as does ire over the arrogance of the U.S. Treasury and the IMF in mandating their aggressive market-economy policies as the best and sole path to sustainable prosperity. Similar policies led to numerous corporate scandals in the United States during the 1990s, increasingly volatile boom-and-bust market cycles across the last decade, and widening imbalances in wealth across the country. For decades, as table 7.1 shows, the share of wealth of the poorest 20 percent of U.S. households has decreased, while the share of the country's richest households has increased.[22]

In no uncertain terms, the fundamental wage and tax structures of the United States have become tilted heavily in favor of the rich and against the poor. In 2006, the average salaries of chief executive officers were three hundred sixty four times those of the average worker, a

TABLE 7.1
Share of Household Income in the United States, 1960–2005 (percent)

Year	Top 20 Percent of Households	Bottom 20 Percent of Households
2005	*50.4*	*3.4*
2000	*49.4*	*3.6*
1990	*46.6*	*3.8*
1980	*44.1*	*4.2*
1970	*43.3*	*4.1*
1960	*41.3*	*4.8*

Source: U.S. Department of Labor, National Compensation Survey, available at http://www.bls.gov/ncs.

jaw-dropping ascent from a ratio of forty-two times in 1980.[23] The U.S. Congress voted for itself seven pay increases from 1998 to 2006, to a hefty $162,500 per year,[24] while it raised the national minimum wage level only once during that same time, from a paltry $5.15 to $5.85 per hour. The U.S. capitalist model widens income disparity and destabilizes societies via the increasingly inequitable treatment of worker classes. Other market economies, such as Sweden, Japan, Germany, and Canada, provide similar standards of living to the United States, but with lower levels of inequality and greater social protections. These models would have been much more appropriate for post-communist countries during the tenuous transitions of the 1990s, but little room was allowed for debate, and the U.S. brand of extreme capitalism has promoted a global civilization that is teetering at the edge of broad-based human, environmental, and moral disaster. The rise in worldwide slavery levels is one of the most reprehensible of these disasters, and sex traffickers in particular have followed the U.S. economic model well: Profits above all, no matter the human cost. The harms that have been caused are incalculable, and the time for massive redress is long overdue.

April 26, 2006

Twenty-eight days after I met Sunee, I returned to her massage parlor. It was not an easy decision, but I thought if I tried once more, she might allow me to call the trafficking hotline for her. When I entered, Chuvit was standing at the reception, chatting on the telephone. The scent of lemongrass still suffused the air. I put on my best customer face and asked for a massage from Sunee.

"You came before?" Chuvit asked.

I nodded.

"Welcome! Sunee is giving massage. You can wait?"

I asked when she might be free. Chuvit said it would be twenty minutes and offered me a cup of tea and apple wedges while I waited. Twenty minutes later, a young Thai man wearing denim suspenders emerged from the massage area. Chuvit went to check on Sunee. When they emerged, my eyes caught her face, and I offered a faint smile. She whispered to Chuvit and returned to her massage room.

"Sunee will take a break now," Chuvit told me. "You take massage from another girl?"

"Can I wait for Sunee?" I asked.

"She is not feeling good. Better for you to take another massage."

My heart sank. I knew Sunee did not want to see me, and there was little I could do to change her mind.

Driving home, my thoughts turned to Panadda in Chiang Mai and the exploitation she endured in exchange for pittances sent to her parents. The children trafficked by Salim in Kamal Daha suffered for the same reason. Slavery was not so simple. Sometimes the scraps tossed at slaves were more valuable than freedom. Sometimes those scraps were what allowed families to survive. I pounded my fist in frustration: Billions of dollars were spent on wars while billions of people eked out existences so squalid that being a slave might be preferable. One mocha latté at the nearby coffee shop cost more than the daily income of almost one-half the planet. As long as the token morsels from the slave owner's hand represented a more filling meal than freedom and democracy could provide, slavery would never end. Never mind the promise of a better life; sometimes slavery was a better life. This was the obscene truth that revealed itself to me with newfound clarity, driving home from my second encounter with Sunee.

8 A Framework for Abolition

Risk and Demand

Live simply, so that others may simply live. —*Gandhi*

A Coalition of Freedom

At the beginning of this book, I enumerated four reasons that efforts to combat sex trafficking remain insufficient: sex trafficking is poorly understood; the organizations dedicated to combating sex trafficking are underfunded and uncoordinated internationally; the laws against sex trafficking are overwhelmingly anemic and poorly enforced; and, despite numerous studies and reports, a systematic business and economic analysis of the industry, conducted to identify strategic points of intervention, has not yet been undertaken. I argued that a business analysis of the sex trafficking industry would reveal its vulnerable points, and further, that those vulnerable points were related to the market force of demand. The best short-term tactics against the industry are those that reduce the aggregate demand of consumers and slave owners. The most effective way to reduce aggregate demand is to attack the industry's immense profitability by inverting its risk-reward economics, that is, by making the risk of operating a sex slave operation far more costly. To ensure that the business of sex trafficking and other forms of modern slavery are eradicated in the long term, the primary conditions that first gave rise to these crimes—poverty and the destructive asymmetries of economic globalization—must also be addressed.

To the extent that my argument for a near-term attack on the aggregate demand for sex slaves is accepted, I am sure that any number of steps could be taken to achieve the desired ends. Analysis and debate should be undertaken to optimize the approach. To commence the process, I offer the suggestions in this chapter as a framework from which to start. I am well aware that there are tremendous hurdles that any short- or long-term antislavery tactics must overcome, not the least of which include global structural economic impediments as well as endemic supply-side drivers, such as bias against minorities and gender. Though the task might prove Sisyphean, it is my hope that the narratives in this book will motivate greater efforts to undertake the task, no matter how imposing the hurdles, however long it takes.

To unify the efforts, resources, and influence required to wage a more effective battle against the business of sex trafficking, I propose the creation of an extra-governmental Coalition of Freedom, dedicated to abolishing all forms of trafficking and slavery, starting with the tactical interventions required to invert the risk-reward economics of the sex trafficking industry.[1] Seven such interventions were listed at the end of chapter 1, each of which will be discussed in the third step of the four-step plan below. For the coalition to succeed, it must exist outside contemporary neoliberal structures of government, because the key steps required to abolish sex trafficking might prove antagonistic to the global economic system that these governments have erected. The coalition would consist of personnel from key anti-trafficking NGOs, economists, business leaders, lawyers, lobbyists, academicians, and law enforcement. To maximize the coalition's effectiveness, these individuals would be allocated across two units. One would focus on victims; the other would focus on policy and tactics. The first unit would be concerned with the second impediment listed above—funding and coordinating the scores of anti-trafficking NGOs worldwide—with an emphasis on implementing standardized, relevant, and robust victim-assistance measures. The second would be concerned with the third and fourth impediments—analysis, advocacy, and enactment of the tactics required to eradicate sex trafficking.[2] With these aims in mind (and this book hopefully helping to address the first impediment), the following pages provide a possible starting point for forming more effective anti-trafficking policies and tactics.

Short-Term Tactics

Accepting the premise that the chief contributor to the success of the contemporary sex slave industry is the combination of immense profitability and minimal risk, a global abolitionist coalition should focus on an aggressive inversion of the industry's economic risks and rewards. The current risk profile of sex trafficking promotes a high level of demand for slave labor among slave owners and consumers alike. Chapter 1's exercise on the elasticity of demand, however, demonstrated that as the retail price of a sex act increases, demand by male consumers decreases at a greater-than-linear rate. If the costs of operating a sex-slave business increase, and a slave owner chooses to maintain the same retail price, profits will decrease, reducing the attractiveness of operating a sex slave business. Altering the market force of demand can be achieved relatively quickly by deploying tactics that assault the profitability of the business of sex trafficking.

Like most businesses, sex trafficking has four components: a product (the victim), a wholesaler (the trafficker), a retailer (the slave owner/exploiter), and a consumer. These business terms are not intended to insult the human face of trafficking crimes or to attenuate the intense suffering of trafficking victims. I use the terms simply to facilitate an analysis of the business that exploits them.

The product, crudely, is the victim. The only associated cost of exploiting the product is to move it from its place of origin to the place of exploitation, where the consumer can consume it. The moving process is the slave-trading portion of the sex trafficking industry. Wholesalers are slave traders, except when they are part of a vertically integrated organized-crime network and are compensated for services in place of the acquisition price of a trafficked slave. Tactics focused on disrupting slave trading are for the most part ineffective: Movement is too easy, inexpensive, and invisible. Wholesalers are always one step ahead of attempts to prevent their movement. Thus, effective anti-trafficking tactics must focus on the stakeholders of demand: retailers and consumers.

Retailers own the brothels, clubs, massage parlors, apartments, or other locations where the product is consumed. Because the business is illegal, retailers employ guards and bribe the police. They keep prices as low as possible to secure as many customers as possible, new and repeat. The operating costs of the business are low. The primary up-front costs include purchasing slaves and perhaps the real estate in which business is conducted. Equipment for business operations must also be purchased: beds, sheets, alcohol, drugs, snacks, condoms, makeup, and clothes. The retailer demands slaves because they elevate profits and expand the customer base by virtue of lower retail prices. The only vulnerability the retailer suffers is the illicit nature of his business. There is a cost if he is caught, but most slave owners are not targeted with aggressive investigation, and a few bribes typically extricate retailers from legal entanglements.

The consumer is the man who buys sex. He is looking for sex, clearly, but also for a way to act out violent, racist, pedophiliac, or other antisocial traits. Thanks to slave labor, he can afford sex from young females that he could not afford before, or he can afford it more often. Demand for sex—be it violent, degrading, or just for "fun"—drives many consumers to prostitutes. Demand for low-cost sex drives them to slaves. The individual may not know he is purchasing a slave, but he knows he is purchasing low-cost sex, which the retailer primarily provides with slaves. Whether or not the consumer is aware he is purchasing a slave is largely irrelevant to the magnitude of demand represented by sex slave consumers. In purchasing sex from slaves, the consumer is fundamentally motivated by the minimal retail price; hence, pricing is the prime driver of consumer demand for sex slaves, not awareness of whether or not the individual is a slave. Table 8.1 summarizes the sex trafficking business chain, including the primary efforts currently deployed to thwart the industry and the tactics that I believe would be more effective.

The table is by no means an exhaustive list of the current efforts to combat sex trafficking, but it summarizes the key initiatives. Each item in the What Should Be Done column can be achieved in the short term except the supply-side (product-victim) initiatives. Issues of bias against gender and minorities also cannot be resolved overnight. However, decreased demand for slave labor will decrease the rate at which these populations are exploited.

Retailer-Slave Owner

Tactics that raise the costs of retail operations create a dilemma for slave owners between, on the one hand, keeping prices static and accepting lower profits, and on the other hand, raising prices and accepting lower consumer demand. In either scenario, aggregate demand for sex slaves decreases. The best way to make a business less profitable is to

TABLE 8.1
Business-Chain Analysis of Sex Trafficking

	What Is Being Done	Impact	Reason	What Should Be Done
Product-victim	1. Awareness campaigns	Small	Need for migration too great	Long-term anti-poverty initiatives and redress of harms of economic globalization
	2. Local education and job training	Small	Too small in scale; limited resources; limited opportunities	
Wholesaler-slave trader	1. Border patrol/security	Small	Impossible to guard borders; corruption facilitates movement; invisibility renders victims impossible to identify	Redirect focus to retailers and consumers
	2. Prosecution	Small	Limited resources; lack of multilateral cooperation; corruption in judiciary; lack of witness protection; weak penalties in the law	
Retailer-slave owner	1. Prosecution	Small	Almost no focus on market force of demand; same problems as with wholesaler prosecutions lead to impunity	Raise real cost of operating a business with slave labor to a profit-compromising level
Consumer	1. Awareness campaigns	Small	Most men who purchase sex from slaves seek low-price sexual gratification and lack moral discrimination between "willing" and "forced"	Higher prices for consumer will decrease demand Optional: increase consumer costs by criminalizing solicitation of sex services

raise the costs of operating it. As mentioned before, there are two key elements to the costs of running a sex-slave business: the costs of acquiring the product and operating costs. In some cases, there are also up-front expenses, such as the large *haftas* (bribes) that brothel owners in Mumbai must pay when they open a new establishment. A third cost element of operating a sex-slave business is not included in a pure profit and loss analysis: risk, or the cost of being caught. Like any form of slavery, sex slavery is illegal. If a retailer is caught, prosecuted, and convicted, there are costs associated with that conviction, including prison time and, in some countries, fines, asset forfeiture, and restitution payments. If the rate and economic costs of conviction are high, the cost of being caught can be detrimental. If not, the cost is negligible.

At present, each of the three categories of costs—acquiring slaves, operating expenses, and economic risks—is minimal. Very little can be done to affect the acquisition costs of products in the short term or the operating costs of a retail sex slave business, but I believe severe upward shocks to the cost of being caught can be imposed very quickly. Every business, whether legal or illegal, attempts to quantify the legal costs associated with doing business. Legitimate companies know that they will be sued for one issue or another, and in their financial planning they allocate a certain amount of money each year for attorney fees, negative judgments, and other economic penalties. Sex slave retailers are no different. They know that slavery is illegal and quantify the costs of running an illegal business (mostly bribes) as part of their overall operations. In doing so, they know that only a miniscule percentage of slave retailers will be prosecuted and convicted in any given year, and that even if they are convicted, the fines are minor compared to the potential economic benefits of sex slavery.

Formulating the best tactics to help eradicate the sex slave industry by elevating the cost of being caught can be thought of as a four-step process: first, calculating the current cost of being caught; second, determining the level at which the cost of being caught compromises profits; third, ascertaining the best strategy to raise the cost of being caught to that profit-compromising level; and fourth, deploying the strategy. The four steps are intended to be a cycle of increasing effectiveness. The first and second steps dictate the tactics to be taken in the third step, followed by the results achieved in the fourth step. As results unfold, the tactics can be refined to improve their effect.

First Step

A simple formula for calculating the cost of being caught would be:

> Cost of being caught = probability of being prosecuted × probability of being convicted × maximum financial penalty in the law.

Simple formulas for the probabilities of being prosecuted and convicted would be:

> Probability of being prosecuted = number of prosecuted criminal acts in a year ÷ number of criminal acts in a year.
>
> Probability of being convicted = number of convictions in a year ÷ number of prosecutions in a year.[3]

Second Step

The level at which the cost of being caught becomes profit compromising requires knowledge of how much profit can be made by exploiting sex slaves. The profit and loss statements in appendix B provide details of the cash profit generated per slave, per year. This information is the first piece of the puzzle.

To ascertain the total profitability of a sex slave, profitability must be determined in terms of some unit, such as months, as well as the average number of those units for which the retailer exploits the slave. The total number of months that retailers exploit sex slaves varies. Some sex slaves are in brothels for a few months, others for years. The churn-rate analysis discussed in chapter 1 provides the computed averages per region.

The term for the total profit that can be generated, on average, by exploiting a sex slave can be considered the "exploitation value" (EV) of the slave. This economic term is not intended to diminish the brutal human cost of these crimes, but rather provide an analytical tool through which the total economic value of a slave to the exploiter for the duration of enslavement can be assessed. I have included the full spreadsheet and explanation of EV calculations in table A.3, but table 8.2 contains a summary.[4]

The numbers in table 8.2 are highly conservative calculations of the total value of a sex slave to a slave owner in each region. To decrease the

TABLE 8.2
Exploitation Value (EV) of Sex Slaves (2006 U.S. dollars)

Region	Net EV of a Sex Slave
South Asia	28,278
East Asia and Pacific	33,049
Western Europe	156,300
Central and Eastern Europe	78,604
Latin America	54,496
Middle East	98,492
Africa	25,454
North America	135,075
Global weighted average	**61,015**

exploitation value of a sex slave, an upward shock to the costs of operating the business must be created. This upward shock relates to the industry's risk economics, and the shock must be applied at a profit-compromising level. To achieve this level, one might argue that the cost of being caught should be greater than the potential economic benefit of slavery, or perhaps at least half the potential economic benefit to materially disrupt the level of demand for sex slaves. While the precise level is open to debate, the concept is clear: The greater the cost of being caught, the lower the profitability of conducting a sex-slave business.[5] At present, those costs are almost nil, as table 8.3 shows.[6]

The real economic cost of being caught for sex-slave violations is miniscule relative to the potential exploitation value of exploiting a slave. The laws in each of the countries in table 8.3 include stipulations for prison time, and there are certainly costs to incarceration; however, by evaluating the strict economic costs in the law, the risk-reward profile of exploiting sex slaves demonstrates the inconsequential nature of current penalties. The United States has the highest real penalty relative to sex slave EV (1.78 percent), a direct result of aggressive fines combined with reasonable prosecution and conviction rates. Of the countries explored in this book, only the United States and Albania stipulate maximum paper penalties greater than the EV of sex slaves in their regions. In the other countries, paper penalties are weak, and in all cases, the real penalties have very little economic impact. To increase the penalty for sex slavery to a profit-compromising level, the real costs must be maximized through a mixture of higher paper penalties and higher prosecution and conviction rates.

TABLE 8.3

Real Penalty to EV Analysis (2006 U.S. dollars)

Country	Maximum Penalty Related to Sex Slavery	Estimated Prosecution Rate (percent)	Estimated Conviction Rate (percent)	Implied "Real" Penalty	Regional EV per Sex Slave	Penalty/ EV (percent)	"Real" Penalty/EV (percent)
India[1]	2,222	*0.6*	*36*	5	28,278	*7.9*	*0.02*
Nepal	2,666	*3.5*	*21*	20	28,278	*9.4*	*0.07*
Italy	0	*5.0*	*55*	0	156,300	*0.0*	*0.00*
Netherlands	54,000	*5.4*	*50*	1,455	156,300	*34.5*	*0.93*
Moldova	2,500	*6.2*	*19*	29	78,604	*3.2*	*0.04*
Albania	80,000	*5.6*	*20*	904	78,604	*101.8*	*1.15*
Thailand	0	*0.7*	*18*	0	33,049	*0.0*	*0.00*
United States[2]	150,000	*4.1*	*39*	2,400	135,075	*111.0*	*1.78*

[1] I have assumed that the ITPA amendment to raise the penalty for a single count of owning a brothel to one hundred thousand rupees will eventually be passed.

[2] There is no maximum fine for the crime of sex trafficking in the United States, though fines have typically ranged from ten thousand to one hundred fifty thousand dollars per victim per trafficker.

Third Step

Derived from the second step, the following is a starting point on how to elevate the economic penalties of sex slavery to a profit-compromising level. To achieve higher paper penalties, raise the penalties prescribed by the law. To achieve higher prosecution rates, increase investigations and address law enforcement and judicial corruption. To achieve higher conviction rates, allow cases to be fast-tracked in specialized trafficking courts, offer better witness protection, and address law enforcement and judicial corruption. The seven tactics listed at the end of chapter 1 are designed to maximize the opportunity to achieve these aims. The logic of the tactics is discussed below.

PAPER LAWS The level to which countries should elevate their paper penalties must be decided in the manner that each country seeks to maximize the real penalty of sex trafficking crimes. One benchmark for more economically meaningful penalties could be drug laws. In every country I visited, the laws against drug trafficking were much more aggressive than were the laws against human trafficking. In India, the Narcotic Drugs and Psychotropic Substances Act of 1985 stipulates a penalty for trafficking in controlled substances of ten to twenty years in prison and a fine of up to two hundred thousand rupees ($4,444). This financial penalty is one hundred times more severe than the current fine for sex trafficking (twice the proposed amendment discussed in chapter 1). In the United States, the 1996 Controlled Substances Act stipulates very severe penalties for cocaine trafficking: up to five million dollars for a first offense of amounts under five kilograms, and up to ten million dollars for a first offense above five kilograms.

I recognize that the per-kilogram profit of cocaine is greater than that of a sex slave, but there is no quantification of the moral outrage of slavery. I see no reason why the penalties for the latter should not be as detrimental as the former. Substituting ten million dollars as the maximum fine for sex trafficking in the United States—with the same prosecution and conviction probabilities—would present a real economic cost of $133,000 to the slave owner, essentially equal to the $135,075 lifetime value of a sex slave. If there is one single effort an extra-governmental abolitionist coalition can start with, it would be to pressure the global community to increase the paper penalties of human slavery to a level at least equal to that of drug trafficking.

PROSECUTION RATES As discussed in chapter 1, the primary barriers to higher prosecution rates in most countries include insufficient law-enforcement resources, untrained or undertrained law enforcement, lack of prioritization of trafficking and slavery investigations, lack of cooperation between origin and destination countries, corruption in law enforcement, corruption in prosecutors, and insufficient witness-protection programs. The first four barriers can be aggregated into law-enforcement issues. The fifth and sixth barriers relate to corruption. The seventh barrier pertains, of course, to protecting victim-witnesses from harm.

To address law-enforcement barriers, the tactical unit of the proposed coalition could liaise with the United Nations to operate an international slavery and trafficking inspection force, similar to the weapons inspectors who search for weapons of mass destruction. The purpose of this force would be to conduct aggressive investigations and raids on suspected locations of forced prostitution and other forms of slavery. The raids would serve four purposes: to identify potential slaves, to free the victims, shut down slave operations, and gather the evidence required to convict criminals. When sex-slave establishments are shut down and slave owners are put out of business, aggregate demand for sex slaves by retailer-slave owners will decrease.[7] For those who wonder how effective such a force could be in finding sex slaves, I submit that if I can find them, an elite police force can. I offer three ways to ensure maximum effectiveness.

Mixes of International and National Inspectors Any country that is serious about ending sex trafficking should not object to an international police force joining its local police to conduct investigations and raids. A convention like COMMIT (see chapter 6) could be signed by all member nations who agree to shared definitions of the inspection force, investigation and enforcement powers, and jurisdiction to apprehend slave criminals for prosecution in the local country. The convention should include multi-lateral extradition relationships. New intelligence could be constantly gathered to refine tactics and assess high-intensity areas of sex slavery, such as Falkland Road in India, the Salaria in Rome, or hotels in Chisinau, Moldova. As those high-intensity areas shift, so could the inspectors. Mixing international and local law enforcement could mitigate issues of corruption, lack of resources, prioritization, and training on how to effectively identify and handle slaves. If countries prefer, a solely international force could be utilized. Investigations would be conducted like organized crime cases, including electronic surveillance, undercover agents, phone tapping, and financial investigation.

Coordination with Community Vigilance Committees The front-line data gathering on trafficked slaves should be conducted by specially trained and formalized community vigilance committees that can be paid by the coalition in poorer countries. These committees would consist of members of the city, town, or village, taxi and *tuk-tuk* drivers, business owners, and specially trained individuals who frequent sex establishments to seek out slaves. Each member would gather information for the slavery inspection force, which would take up investigations and plot the best way to bring down the establishment and free its victims. Volunteer committees consisting of individuals who wish to contribute without needing compensation can further expand these efforts. The moral rigor of tens of thousands of committed citizens would vastly expand the reach of law enforcement and leave slave owners scrambling to stay in business.

Raids Raids must be handled delicately. Sex slaves rarely trust the police, and when they are suddenly rescued in a blaze of guns and shouting, they are often too traumatized to participate in the jurisprudence process. Raids should be conducted in conjunction with a designated, local NGO that belongs to the coalition, with protections in place to minimize adverse effects against the individuals—slaves or otherwise—living in those establishments. A common criticism of aggressive raids is that they push the exploitation of sex slaves deeper underground, however, there is only so far underground a sex-slave establishment can go before it is too far underground for consumers to find it. Sex-slave retailers require visibility and impunity to function. This is why bribes have been the operating tactic of choice for slave owners, but bribes will not work with a well-paid, international police force and community vigilance committees dedicated to abolishing slavery.

Corruption Corruption in the judiciary could be mitigated by providing higher salaries to prosecutors and judges, making them less vulnerable to bribes. The coalition would fund these salaries. International prosecutors and judges whom the coalition appoints could observe and participate in sex trafficking cases. Special fast-track courts could be established that solely handle trafficking cases to ensure swift decisions. Judicial reviews could be conducted each year to ensure that particular prosecutors were not always losing cases, or particular judges always lessening charges. Paying fines to reduce prison terms would have to be disallowed at least for slave-related crimes. Laws would have to be amended to provide restitution to the victims, whether as part of the fines or through asset forfeiture. Funding by the coalition would also be provided to expand local economic-development initiatives, especially those that focus on women and minorities. The return of slaves to conditions of poverty and disenfranchisement has been a primary reason for the deplorable increase in re-trafficking.

CONVICTION RATES In most countries, conviction rates are insufficient due to a lack of law-enforcement resources for gathering evidence, poor multi-lateral cooperation between origin and destination countries, judicial corruption, and poor, unrealistic, and unfunded witness-protection programs. The first three causes are addressed through the programs discussed above. Remedying witness-protection programs would require elevated funding. The coalition could be mandated to fund twelve months of remittances to families so that the victim's liberation does not have ill effects on poor families depending on a share of their earnings. Guarded accommodation for witnesses and family, especially in small countries such as Moldova and Albania, should be provided. Witness-relocation programs should be included so that individuals and their families are given new identities and vocations after a trial, thereby minimizing the risk of retaliation from vengeful traffickers. In a broader sense, states should disaggregate cooperation with law enforcement and the receipt of human rights benefits. Secure and confident victims would be better allies to prosecutors than frightened individuals forced to cooperate under threat of deportation.

Fourth Step

Inverting the risk-reward economics of sex-slave operations should tangibly reduce demand by retailers and consumers for sex slaves. It is impossible to know precisely by how much demand will be reduced, but basic economic theory can provide a sense. In chapter 1, I asked how low the price for sex from a slave was, relative to wages. The answer for India was 2.5 hours of work at the national per-capita income, 2.2 hours in Italy, and 1.4 hours in the United States. These numbers demonstrated that using slaves allowed retailers to drop prices to such a level that most men on the planet could afford to purchase sex. In addition to elevating the cost of being caught, which affects both retail and consumer demand, countries might opt to criminalize the solicitation of such services, which additionally affects consumer demand. Some countries argue against such sanctions, citing the fact that up to one-third of sex trafficking victims escape with the assistance of "kind" consumers. With community vigilance committees and a special trafficking inspection force, the need for such consumers would be attenuated, and criminalizing sex-service solicitation would thus reduce consumer demand without ill effects. Issues related to consumer demand, as driven by male demand for commercial sex, should also be considered. However, I believe that an economic approach would prove more effective in the short-term at lowering consumer demand than would attempts to educate men that they are not entitled to gratify their sexual needs by purchasing female bodies.

Table 8.4 offers a theoretical analysis of the price and consumer-demand effects of possible shocks to the cost structure of a retail sex business, achieved by increasing the cost of being caught.

The data in the upper half describe the present unit economics of sex-slave operations in India and the United States, wherein the cost of being caught is negligible. In the lower half of the table, I offer two scenarios that would result in an upward shock to the cost of being caught: a small impact and a large impact. Both scenarios could be achieved by implementing the measures described in the third step, above. The first assumption in the first scenario is that countries pass legislation mandating maximum trafficking fines equal to twice the calculated EV of a sex slave. In the second scenario, I assume that fines are at five times a slave's EV, which would still be one-half the fine for a first offense of cocaine trafficking in the United States. The prosecution and conviction rates are also fully achievable. Italy and the Netherlands already achieve over 50 percent conviction rates and the United States is not far behind. Aggressive anti-trafficking tactics could easily result in 20 percent prosecution rates in each country. There are 1.2 million trafficked sex slaves in the world, and prosecuting the exploiters of one in five is well within reach.

In the first scenario, both regions suffer 8 to 10 percent drops in net profit. Net profit erodes because the amortized cost of being caught per sex act increases considerably. A 10 percent drop in net profit may not sound impressive, but if a brothel owner wanted to maintain the same profit margin, he would have to increase prices by 36 and 24 percent in India and the United States, respectively. Doing so would result in a retail

TABLE 8.4
Impact Analysis: Retail Price and the Cost of Being Caught (2006 U.S. dollars)

Current Conditions:

	India	United States
Price of sex act[1]	**4.50**	**30.00**
Less unit allocation of:[2]		
Operating expenses	1.12	9.03
Acquisition price	0.11	0.67
Up-front bribe	0.02	0.00
Cost of being caught	0.00	0.53
Total	**1.25**	**10.22**
Net Profit	**3.25**	**19.78**
Net Profit Margin (percent)	*72*	*66*

With Increased Cost of Being Caught:

	Scenario 1: Small Impact		*Scenario 2: Large Impact*	
	India	**U.S.**	**India**	**U.S.**
Price of sex act[1]	**4.50**	**30.00**	**4.50**	**30.00**
Less unit allocation of:[2]				
Operating expenses	1.12	9.03	1.12	9.03
Acquisition price	0.11	0.67	0.11	0.67
Up-front bribe	0.02	0.00	0.02	0.00
Cost of being caught	0.45	3.00	3.02	20.10
Total	**1.70**	**12.69**	**4.27**	**29.79**
Net Profit	**2.80**	**17.31**	**0.23**	**0.21**
Net Profit Margin (percent)	*62*	*58*	*5*	*1*
Implied retail price to maintain profit margin	6.10	37.25	15.40	87.50
Percent increase	*36*	*24*	*242*	*192*
Implied work hours at per capita income	3.7	1.9	9.5	4.4
Implied consumer demand reduction (percent)	*–50*	—	*–90+*	—

Note: In Scenario 1, fines are raised to twice the EV of a sex slave, a 10 percent prosecution rate is achieved, and a 50 percent conviction rate is achieved. In Scenario 2, fines are raised to five times the EV of a sex slave, a 20 percent prosecution rate is achieved, and a 67 percent conviction rate is achieved.

[1] Bungalow brothel for India, apartment brothel for United States.

[2] Monthly operating expenses do not include costs associated with sale of items other than commercial sex (alcohol, food, etc.).

price of $6.10 for a sex act in India, just above the threshold at which the day laborers from Silpa's brothel (see chapter 2) were priced out the market. If Silpa kept prices the same, profits would erode and the risks associated with exploiting sex slaves would render the business much less compelling.

In the second scenario, the impact on brothel profits is extreme. Profit margins drop to almost nil, and retail price increases to $15.40 in India and $87.50 in the United States would be required to recapture the original profit levels. I can only estimate that demand among the four Kamathipura consumers would drop by over 90 percent because I only procured data for price increases of up to eight dollars. Assuming that brothel owners were willing to operate with half their original margin, prices would still be high and sex slavery would not be nearly as desirable a business. Either way, aggregate demand for slaves from brothel owners and consumers would decrease.

I have not adjusted one variable in both scenarios, and it is perhaps the most important variable in the economics of the entire sex trafficking industry. The fundamental reason that sex slavery is immensely profitable is because of the lengthy duration of enslavement. In economic terms, this means that the unit costs of operating a sex-slave business are minor because they are amortized across thousands of profit-generating sex acts during years of enslavement.

The totality of the above reasoning leads to the most important premise of this book: the two measures most likely to invert the risk-reward economics of sex slavery, and thereby reduce aggregate demand for sex slaves, are raising the costs of being caught and shortening the average duration of enslavement. If the unit costs of a sex slave must be amortized across substantially fewer sex acts, the profit margin evaporates. Put another way, if a sex slave is freed by a slavery inspection force just a few months after being enslaved, the slave owner faces a much shorter time frame of revenue generation relative to the same level of costs (acquisition, operating, risk) per slave, and thus much lower profits. If the inspection force acts quickly enough, the slave owner might not even be able to recoup the initial acquisition cost of the slave. If convicted under an elevated penalty regime, the slave owner would also face sizable fines per slave that would render his criminal operation unsustainable. Raising the costs of being caught and shortening the average duration of enslavement are intricately linked, as the latter would perforce decrease by virtue of higher prosecution and conviction rates—two of the three variables that, when elevated, increase the cost of being caught. In the first scenario, halving the average duration of enslavement reduces profitability to 25 and 16 percent in India and the United States, respectively, requiring price increases to $12.15 and $73.80 to maintain margin. In the second scenario, the industry is ruined. Concerns that reducing the average duration of enslavement would result in higher levels of trafficking in sex slaves should be allayed, for the entire system would be besieged by substantially more risk, rendering the totality of the sex trafficking industry a less rewarding and more perilous pursuit. A relentless slavery inspection force and thousands of rigorous community vigilance committees will make sure of it.

I do not for a moment suggest that this theoretical analysis would be actualized in reality in the exact manner outlined above, or that the tactics suggested would provide the required inversion in the risk-reward profile of sex slavery. However, even if only half the predicted effect were achieved, and that so by deploying tactics completely different from those suggested, the sex slave industry would be far less profitable, and aggregate demand by slave owners and consumers would decrease appreciably. For these reasons, I believe tactics that target the sex trafficking industry like a business, by attacking the vulnerabilities in the economics of sex slave operations, will have the best chance of ridding the world of this disease. The highly elastic market force of demand is the aspect of the sex trade most vulnerable to attack, and only a global coalition, with sufficient unity, expertise, and influence, will be able to pressure the countries of the world into adopting effective measures.

A Child Named Aye

Before I end this book, there is one more person I would like you to meet. She was not a sex slave, but a child slave, named Aye. In all my travels, I experienced no emotion more devastating than peering into the eyes of an enslaved human child. Where one expects to see the spark of innocence, one discovers instead the abyss of humankind's most savage cruelty. I met scores of child slaves during my research, but none was more haunting than Aye.

I cannot explain why meeting Aye was so difficult for me. Perhaps because our meeting was toward the end of my final research trip. Perhaps because even though she was fifteen, the depraved exploitation she suffered stunted her development, so that she behaved like a meek, five-year-old child. Or perhaps it was because after she suffered ten years of slavery, I was the first person with whom she shared her story.

Aye was a member of the Shan hill tribe of Burma. When she was four years old, she and her mother fled government soldiers who destroyed their village. From the ages of four to fourteen, she was a slave near Chiang Mai. When we met at her shelter, Aye entered the interview room with a severe hunch. She constantly plucked the skin from her fingers, and she spoke in a voice just barely above a whisper. Because she had been virtually starved for years, she did not understand that she would receive three meals a day in the shelter, so she often overate and had to be taken to the hospital to avoid a ruptured stomach. Her story revealed the darkest cruelties of humankind—callous exploitation and unconscionable violence committed against a child, solely for the sake of profit. As Aye shared her story, the bleakness in her eyes shook me to my core.

> When I was four years old, soldiers came to our village late in the night. They shot people and burned our homes. My mother and I ran into the forest for many days, until we came to Thailand.
>
> We were hungry, and my mother looked for work. We came to a factory in a town called Sarapee, in Chiang Mai district. A Burmese husband and wife owned this factory. We thought we would be safe with them. They said my mother could work and I could be kept with her because I was too young to be on my own. The wife said we must call her Jay, which is a term for a rich woman. Two hundred people worked in her factory. They were all Shan Burmese.
>
> The next day we came to the factory and the owners beat me very badly. They pulled out my hair and I was bleeding. They told my mother if she did not work, they would beat me again. They separated me from my mother and also made me work. Even though we worked in the same factory, I never saw my mother. The work was very bad. We woke at four in the morning and worked until one in the morning. I do not remember sleeping. I would separate good fruits from bad fruits; I would mash dry peppers; I would cut bamboo shoots. Every day, a truck came and took the goods to a market in Chiang Mai. I also had to clean the toilets and wipe the spit on the floor from men who chewed betel nut. I was so tired doing this work. I would try to sleep on the staircase for a few minutes when the owners were not watching. We were not given beds, so I slept with my head on one step and my body on the step below. We were

also not given food. Sometimes I would go two days without eating, only water.

Every night, the owner's wife would make me massage her until she fell asleep. Sometimes I would fall asleep, and if she woke up and found me, she would beat me on the shoulders with a bamboo stick. If she did not like the work I did, she would make me get on my knees and beat me until I fell over. If she found me sleeping on the stairs, she would stab me with scissors in the shoulder until I bled very badly. Even when I was bleeding, she would make me go back to work.

I worked in the factory until I was fourteen years old. One day, the owner caught me sleeping on the stairs and she stabbed me in the head with scissors. There was so much blood I thought I might die. I was given a bandage and sent back to work, but I was too dizzy. That night, I ran away. I wanted to run away before, but I had seen other people try, and the guards always caught them. The owner would pull their fingernails or burn them with torches for punishment. When I escaped, I wanted to call the police, but I did not know how to dial a telephone. I found an adult to help me and he filed a police report. I went to the hospital and was taken to a shelter. They helped me file a court case against the owners. The judge sent the owners to prison for six months and fined them forty thousand baht [$1,000]. They served their sentence and they are back at the market. They are very upset at me, and I am afraid they will come after me.

When I first came to this shelter, I was very angry. I did not understand why something like this happened to me. I wanted to go to school so badly, but I could not. The owner had three children, and they went to school. One was in Bangkok, and the other two went to university in America.

I recently met my mother for the first time in many years. She is working in a second factory owned by Jay. I miss my mother, but I cannot see her again because the shelter is worried the owners will find out where I am, and they will do harm to me.

I asked the shelter personnel for the names of the owners, but they could not tell me because of a confidentiality agreement they signed during Aye's legal case. They did, however, tell me the location of the market in which the goods from the factory were sold. I visited the market and saw the fruits, spices, and other trinkets Aye was forced to process for ten of her fifteen years of life. The market was not more than a stone's throw from the U.S. embassy. I wanted to burn it to the ground.

Though Aye suffered nightmares, fits of anger, and an acute eating disorder, after a few months in the shelter she had discovered a genuine enjoyment for art. At the end of her story, I asked if she would like to share her work. Her eyes lit up and she hurried to retrieve it. When she returned, she proudly presented a painted pencil holder, a beanbag key-chain, and a greeting card with yellow and pink flowers drawn inside. I told her they were beautiful. She bowed her head and giggled bashfully.

Before I left, I asked Aye how she felt about sharing her story for the first time. This is what she said:

> I want to tell people my life story, so they know what happens to people like me. I want other people who have suffered like me to know they are not alone.

Appendix A
Selected Tables and Notes

Slaves are broadly defined as individuals who are held captive and coerced to work against their will without compensation. There are many modes by which slaves are exploited, which I have aggregated into three categories in table A.1: bonded labor, trafficked slaves, and forced-labor slaves.

The overwhelming majority of bonded laborers live in South Asia, with smaller numbers spread across other regions. The economic model of debt bondage dates back centuries, with various forms including peonage, serfdom, and sharecropping. In each modality, individuals borrow money or assets and are bound in

TABLE A.1
Breakdown of Contemporary Slavery: End of 2006

	Number of Slaves (millions)	Percent of Total
Bonded labor[1]	18.1	*63.7*
Trafficked slaves:		
Sexual exploitation	1.2	*4.2*
Other forced labor	1.5	*5.3*
Total trafficked slaves	2.7	*9.5*
Forced labor	7.6	*26.8*
Total	28.4	***100.0***

[1] Includes debt bondage.

servitude until the debts are repaid. The accounting of such debts invariably disfavors the laborer, and the work is essentially extracted for free. Following the abolition of slavery in most countries during the nineteenth century, debt bondage became a substitute method for procuring slave-like labor for agriculture plantations in Africa, the Americas, and the Caribbean. Bonded laborers currently toil in numerous industries, including carpet weaving, brick molding, jewelry, pottery, stone quarrying, cigarettes, timber, fireworks, and numerous agricultural products.

Unlike bonded laborers, forced laborers are more evenly spread throughout the world. They are coerced to work without pay through violence, the threat of violence, or a similar penalty. The line between bonded labor and forced labor can be easily blurred. The more farcical a debt becomes, the more the bonded laborer is actually a forced laborer. Like bonded laborers, forced laborers are exploited in numerous industries; the primary of these include construction, logging, charcoal production, dairy farms, coffee harvesting, cocoa harvesting, domestic work, and child soldiers.

Estimates of the number of slaves in the world vary. On the low end, the ILO estimated that there were 12.3 million forced laborers in 2005.[1] The ILO admits that its estimate represents a "bare minimum" and that the number could be much higher. At issue in determining the number of slaves in the world is the number of bonded laborers, wherein credible estimates range from 10 to 60 million. My estimate of 18.1 million bonded laborers is based on conservative, bottom-up calculations that I cross-checked with numerous academic and NGO estimates, including the most authoritative assessment of the number of bonded laborers in India conducted by the Gandhi Peace Foundation in 1981. This study determined that at the time, there were 26.2 million bonded laborers in India,[2] a number some experts feel has doubled since that time; others argue that bonded labor in India has been virtually eliminated. My calculations on the total number of slaves in the world are slightly greater than those of Kevin Bales, who estimated 27 million slaves in his 1999 publication *Disposable People: New Slavery in the Global Economy*.

Estimates of the number of slaves should not be treated as static numbers. Every year, the world's population grows, especially in poor, developing countries, where individuals are more vulnerable to enslavement. Even if the net number of slaves grew by only 1.0 percent per year, the total number of slaves in 2010 would be 29.6 million. In 2020 it would be 32.6 million. The total profits generated by slave labor would be correspondingly greater (see table A.2).

Slave labor generated revenues of $152.3 billion during 2007, with total profits of $91.2 billion accruing to the exploiters of these slaves—$17.3 billion from bonded labor, $39.7 billion from trafficked slaves, and $34.2 billion from forced labor.[3]

Worldwide, the average slave generated $3,175 in net profits during 2007, at a weighted average net profit margin of 60 percent. These numbers are weighted downward due to the large number of bonded laborers.

As a criminal illicit enterprise, the slave industry is second only to the drug industry, which generated revenues of $322 billion in 2004, according to the latest data available from the UNODC,[4] compared to $152.3 billion for slaves.

TABLE A.2

Summary of Global Slavery Profits, 2007

	Weighted Average Annual Revenues per Slave (U.S. dollars)	Implied Annual Revenues from Slave Labor (billions of U.S. dollars)[1]	Average Estimated Net Profit Margin (percent)[2]	Weighted Average Annual Profits per Slave	Implied Annual Profits from Slave Labor (billions of U.S. dollars)	Percent of Total
Bonded labor[3]	1,810	32.9	*52.5*	950	17.3	*19.0*
Trafficked slaves:						
Sexual exploitation	42,030	51.3	*69.5*	29,210	35.7	*39.1*
Other forced labor	4,800	7.2	*55.0*	2,640	4.0	*4.4*
Total trafficked slaves		58.6			39.7	*43.5*
Forced labor[4]	7,960	60.8	*56.3*	4,482	34.2	*37.5*
Total		**152.3**			**91.2**	***100.0***
	per slave	5,304		per slave	3,175	
		Global Slavery Net Profit Margin (percent)	*60.0*			

[1] Based on average of starting and ending number of slaves during 2007; the number of bonded laborers and forced laborers is assumed to grow by a net of 1.0 percent during 2007.

[2] For bonded labor and some forms of forced labor, this is a pretax profit margin, though it includes an assumption of bribes paid to avoid full tax rates.

[3] Includes debt bondage.

[4] Includes forced commercial sex work of individuals not trafficked.

TABLE A.3

Exploitation Value of a Sex Slave: Brothels (2006 U.S. dollars)

Monthly Unit Economics	South Asia	East Asia and Pacific	Western Europe	Central and Eastern Europe	Latin America	Middle East	Africa	North America	Global Weighted Average
Revenues									
Sale of sex	1,350	1,620	10,080	5,040	3,200	6,510	1,300	9,000	
Alcohol	90	144	202	115	80	102	110	—	
Condoms	12	14	58	23	15	25	10	60	
Cigars, snacks, other	—	—	230	115	75	—	—	—	
Total Revenues	**1,452**	**1,778**	**10,570**	**5,293**	**3,370**	**6,637**	**1,420**	**9,060**	**3,831**
Variable Costs									
Food and beverage for slaves	105	113	900	360	240	500	120	540	
Police bribe	33	30	—	216	90	124	30	—	
Rent	27	27	180	90	65	140	25	263	
Clothing, makeup, grooming	45	60	288	144	100	265	44	240	
Organized crime payment	—	—	504	—	—	—	—	—	
Bouncers/guards	36	45	720	288	120	345	35	900	
Madam/cashier	18	18	180	90	40	100	20	—	
Cost of retail products	42	72	274	144	100	80	55	15	
Bail	6	—	—	—	—	—	—	—	
Medical	15	30	108	60	45	81	20	300	
Occasional payment/"tip"	23	27	252	126	80	102	22	225	
Marketing/advertising	—	—	—	—	—	—	—	90	

Utilities and miscellaneous	30	38	216	108	75	202	30	150	
Total Variable Costs	**379**	**459**	**3,622**	**1,626**	**955**	**1,939**	**401**	**2,723**	**1,176**
Recurring contribution	**1,073**	**1,319**	**6,948**	**3,667**	**2,415**	**4,698**	**1,019**	**6,338**	**2,655**
Average monthly churn rate (percent)	*2.5*	*2.7*	*3.1*	*3.3*	*3.1*	*3.4*	*2.7*	*3.3*	*3.0*
Operating EV	**28,928**	**33,799**	**161,100**	**81,204**	**55,996**	**101,492**	**26,104**	**140,325**	**62,910**
Fixed Costs									
Average acquisition cost	650	750	4,800	2,600	1,500	3,000	650	5,250	1,895
Total Fixed Costs	**650**	**750**	**4,800**	**2,600**	**1,500**	**3,000**	**650**	**5,250**	**1,895**
Net EV	**28,278**	**33,049**	**156,300**	**78,604**	**54,496**	**98,492**	**25,454**	**135,075**	**61,015**
Implied return on investment (percent)	*4,350*	*4,407*	*3,256*	*3,023*	*3,633*	*3,283*	*3,916*	*2,573*	*3,220*
Implied annual return (percent)	*1,323*	*1,428*	*1,211*	*1,190*	*1,351*	*1,339*	*1,271*	*1,019*	*1,171*
Relative to regional per capita income	2.9x	1.9x	1.6x	3.9x	2.5x	2.1x	4.2x	1.3x	2.5x

The EV (see table A.3) is calculated by deducting variable costs from revenues, which provides a monthly recurring contribution. This figure is multiplied by the average number of months of enslavement to generate an operating EV. Deducting the acquisition cost of the slave from operating EV provides the net exploitation value of a sex slave.

Two finance concepts must be considered when multiplying monthly recurring contribution by the average duration of enslavement: the time value of money and the risk of future cash flows. The time value of money considers the fact that a dollar today is worth more than a dollar a year from now, primarily because of inflation. The risk of future cash flows is the risk that the slave owner will not possess the slave for as long as expected. Theoretically, the churn rate captures these risks, but to be conservative, the slave owner's likelihood of achieving the average duration of enslavement can still be discounted. This discount rate is applied when calculating the operating EV to depreciate the value of future cash flows in relation to the time value of money and the risk of future cash flows.

Most models used to calculate discount rates include applying a country's inflation rate to capture the time value of money as well as a risk premium on future cash flows. For sex slaves, one could argue that discount rates should be higher in developing countries than in developed countries as a result of higher inflation. On the other hand, sex slavery is riskier in most developed countries as a result of less corruption and better-enforced laws. To simplify, I have applied hefty discount rates of 25 percent to all regions.

After calculating the net EV of a brothel sex slave in each region, I provide a return on investment (ROI) calculation, which is the net EV divided by the acquisition cost. The numbers are staggering. Sex slaves in South and East Asia provide the highest ROIs of 4,350 percent and 4,186 percent, respectively, compared to a low of 2,573 percent in North America. High rates of sex acts per day, the cultivation of sex as a business, and the longer average duration of enslavement in Asia are responsible for the higher returns on investment. Annualizing these returns leads to a range of 1,356 percent per year in East Asia and 1,019 percent in North America.

The global weighted average column offers a snapshot of the EV of brothel sex slaves for the entire world. The global average brothel sex slave provides an ROI of 3,220 percent (1,171 percent annualized), with an annual cash profit that is 2.5 times the global per capita income. If the global average EV of a brothel sex slave ($61,015) were applied to the total number of trafficked sex slaves in the world, the total EV of the global sex slave industry would be $73.2 billion. This number represents the total present value of all future profits that will end up in the pockets of the exploiters of today's 1.2 million trafficked sex slaves.

Appendix B
Contemporary Slavery Economics

TABLE B.1

Bungalow Brothel Economics: Mumbai, India (2006 U.S. dollars)

General Assumptions

20 slaves per *Malik*
Average 10 sex acts per day
1 of 5 customers buys 1 alcoholic drink
1 of 5 customers buys 1 condom
1 slave per month requires bail
50 percent "tip" per 30 sex acts
1 slave re-trafficked every 4 months

Unit Assumptions

Revenues	**Unit Prices**	
Sale of sex	4.50	
Alcohol	1.50	
Condoms	0.20	
Re-trafficking	3,000.00	
Variable Costs		
Food, beverage, drugs for slave	3.50	per slave per day
Police *Hafta* (bribe)	1.10	per slave per day
Rent	18.00	per day
Clothing, makeup, grooming	1.50	per slave per day
Bouncer/guard (2)	12.00	per day
Gharwali	12.00	per day
Cost of alcohol, condoms	0.70	per unit
Bail	110.00	per month
Medical	0.50	per slave per day
"Tip"	2.25	per slave per 30 sex acts
Re-trafficking	1,200.00	per slave per re-trafficking
Utilities and miscellaneous	1.00	per slave per day
Fixed Costs		
Up-front *Hafta*	2,000.00	
Average acquisition cost of slave	700.00	

Monthly Profit and Loss

Revenues	
	27,000
	1,800
	240
	750
Total Monthly Revenues	**29,790**
Operating Expenses	
	2,100
	660
	540
	900
	720
	360
	840
	110
	300
	450
	300
	600
Total Operating Expenses	**7,880**
Gross Profit	**21,910**
Gross Profit Margin (percent)	*73.5*
Depreciation and Amortization	
Up-front *Hafta*	17
Acquisition cost of slave	350
Total Depreciation and Amortization	**367**
Net Profit	**21,543**
Net Profit Margin (percent)	*72.3*
Annual Revenues	**357,480**
Annual Net Profit	**258,516**
per slave	12,926

TABLE B.2

Pinjara Economics: Mumbai, India (2006 U.S. dollars)

General Assumptions

- 20 slaves per *Malik*
- Average 12 sex acts per day
- 1 of 10 customers buys 1 condom
- 2 slaves per month require bail
- 50 percent "tip" per 30 sex acts
- 1 slave re-trafficked every 4 months

Unit Assumptions			Monthly Profit and Loss	
Revenues	**Unit Prices**		**Revenues**	
Sale of sex	3.33			24,000
Condoms	0.20			144
Re-trafficking	3,000.00			750
			Total Monthly Revenues	**24,894**
Variable Costs			**Operating Expenses**	
Food, beverage, drugs for slave	3.50	per slave per day		2,100
Police *Hafta* (bribe)	1.10	per slave per day		660
Rent (*Pinjara*)	12.00	per day		360
Clothing, makeup, grooming	1.50	per slave per day		900
Bouncer/guard (2)	12.00	per day		720
Gharwali	12.00	per day		360
Cost of condom	0.05	per unit		36
Bail	110.00	per slave per month		220
Medical	0.50	per slave per day		300
"Tip"	1.67	per slave per 30 sex acts		400
Re-trafficking	1,200.00	per slave per re-trafficking		300
Utilities and miscellaneous	1.00	per slave per day		600
			Total Operating Expenses	**6,956**
Fixed Costs			**Gross Profit**	**17,938**
Up-front *Hafta* for *Pinjara*	1,500.00		*Gross Profit Margin (percent)*	*72.1*
Average acquisition cost of slave	700.00		**Depreciation and Amortization**	
			Up-front *Hafta*	13
			Acquisition cost of slave	350
			Total Depreciation and Amortization	**363**
			Net Profit	**17,575**
			Net Profit Margin (percent)	*70.6*
			Annual Revenues	**298,728**
			Annual Net Profit	**210,902**
			per slave	10,545

TABLE B.3

Massage Parlor Economics: Kathmandu, Nepal (2006 U.S. dollars)

General Assumptions

4 slaves per parlor
Average 10 sex acts per day
1 of 10 customers buys 1 condom
1 slave re-trafficked every 6 months
50 percent "tip" per 30 sex acts

Unit Assumptions			Monthly Profit and Loss	
Revenues	**Unit Prices**		**Revenues**	
Sale of sex	3.33			3,996
Condoms	0.20			24
Re-trafficking	800.00			133
			Total Monthly Revenues	**4,020**
Variable Costs			**Operating Expenses**	
Food, beverage, drugs for slave	2.25	per slave per day		270
Police bribe	0.50	per slave per day		60
Allocated rent	3.00	per day		90
Clothing, makeup, grooming	1.00	per slave per day		120
Bouncer/guard	8.00	per day		240
Madam/cashier	8.00	per day		240
Cost of condom	0.05	per unit		6
Medical	0.30	per slave per day		36
"Tip"	1.67	per slave per 30 sex acts		67
Re-trafficking	340.00	per slave per re-trafficking		57
Utilities and miscellaneous	0.60	per slave per day		72
			Total Operating Expenses	**1,257**
Fixed Costs			**Gross Profit**	**2,763**
			Gross Profit Margin (percent)	68.7
Average acquisition cost of slave	450.00		**Depreciation and Amortization**	
Massage equipment	300.00		Acquisition cost of slave	45
			Massage equipment	5
			Total Depreciation and Amortization	**50**
			Net Profit	**2,713**
			Net Profit Margin (percent)	67.5
			Annual Revenues	**48,240**
			Annual Net Profit	**32,552**
			per slave	8,138

TABLE B.4

International Slave-Trading Economics: Slave-Trading Route from Sindhupalchok, Nepal to Mumbai, India (2006 U.S. dollars)

General Assumptions

1 victim for each modality
4-day journey from Sindhupalchok to Mumbai

	Purchased from Family	Abducted[1]	Deceit (False Job Offer, Marriage Offer, etc.)	Recruited by Former Sex Slave	Total		Re-trafficked to Middle East
Acquisition cost	100	0	30	30	160		
Food and beverage	25	10	25	25	85		
Border bribe[2]	25	0	25	25	75		
Transport by bus	30	30	30	30	120		
Three nights "safe house"	25	25	25	25	100		
Presale clothing and grooming	25	25	25	25	100	False documents	300
Break-in cost[4]	30	30	30	30	120	Round-trip air travel[3]	300
Miscellaneous (extra bribe, medical, etc.)	30	30	30	30	120	Miscellaneous (clothing, food, etc.)	100
Allocated trafficker's cost[5]	120	120	120	120	480	Allocated trafficker's cost[5]	500
Total Cost	**410**	**270**	**340**	**340**	**1,360**		**1,200**
Average sale price	800	800	800	800	3,200		3,000
Net Profit	**390**	**530**	**460**	**460**	**1,840**		**1,800**
Net Profit Margin (percent)	*48.8*	*66.3*	*57.5*	*57.5*	*57.5*		*60.0*

Note: Victims may be re-trafficked from Mumbai to international destinations, such as the Middle East, Western Europe, and East Asia.

[1] In the case of abduction, the trafficker smuggles the victim across the border, offers very little food, and possibly drugs the victim for transport by train or bus.

[2] Very often traffickers cross the border at a place without border guards, or the guards may simply let them pass without questioning.

[3] A round-trip ticket is purchased to avoid suspicion, though it is used for one-way travel.

[4] I only witnessed formal break-in processes in India; while such efforts occur in other countries, none manifested regular, formal processes.

[5] Includes return journey and allocation of 10 percent trafficking cost for victims lost or killed en route.

TABLE B.5

Internal Slave-Trading Economics: Slave-Trading Route from Punjab to Mumbai, India (2006 U.S. dollars)

General Assumptions

1 victim for each modality
3-day journey from Punjab to Mumbai

	Purchased from Family	Abducted[1]	Deceit (False Job Offer, Marriage Offer, etc.)	Recruited by Former Sex Slave	Total
Acquisition cost	100	0	30	30	160
Food and beverage	18	6	18	18	60
Border bribe	0	0	0	0	0
Transport by bus	20	20	20	20	80
Two nights "safe house"	20	20	20	20	80
Pre-sale clothing and grooming	25	25	25	25	100
Break-in cost[2]	30	30	30	30	120
Miscellaneous (extra bribe, medical, etc.)	25	25	25	25	100
Allocated trafficker's cost[3]	100	100	100	100	400
Total Cost	**338**	**226**	**268**	**268**	**1,100**
Average sale price	650	650	650	650	2,600
Net Profit	**312**	**424**	**382**	**382**	**1,500**
Net Profit Margin (percent)	*48.0*	*65.2*	*58.8*	*58.8*	*57.7*

[1] In the case of abduction, the trafficker smuggles the victim across the border, offers very little food, and possibly drugs the victim for transport by train or bus.

[2] I only witnessed formal break-in processes in India; while such efforts occur in other countries, none manifested regular, formal processes.

[3] Includes return journey and allocation of 10 percent trafficking cost for victims lost or killed en route.

TABLE B.6

Club/House-Brothel Economics: Outskirts of Italian Urban Center (2006 U.S. dollars)

General Assumptions

10 slaves per house/club-brothel
Average of 8 sex acts per day
1 of 5 customers buys 1 alcoholic drink
1 of 5 customers buys 1 condom
1 of 10 customers buys 1 cigar or snack
5 percent of sex revenues to local mafia
50 percent "tip" per 20 sex acts
1 slave re-trafficked every 3 months

Unit Assumptions			Monthly Profit and Loss	
Revenues	**Unit Prices**		**Revenues**	
Sale of sex	42.00			100,800
Alcohol	4.20			2,016
Condoms	1.20			576
Cigars, snacks, other	9.60			2,304
Re-trafficking	4,800.00			1,600
			Total Monthly Revenues	**107,296**
Variable Costs			**Operating Expenses**	
Food, beverage, drugs for slave	30.00	per slave per day		9,000
Allocated rent	60.00	per day		1,800
Clothing, makeup, grooming	9.60	per slave per day		2,880
Organized crime/police payment	2.10	per sex act		5,040
Bouncer/guard (2)	120.00	per day		7,200
Cashier	60.00	per day		1,800
Cost of alcohol, condom, snacks	8.40	per unit		2,736
Medical	3.60	per slave per day		1,080
"Tip"	21.00	per slave per 20 sex acts		2,520
Re-trafficking	1,800.00	per slave per re-trafficking		600
Utilities and miscellaneous	7.20	per slave per day		2,160
			Total Operating Expenses	**36,816**
Fixed Costs			**Gross Profit**	**70,480**
Average acquisition cost of slave	4,800.00		*Gross Profit Margin (percent)*	*65.7*
			Depreciation	
			Acquisition cost of slave	1,498
			Total Depreciation	**1,498**
			Net Profit	**68,982**
			Net Profit Margin (percent)	*64.3*
			Annual Revenues	**1,287,552**
			Annual Net Profit	**827,782**
			per slave	82,778

TABLE B.7

Apartment Brothel Economics: West European Urban Center (2006 U.S. dollars)

General Assumptions

4 slaves per apartment
Average 10 sex acts per day
1 of 10 customers buys 1 condom
50 percent tip per 30 sex acts
1 slave re-trafficked every 3 months

Unit Assumptions			**Monthly Profit and Loss**	
Revenues	**Unit Prices**		**Revenues**	
Sale of sex	30.00			36,000
Condoms	1.20			144
Re-trafficking	4,800.00			1,600
			Total Monthly Revenues	**37,744**
Variable Costs			**Operating Expenses**	
Food, beverage, drugs for slave	21.60	per slave per day		2,592
Rent	36.00	per day		1,080
Clothing, makeup, grooming	6.00	per slave per day		720
Bouncer/guard (2)	96.00	per day		5,760
Cost of condom	0.30	per unit		36
Medical	3.00	per slave per day		360
"Tip"	15.00	per slave per 30 sex acts		600
Re-trafficking	1,800.00	per slave per re-trafficking		600
Utilities and miscellaneous	6.00	per slave per day		720
			Total Operating Expenses	**12,468**
Fixed Costs			**Gross Profit**	**25,276**
Average acquisition cost of slave	4,800.00		*Gross Profit Margin (percent)*	*67.0*
			Depreciation	
			Acquisition cost of slave	599
			Total Depreciation	**599**
			Net Profit	**24,677**
			Net Profit Margin (percent)	*65.4*
			Annual Revenues	**452,928**
			Annual Net Profit	**296,121**
			per slave	74,030

TABLE B.8

Forced Street Prostitution Economics: West European Urban Center (2006 U.S. dollars)

General Assumptions

6 slaves per pimp
Average 10 sex acts per day
50 percent tip per 20 sex acts
1 slave re-trafficked every 3 months

Unit Assumptions			**Monthly Profit and Loss**	
Revenues	**Unit Prices**		**Revenues**	
Sale of sex	27.00			48,600
Re-trafficking	4,800.00			1,600
			Total Monthly Revenues	**50,200**
Variable Costs			**Operating Expenses**	
Food, beverage, drugs for slave	21.60	per slave per day		3,888
Police bribe	8.40	per slave per day		1,512
Rent	36.00	per day		1,080
Clothing, makeup, grooming	7.20	per slave per day		1,296
Medical	3.00	per slave per day		540
"Tip"	13.50	per slave per 20 sex acts		1,215
Re-trafficking	1,800.00	per slave per re-trafficking		600
Utilities and miscellaneous	6.00	per slave per day		1,080
			Total Operating Expenses	**11,211**
Fixed Costs			**Gross Profit**	**38,989**
Average acquisition cost of slave	4,800.00		*Gross Profit Margin (percent)*	*77.7*
			Depreciation	
			Acquisition cost of slave	899
			Total Depreciation	**899**
			Net Profit	**38,090**
			Net Profit Margin (percent)	*75.9*
			Annual Revenues	**602,400**
			Annual Net Profit	**457,081**
			per slave	76,180

TABLE B.9

International Slave-Trading Economics: Slave-Trading Route from Albania to Italy via Greece (2006 U.S. dollars)

General Assumptions

1 victim romance/seduction, 1 victim abducted, 7 victims deceived, 1 victim recruited
6-day journey from Albania to Italy

Number of Victims	1	1	7	1	10		1
	Romance or Seduction	**Abducted[1]**	**Deceit (false job offer, travel or study, etc.)**	**Recruited by Former Sex Slave**	**Total**		**Re-Trafficked to Netherlands**
Acquisition cost	200	0	350	150	700		
Food and beverage	120	60	840	120	1,140		
False documents	500	500	3,500	500	5,000		
Border bribe[2]	100	100	700	100	1,000		
Allocated speedboat lease[3]	250	250	1,750	250	2,500		
5 nights in motel/"safe house"	120	120	840	120	1,200		
Ground transport and delivery	150	150	1,050	150	1,500	False Documents	500
Presale clothing and grooming	75	75	525	75	750	4-day land journey	350
Miscellaneous (extra bribe, medical, etc.)	100	100	700	100	1,000	Miscellaneous (clothing, food, etc.)	200
Allocated trafficker's cost[4]	600	600	4,200	600	6,000	Allocated Trafficker's cost[4]	750
Unit Cost	2,215	1,955	2,065	2,165			
Total Cost	**2,215**	**1,955**	**14,455**	**2,165**	**20,790**		**1,800**
Average sale price	4,800	4,800	4,800	4,800			
Total sale price	**4,800**	**4,800**	**33,600**	**4,800**	**48,000**		**4,800**
Net Profit	**2,585**	**2,845**	**19,145**	**2,635**	**27,210**		**3,000**
Net Profit Margin (percent)	*53.9*	*59.3*	*57.0*	*54.9*	*56.7*		*62.5*

[1] With abduction, the trafficker smuggles the victim across the border, offers very little food, and takes a boat to Southern Italy or truck to northeastern Italy on his own, in which case petrol would not quite cost as much as leasing a boat.

[2] More recently, much of the trafficking from Eastern to Western Europe involves false documents, as opposed to border bribes, though some border bribes are still required to avoid excessive questioning; for this example I have assumed no bribe at the Albania-Greece border, a bribe to depart Greece via speedboat, and no bribe at the Italian shore.

[3] Most trafficking from Greece to Italy is via regular ferry, though to be conservative I have assumed the use of a more expensive speedboat.

[4] Includes return journey and allocation of 10 percent trafficking cost for victims lost or killed en route.

TABLE B.10

Club-Brothel Economics: East European Urban Center (2006 U.S. dollars)

General Assumptions

10 slaves per brothel
Average 8 sex acts per day
1 of 5 customers buys 1 alcoholic drink
1 of 5 customers buys 1 condom
1 of 10 customers buys 1 cigar or snack
50 percent "tip" per 20 sex acts
1 slave re-trafficked every 3 months

Unit Assumptions			Monthly Profit and Loss	
Revenues	**Unit Prices**		**Revenues**	
Sale of sex	21.00			50,400
Alcohol	2.40			1,152
Condoms	0.48			230
Cigars, snacks, other	4.80			1,152
Re-Trafficking	3,300.00			1,100
			Total Monthly Revenues	**54,034**
Variable Costs			**Operating Expenses**	
Food, beverage, drugs for slave	12.00	per slave per day		3,600
Police bribe	7.20	per slave per day		2,160
Allocated rent	30.00	per day		900
Clothing, makeup, grooming	4.80	per slave per day		1,440
Bouncer/guard (2)	48.00	per day		2,880
Cashier	30.00	per day		900
Cost of alcohol, condom, snacks	4.20	per unit		1,440
Medical	2.00	per slave per day		600
"Tip"	10.50	per slave per 20 sex acts		1,260
Re-trafficking	1,300.00	per slave per re-trafficking		433
Utilities and miscellaneous	3.60	per slave per day		1,080
			Total Operating Expenses	**16,693**
Fixed Costs			**Gross Profit**	**37,341**
Average acquisition cost of slave	2,600.00		*Gross Profit Margin (percent)*	*69.1*
			Depreciation	
			Acquisition cost of slave	867
			Total Depreciation	**867**
			Depreciation	
			Net Profit	**36,474**
			Net Profit Margin (percent)	*67.5*
			Annual Revenues	**648,413**
			Annual Net Profit	**437,693**
			per slave	43,769

TABLE B.11

Apartment Brothel Economics: East European Urban Center (2006 U.S. dollars)

General Assumptions

4 slaves per apartment
Average 10 sex acts per day
1 of 10 customers buys 1 condom
50 percent "tip" per 30 sex acts
1 slave re-trafficked every 3 months

Unit Assumptions			Monthly Profit and Loss	
Revenues	**Unit Prices**		**Revenues**	
Sale of sex	15.00			18,000
Condoms	0.48			58
Re-trafficking	3,300.00			1,100
			Total Monthly Revenues	**19,158**
Variable Costs			**Operating Expenses**	
Food, beverage, drugs for slave	9.00	per slave per day		1,080
Rent	18.00	per day		540
Clothing, makeup, grooming	3.00	per slave per day		360
Bouncer/guard (2)	42.00	per day		2,520
Cost of condom	0.12	per unit		14
Medical	2.00	per slave per day		240
"Tip"	7.50	per slave per 30 sex acts		300
Re-trafficking	1,300.00	per slave per re-trafficking		433
Utilities and miscellaneous	3.00	per slave per day		360
			Total Operating Expenses	**5,848**
Fixed Costs			**Gross Profit**	**13,310**
Average acquisition cost of slave	2,600.00		*Gross Profit Margin (percent)*	*69.5*
			Depreciation	
			Acquisition cost of slave	347
			Total Depreciation	**347**
			Net Profit	**12,963**
			Net Profit Margin (percent)	*67.7*
			Annual Revenues	**229,891**
			Annual Net Profit	**155,558**
			per slave	38,890

TABLE B.12

Forced Street Prostitution Economics: East European Urban Center (2006 U.S. dollars)

General Assumptions

6 slaves per pimp
Average 10 sex acts per day
50 percent "tip" per 20 sex acts
1 slave re-trafficked every 3 months

Unit Assumptions			**Monthly Profit and Loss**	
Revenues	**Unit Prices**		**Revenues**	
Sale of sex	12.00			21,600
Re-trafficking	3,300.00			1,100
			Total Monthly Revenues	**22,700**
Variable Costs			**Operating Expenses**	
Food, beverage, drugs for slave	9.00	per slave per day		1,620
Police bribe	3.60	per slave per day		648
Rent	18.00	per day		540
Clothing, makeup, grooming	3.00	per slave per day		540
Medical	2.00	per slave per day		360
"Tip"	6.00	per slave per 20 sex acts		540
Re-trafficking	1,300.00	per slave per re-trafficking		433
Utilities and miscellaneous	3.00	per slave per day		540
			Total Operating Expenses	**5,221**
Fixed Costs			**Gross Profit**	**17,479**
Average acquisition cost of slave	2,600.00		*Gross Profit Margin (percent)*	*77.0*
			Depreciation	
			Acquisition cost of slave	520
			Total Depreciation	**520**
			Net Profit	**16,959**
			Net Profit Margin (percent)	*74.7*
			Annual Revenues	**272,400**
			Annual Net Profit	**203,504**
			per slave	33,917

TABLE B.13

International Slave-Trading Economics: Slave-Trading Route from Rural Moldova to Moscow, Russia (2006 U.S. dollars)

General Assumptions

1 victim romance/seduction, 7 victims deceived, 2 victims recruited
4-day journey from Moldova to Russia

Number of Victims	1	7	2	10		1
	Romance or Seduction	**Deceit (False Job Offer, Travel, or Study, etc.)**	**Recruited by Former Sex Slave**	**Total**		**Re-Trafficked to Turkey**
Acquisition cost	100	175	100	375		
Food and beverage	60	420	120	600		
False documents	500	3,500	1,000	5,000		
Border bribe[1]	100	700	200	1,000		
3 nights in motel/"safe house"	30	210	60	300		
Ground transport and delivery	125	875	250	1,250	False documents	300
Presale clothing and grooming	50	350	100	500	Round-trip air travel[2]	350
Miscellaneous (extra bribe, medical, etc.)	60	420	120	600	Miscellaneous (clothing, food, etc.)	150
Allocated trafficker's cost[3]	350	2,450	700	3,500	Allocated trafficker's cost[3]	500
Unit Cost	1,375	1,300	1,325			
Total Cost	**1,375**	**9,100**	**2,650**	**13,125**		**1,300**
Average sale price	3,300	3,300	3,300			
Total sale price	**3,300**	**23,100**	**6,600**	**33,000**		**3,300**
Net Profit	**1,925**	**14,000**	**3,950**	**19,875**		**2,000**
Net Profit Margin (percent)	*58.3*	*60.6*	*59.8*	*60.2*		*60.6*

Note: Victims may be re-trafficked to Western Europe, Eastern Europe, or the Middle East.

[1] Most trafficking from Eastern Europe involves false documents, as opposed to border bribes, though some border bribes may still be required to avoid excessive questioning; for this example I have assumed a bribe from Moldova to Transdniester and no bribe from Transdniester to Ukraine, Ukraine to Belarus, and Belarus to Russia.

[2] Round-trip ticket is purchased to avoid suspicion, though used for one-way travel.

[3] Includes return journey and allocation of 10 percent trafficking cost for victims lost or killed en route.

TABLE B.14

Internal Slave-Trading Economics: Slave-Trading Route from Rural Eastern Europe to Urban Center (2006 U.S. dollars)

General Assumptions

1 victim romance/seduction, 7 victims deceived, 2 victims recruited
2-day journey

Number of Victims	1	7	2	10
	Romance or Seduction	**Deceit (false job offer, marriage offer, etc.)**	**Recruited by Former Sex Slave**	**Total**
Acquisition cost	100	175	100	375
Food and beverage	30	210	60	300
Identity card[1]	100	700	200	1,000
Border bribe	0	0	0	0
1 night in motel/"safe house"	10	70	20	100
Ground transport and delivery	50	350	100	500
Presale clothing and grooming	50	350	100	500
Miscellaneous (extra bribe, medical, etc.)	30	210	60	300
Allocated trafficker's cost[2]	150	1,050	300	1,500
Unit Cost	520	445	470	
Total Cost	**520**	**3,115**	**940**	**4,575**
Average sale price	1,200	1,200	1,200	
Total sale price	**1,200**	**8,400**	**2,400**	**12,000**
Net Profit	**680**	**5,285**	**1,460**	**7,425**
Net Profit Margin (percent)	*56.7*	*62.9*	*60.8*	*61.9*

[1] Identification cards are provided in the case of police questioning during travel, or during street prostitution.
[2] Includes return journey and allocation of 10 percent trafficking cost for victims lost or killed en route.

TABLE B.15

Brothel Economics: Chiang Mai, Thailand (2006 U.S. dollars)

General Assumptions

20 slaves per brothel
Average 12 sex acts per day
1 of 5 customers buys 1 alcoholic drink
1 of 5 customers buys 1 condom
50 percent "tip" per 30 sex acts
1 slave re-trafficked every 4 months

Unit Assumptions			**Monthly Profit and Loss**	
Revenues	**Unit Prices**		**Revenues**	
Sale of sex	4.50			32,400
Alcohol	2.00			2,880
Condoms	0.20			288
Re-trafficking	750.00			188
			Total Monthly Revenues	**35,756**
Variable Costs			**Operating Expenses**	
Food, beverage, drugs for slave	3.75	per slave per day		2,250
Polie bribe	1.00	per slave per day		600
Rent	18.00	per day		540
Clothing, makeup, grooming	2.00	per slave per day		1,200
Bouncer/guard (2)	15.00	per day		900
Madam/cashier	12.00	per day		360
Cost of alcohol, condom	1.00	per unit		1,440
Medical	1.00	per slave per day		600
"Tip"	2.25	per slave per 30 sex acts		540
Re-trafficking	325.00	per slave per re-trafficking		81
Utilities and miscellaneous	1.25	per slave per day		750
			Total Operating Expenses	**9,261**
Fixed Costs			**Gross Profit**	26,494
Up-front bribe for new brothel	2,500.00		*Gross Profit Margin (percent)*	*74.1*
Average acquisition cost of slave	750.00		**Depreciation and Amortization**	
			Up-front bribe	21
			Acquisition cost of slave	417
			Total Depreciation and Amortization	**438**
			Net Profit	**26,057**
			Net Profit Margin (percent)	*72.9*
			Annual Revenues	**429,066**
			Annual Net Profit	**312,681**
			per slave	15,634

TABLE B.16

Massage Parlor Economics: Bangkok, Thailand (2006 U.S. dollars)

General Assumptions

6 slaves per parlor
Average 10 sex acts per day
1 of 5 customers buys 1 condom
1 slave re-trafficked every 4 months
50 percent "tip" per 30 sex acts

Unit Assumptions			Monthly Profit and Loss	
Revenues	**Unit Prices**		**Revenues**	
Sale of sex	4.25			7,650
Condoms	0.20			72
Re-trafficking	750.00			188
			Total Monthly Revenues	**7,722**
Variable Costs			**Operating Expenses**	
Food, beverage, drugs for slave	3.25	per slave per day		585
Police bribe	1.00	per slave per day		180
Allocated rent	6.00	per day		180
Clothing, makeup, grooming	1.50	per slave per day		270
Bouncer/guard	15.00	per day		450
Madam/cashier	10.00	per day		300
Cost of condom	0.05	per unit		18
Medical	0.75	per slave per day		135
"Tip"	2.13	per slave per 30 sex acts		128
Re-trafficking	325.00	per slave per re-trafficking		81
Utilities and miscellaneous	1.00	per slave per day		180
			Total Operating Expenses	**2,507**
Fixed Costs			**Gross Profit**	**5,215**
			Gross Profit Margin (percent)	*67.5*
Average acquisition cost of slave	750.00			
Massage equipment	500.00			
			Depreciation and Amortization	
			Acquisition cost of slave	125
			Massage equipment	8
			Total Depreciation and Amortization	**133**
			Net Profit	**5,082**
			Net Profit Margin (percent)	*65.8*
			Annual Revenues	**92,664**
			Annual Net Profit	**60,983**
			per slave	10,164

TABLE B.17

International Slave-Trading Economics: Slave-Trading Route from Karen Region, Myanmar to Bangkok, Thailand (2006 U.S. dollars)

General Assumptions

1 victim for each modality
4-day journey from Karen to Bangkok

	Purchased from Family	Abducted[1]	Deceit (false job offer, marriage offer, etc.)	Recruited by Former Sex Slave	Total		Re-Trafficked to United States
Acquisition cost	100	0	30	30	160		
Food and beverage	30	15	30	30	105		
Border bribe[2]	30	0	30	30	90		
Transport by bus	35	35	35	35	140		
3 nights "safe house"	30	30	30	30	120	False documents	500
Presale clothing and grooming	30	30	30	30	120	Round-trip air travel[3]	1,200
Miscellaneous (extra bribe, medical, etc.)	40	40	40	40	160	Miscellaneous (clothing, food, etc.)	150
Allocated trafficker's cost[4]	120	120	120	120	480	Allocated trafficker's cost[4]	1,500
Total Cost	**415**	**270**	**345**	**345**	**1,375**		**3,350**
Average sale price	850	850	850	850	3,400		7,500
Net Profit	**435**	**580**	**505**	**505**	**2,025**		**4,150**
Net Profit Margin (percent)	*51.2*	*68.2*	*59.4*	*59.4*	*59.6*		*55.3*

Notes: Victims may be re-trafficked to East Asia, the Middle East, Western Europe, or the United States.

[1] In the case of abduction, the trafficker smuggles the victim across the border, offers very little food, and drives to Bangkok in his own vehicle, in which case petrol costs about the same as several bus tickets.

[2] Very often traffickers may cross the border at a place without border guards, or the guards may simply let them pass without questioning.

[3] A round-trip ticket is purchased to avoid suspicion, though used for one-way travel.

[4] Includes return journey.

TABLE B.18

Internal Slave-Trading: Slave-Trading Route from Chiang Rai to Bangkok, Thailand (2006 U.S. dollars)

General Assumptions

1 victim for each modality
3-day journey from Chiang Rai to Bangkok

	Purchased from Family	Abducted[1]	Deceit (false job offer, marriage offer, etc.)	Recruited by Former Sex Slave	Total		Re-Trafficked to Malaysia
Acquisition cost	100	0	30	30	160		
Food and beverage	25	10	25	25	85		
Border bribe	0	0	0	0	0		
Transport by bus	25	25	25	25	100		
2 nights "safe house"	20	20	20	20	80	Border bribe	25
Presale clothing and grooming	30	30	30	30	120	Tourist bus and bribe for transport	100
Miscellaneous (extra bribe, medical, etc.)	35	35	35	35	140	Miscellaneous (clothing, food, etc.)	75
Allocated trafficker's cost[2]	100	100	100	100	400	Allocated trafficker's cost[2]	125
Total Cost	**335**	**220**	**265**	**265**	**1,085**		**325**
Average sale price	650	650	650	650	2,600		750
Net Profit	**315**	**430**	**385**	**385**	**1,515**		**425**
Net Profit Margin (percent)	*48.5*	*66.2*	*59.2*	*59.2*	*58.3*		*56.7*

[1] In the case of abduction, the trafficker smuggles the victim across the border, offers very little food, and drives to Bangkok in his own vehicle, in which case petrol costs about the same as several bus tickets.
[2] Includes return journey.

TABLE B.19

Apartment Brothel Economics: Queens, New York (2006 U.S. dollars)

General Assumptions

- 8 slaves per apartment brothel
- Average 10 sex acts per day
- 1 of 5 customers buys 1 condom
- 50 percent "tip" per 20 sex acts

Unit Assumptions			**Monthly Profit and Loss**	
Revenues	**Unit Prices**		**Revenues**	
Sale of Sex	30.00			72,000
Condoms	1.00			480
			Total Monthly Revenues	**72,480**
Variable Costs			**Operating Expenses**	
Food, beverage, drugs for slave	18.00	per slave per day		4,320
Rent	70.00	per day		2,100
Clothing, makeup, grooming	8.00	per slave per day		1,920
Bouncer/guard (2)	120.00	per day		7,200
Cost of condom	0.25	per unit		120
Medical (includes abortions)	10.00	per slave per day		2,400
"Tip"	15.00	per slave per 20 sex acts		1,800
Marketing/advertising	3.00	per slave per day		720
Utilities and miscellaneous	5.00	per slave per day		1,200
			Total Operating Expenses	**21,780**
Fixed Costs			**Gross Profit**	**50,700**
Average acquisition cost of slave	3,000.00		*Gross Profit Margin (percent)*	*70.0*
			Depreciation	
			Acquisition cost of slave	800
			Total Depreciation	**800**
			Net Profit	**49,900**
			Net Profit Margin (percent)	*68.8*
			Annual Revenues	**869,760**
			Annual Net Profit	**598,800**
			per slave	74,850

TABLE B.20

Massage Parlor Economics: Los Angeles, California (2006 U.S. dollars)

General Assumptions

4 slaves per parlor
Average 8 sex acts per day
1 of 5 customers buys 1 condom
30 percent "tip" per 20 sex acts

Unit Assumptions			**Monthly Profit and Loss**	
Revenues	**Unit Prices**		**Revenues**	
Sale of sex	25.00			24,000
Condoms	1.00			192
			Total Monthly Revenues	**24,192**
Variable Costs			**Operating Expenses**	
Food, beverage, drugs for slave	18.00	per slave per day		2,160
Allocated rent	45.00	per day		1,350
Clothing, makeup, grooming	3.50	per slave per day		420
Manager/cashier	100.00	per day		3,000
Cost of condom	0.25	per unit		48
Medical	5.00	per slave per day		600
"Tip"	8.33	per slave per 20 sex acts		400
Utilities, promotional, and miscellaneous	7.50	per slave per day		900
			Total Operating Expenses	**8,878**
Fixed Costs			**Gross Profit**	**15,314**
			Gross Profit Margin (percent)	*63.3*
Average acquisition cost of slave	7,500.00			
Massage equipment	1,500.00			
			Depreciation	
			Acquisition cost of slave	1,000
			Massage equipment	25
			Total Depreciation	**1,025**
			Net Profit	**14,289**
			Net Profit Margin (percent)	*59.1*
			Annual Revenues	**290,304**
			Annual Net Profit	**171,468**
			per slave	42,867

TABLE B.21

International Slave-Trading Economics: Slave-Trading Route from Chiang Mai, Thailand to Los Angeles, California (2006 U.S. dollars)

General Assumptions

1 victim for each modality
3-day journey from Thailand to United States

	Purchased from Family	Deceit (false job offer, study abroad, etc.)	Recruited by Former Sex Slave	Total
Acquisition cost	100	30	30	160
Food and beverage	40	40	40	120
Bus to Bangkok	25	25	25	75
False documents	500	500	500	1,500
Round-trip air travel[1]	1,200	1,200	1,200	3,600
2 nights "safe house"	40	40	40	120
Presale clothing and grooming	75	75	75	225
Miscellaneous (medical, etc.)	100	100	100	300
Allocated trafficker's cost[2]	1,750	1,750	1,750	5,250
Total Cost	**3,830**	**3,760**	**3,760**	**11,350**
Average sale price	7,500	7,500	7,500	22,500
Net Profit	**3,670**	**3,740**	**3,740**	**11,150**
Net Profit Margin (percent)	*48.9*	*49.9*	*49.9*	*49.6*

Note: There is no evidence of significant re-trafficking from the United States.

[1] Round-trip ticket is purchased to avoid suspicion, though used for one-way travel.

[2] Includes return journey.

TABLE B.22

International Slave-Trading Economics: Slave-Trading Route from Rural Mexico to New York, New York (2006 U.S. dollars)

General Assumptions

1 victim for each modality
3-day journey from Mexico to United States

	Abducted	Deceit (false job offer, study abroad, etc.)	Romance or Seduction	Total
Acquisition cost	0	50	200	250
Food and beverage	20	40	40	100
Coyote	1,250	1,250	1,250	3,750
False documents	0	50	0	50
Truck transport	70	70	70	210
2 nights "safe house"	60	60	60	180
Presale clothing and grooming	75	75	75	225
Miscellaneous (medical, etc.)	50	50	50	150
Allocated trafficker's cost[1]	150	150	150	450
Total Cost	**1,675**	**1,795**	**1,895**	**5,365**
Average sale price	3,000	3,000	3,000	9,000
Net Profit	1,325	1,205	1,105	3,635
Net Profit Margin (percent)	*44.2*	*40.2*	*36.8*	*40.4*

Note: There is no evidence of significant re-trafficking from the United States.

[1] Includes return journey and allocation of 10 percent trafficking cost for victims lost or killed en route.

TABLE B.23

Trafficking for Forced Begging: Greece (2006 U.S. dollars)

General Assumptions

6 forced beggars per owner
30 donations received per beggar per day
1 beggar re-trafficked every 12 months

Unit Assumptions

Revenues	Unit Prices	
Donation	0.30	
Re-trafficking	1,200.00	
Variable Costs		
Food and beverage	2.00	per forced beggar per day
Allocated rent[1]	5.00	per day
Medical	0.30	per forced beggar per day
Re-trafficking	480.00	per forced beggar per re-trafficking
Miscellaneous	0.50	per forced beggar per day
Fixed Costs		
Average acquisition cost of beggar	1,200.00	

Monthly Profit and Loss

Revenues	
	1,620
	100
Total Monthly Revenues	**1,720**
Operating Expenses	
	360
	150
	54
	40
	90
Total Operating Expenses	**694**
Gross Profit	**1,026**
Gross Profit Margin (percent)	*59.7*
Depreciation	
Acquisition cost of beggar	150
Total Depreciation	**150**
Net Profit	**876**
Net Profit Margin (percent)	*50.9*
Annual Revenues	**20,640**
Annual Net Profit	**10,512**
per beggar	1,650

[1] The exploiter of forced beggars often keeps individuals locked in a room in his/her apartment or houses them with other forced beggars in a separate apartment. In some cases, forced beggars are left to sleep in slums or on the street.

TABLE B.24

Trafficking for Forced Carpet Weaving: Uttar Pradesh, India (2006 U.S. dollars)

General Assumptions

30 forced laborers, 3 groups for each size of carpet

Carpets made:	*Carpets sold:*
15: 2′×5′ (small)	15: 2′× 5′ (small)
4.5: 2′× 8′ (medium)	4.5: 2′× 8′ (medium)
0.5: 12′× 15′ (large)	0.5: 12′× 15′ (large)

Wholesale rate: $10 per square foot
Cost of thread: $0.89 per square foot
5 percent of thread lost each month

Unit Assumptions			Monthly Profit and Loss	
Revenues	**Unit Prices**		**Revenues**	
Carpets, small	100.00			1,500
Carpets, medium	400.00			1,800
Carpets, large	1,800.00			900
			Total Monthly Revenues	**4,200**
Operating Costs			**Operating Expenses**	
Thread	0.89	per square foot		392
Guards (2)	7.78	per day		467
Food and beverage	0.56	per laborer per day		500
Commission to traffickers	3.33	per square meter of carpet		141
Repair and miscellaneous	0.25	per laborer per day		375
			Total Operating Expenses	**1,875**
Fixed Costs			**Gross Profit**	**2,325**
			Gross Profit Margin (percent)	*55.4*
Looms	1,800.00			
Tools and other equipment	400.00			
Acquisition cost of laborer	150.00			
			Depreciation	
			Looms	15
			Tools and other equipment	11
			Acquisition cost of laborer	125
			Total Depreciation	**151**
			Net Profit	**2,174**
			Net Profit Margin (percent)	*51.8*
			Annual Revenues	**50,400**
			Annual Net Profit	**26,086**
			per forced laborer	870

TABLE B.25

Bonded Labor for Carpet Weaving: Uttar Pradesh, India (2006 U.S. dollars)

General Assumptions

30 bonded laborers, 3 groups for each size of carpet	
Carpets made:	*Carpets sold:*
15: 2′×5′ (small)	15: 2′×5′ (small)
4.5: 2′×8′ (medium)	4.5: 2′×8′ (medium)
0.5: 12′×15′ (large)	0.5: 12′×15′ (large)
Wholesale rate: $10 per square foot	
Cost of thread: $0.89 per square foot	
5 percent of thread lost each month	

Unit Assumptions			Monthly Profit and Loss	
Revenues	**Unit Prices**		**Revenues**	
Carpets, small	100.00			1,500
Carpets, medium	400.00			1,800
Carpets, large	1,800.00			900
Wage deduction	0.55			495
			Total Monthly Revenues	**4,695**
Operating Costs			**Operating Expenses**	
Wages	1.10	per laborer per day		990
Thread	0.89	per square foot		392
Repair and miscellaneous	0.25	per laborer per day		375
			Total Operating Expenses	**1,757**
Fixed Costs			**Gross Profit**	**2,938**
			Gross Profit Margin (percent)	*62.6*
Looms	1,800.00			
Tools and other equipment	400.00			
			Depreciation	
			Looms	15
			Tools and other equipment	11
			Total Depreciation	**26**
			Taxes/tax bribe[1]	420
			Net Profit	**2,492**
			Net Profit Margin (percent)	*53.1*
			Annual Revenues	**56,340**
			Annual Net Profit	**29,903**
			per bonded laborer	997

[1] Theoretically, carpet weaving is a legitimate business that requires taxes paid at the national and local tax rates; however, almost all carpet-loom owners offer bribes to local tax officials to avoid paying full business taxes. These rates vary, but the figure tends to hover around 10 percent.

TABLE B.26

Bonded Labor for Brick Making: Bihar, India (2006 U.S. dollars)

General Assumptions

50 bonded laborers per brick kiln
500,000 bricks made each month
90 percent of bricks sold (10 percent lack of demand and breakage)
Weighted average brick unit sale price: 1.75 rupees
Bricks made 8 months of year
Extra capacity sold during rainy season
Transportation costs paid by buyer

Unit Assumptions			Monthly Profit and Loss	
Revenues	**Unit Prices**		**Revenues**	
Bricks	0.04			17,500
Wage deduction	0.64			967
			Total Monthly Revenues	**18,467**
Operating Costs			**Operating Expenses**	
Wages	1.29	per laborer per day		1,933
Foreman/manager (2)	7.78	per day		467
Accountant	10.00	per day		300
Government royalty[1]	370.00	per month		370
Fuel (coal, oil, diesel)	5,333.00	per month		5,333
Utilities, repairs, and miscellaneous	1.00	per laborer per day		1,500
			Total Operating Expenses	**9,904**
Fixed Costs			**Gross Profit**	**8,563**
Kiln construction	33,333.33		*Gross Profit Margin (percent)*	*46.4*
Tools, molds, pump, equipment	3,000.00			
			Depreciation	
			Kiln construction	139
			Tools, molds, pump, equipment	50
			Total Depreciation	**189**
			Taxes/tax bribe[2]	1,750
			Net Profit	**6,624**
			Net Profit Margin (percent)	*35.9*
			Annual Revenues	**217,733**
			Annual Net Profit[3]	**110,689**
			Net Profit (percent)	*50.8*
			per bonded laborer	2,214

[1] The precise royalty depends on the state in India in which the kiln is located. Some are fixed sums for the year; others are fixed sums plus variable amounts per thousand bricks made. In variable scenarios, the brick kiln owners can pay bribes to reduce the royalty, and they often cook the books to show a lower number of bricks produced and sold. A review of numerous kilns in three states revealed that the average royalty is approximately 200,000 rupees per year, or about 4,450 U.S. dollars.

[2] Theoretically, brick making is a legitimate business that would require taxes paid at the national and local tax rates; however, almost all kiln owners offer bribes to local tax officials to avoid paying full business taxes. These rates vary, but the figure tends to hover around 10 percent.

[3] Assumes 360,000 of 400,000 (90 percent) bricks not sold during the season are sold during the off-season; the only associated expenses with these sales are government royalty, tax bribe, depreciation, and wages for the foremen and accountant.

TABLE B.27

Forced Labor for Charcoal *Batteria*: Carajas Region, Brazil (2006 U.S. dollars)

General Assumptions

14 forced laborers per *Batteria* (4 clay packers)
30 ovens per *Batteria*
Each ton of charcoal wholesales for 2,500 reales
12 tons produced per month

Unit Assumptions

Revenues	**Unit Prices**	
Charcoal	1,250.00	
Operating Costs		
Gato	450.00	per month
Guards (2)	300.00	per month
Transport	1,900.00	per month
Food and beverage	3.00	per laborer per day
Utilities, repairs, and miscellaneous	4.00	per laborer per day
Fixed Costs		
Batteria construction	6,750.00	
Tools and equipment	2,500.00	

Monthly Profit and Loss

Revenues	
	15,000
Total Monthly Revenues	**15,000**
Operating Expenses	
	450
	600
	1,900
	1,260
	1,680
Total Operating Expenses	**5,890**
Gross Profit	**9,110**
Gross Profit Margin (percent)	*60.7*
Depreciation	
Batteria construction	188
Tools and equipment	69
Total Depreciation	**257**
Net Profit	**8,853**
Net Profit Margin (percent)	59.0
Annual Revenues	**180,000**
Annual Net Profit	**106,237**
per forced laborer	7,588

TABLE B.28

Forced Labor for Coffee: Rural Kenya (2006 U.S. dollars)

General Assumptions

10-acre coffee plantation
2 harvests per year (3-month season,3-month off-season)
4 forced laborers per acre
$25 per acre fertilizer and pesticide
1,000-pound yield per acre
Wholesale spot price: $1.00 per pound
90 percent of each harvest sold

Unit Assumptions

Revenues	Unit Prices	
Coffee Beans	1.00	
Operating Costs		
Food and beverage for laborer	0.33	per laborer per day
Guards (2)	1.50	per day
Fertilizer and pesticide	25.00	per acre per harvest
Off-season planting and maintenance	200.00	per harvest
Utilities, repairs, and miscellaneous	0.20	per laborer per day
Fixed Costs		
Tools and equipment	1,000.00	

Harvest Profit and Loss

Revenues	
	9,000
Total Monthly Revenues	**9,000**
Operating Expenses	
	2,376
	540
	250
	200
	1,440
Total Operating Expenses	**4,806**
Gross Profit	**4,194**
Gross Profit Margin (percent)	*46.6*
Depreciation	
Tools and equipment	17
Total Depreciation	**17**
Net Profit	**4,177**
Net Profit Margin (percent)	*46.4*
Annual Revenues	**18,000**
Annual Net Profit	**8,355**
per forced laborer	209

Table B.1: For those tables in appendix B that calculate the profits generated by exploiting sex slaves in each mode and region, unit economic assumptions are listed to the left, monthly profit and loss numbers to the right. Revenues are generated from the sale of items such as commercial sex, food, alcohol, condoms, and re-trafficking. The relatively low assumption for the average number of daily sex acts performed accounts for the fact that a slave might fall ill, be injured by a consumer or owner, escape for a few days, or be killed with a few days passing before a replacement can be acquired. Operating costs can include food, beverages, drugs, police bribes, rent, a bouncer or guard, and medical expenses.[1] Fixed costs are also included. In the case of a bungalow brothel in Mumbai, these include the up-front bribe (*hafta*) to police and the acquisition cost of each slave. I have depreciated the acquisition cost of the slaves in all regions and modes across their respective average durations of exploitation. For simplicity, I have assumed that all slaves are acquired at once.

The bottom right of each table shows the resulting profit margin and cash profit per slave. In this table, the owner of a bungalow brothel in Mumbai enjoys over $12,900 in profits per slave per year, on a profit margin just over 72 percent. Bungalow brothels will always contain a mix of slaves and working prostitutes. The economics in the spreadsheet reflect solely the economic contribution of the slaves.

Tables B.2–B.3: *Pinjara* slaves perform more average sex acts per day than bungalow slaves do, though at lower price points. *Pinjaras* and massage parlors typically do not contain merchants who sell alcohol or snacks. Acquisition costs for slaves, as well as bribes and other operating costs, are lower in these venues.

Table B.4: One *dalal* would never recruit victims in each of the four modes in the same journey, but assuming equality among modes and representing them as part of one movement allows for a clearer overall profit picture.

Table B.5: I have specified an Italian club-brothel to portray the economics of sex-slave establishments in Western Europe that are required to make organized-crime payments. Italian house-brothels operate under a similar economic structure. Each has fewer slaves than Indian brothels have, with a lower number of average daily sex acts. As any club or house-brothel will contain a mix of slaves and prostitutes, the economics in this table apply solely to the contribution of the slaves.

Tables B.6–B.7: The price of a sex act for apartment and street prostitutes is typically 25 to 30 percent lower than it is in a club-brothel, and for the same reason, these slaves typically perform more sex acts per day. There are fewer revenue and cost items for apartments and street prostitutes, and operating expenses are also lower than club-brothels, which invest more in the overall well being, appearance, and medical care of sex slaves to entice customers to pay higher prices.

Table B.8: Along the top axis, the table includes the four primary modes of trafficking from Eastern to Western Europe, with the number of slaves trafficked under each modality representing the ratio in which these modalities actually occur, as of 2006.

Tables B.9–B.11: In general, forced prostitution in Central and Eastern Europe is slightly more profitable than it is in Western Europe, as a sizeable proportion of the clientele are sex tourists, who are willing to pay higher prices for sex relative to local operating costs. I do not have sufficient data to plot the profitability of hotel prostitution in Eastern Europe, though I expect this to be the least profitable mode due to hefty revenue shares with the hotel in exchange for access to male guests. I also suspect that most hotel prostitutes are not slaves.

Tables B.12–B.13: These spreadsheets include the three primary modes of trafficking in Eastern Europe, with the number of slaves trafficked under each modality representing the ratio in which these modalities actually occur, as of 2006.

Tables B.14–B.15: Similar to Indian sex establishments, Thai sex establishments contain a mix of trafficked sex slaves as well as working prostitutes. Like European club-brothels, Thai sex establishments invest more in the overall well being and appearance of their slaves. The economics in the spreadsheet reflect solely the economic contribution of the slaves.

Tables B.18–B.19: These spreadsheets capture the economics of the two primary modes of sex slavery in the United States as well as the two primary nationalities of the victims: East Asian and Hispanic. African and East European individuals are also trafficked for commercial sexual exploitation in the United States, including in strip clubs and pornography.

U.S. apartment brothels usually entail heavy bouncer or guard costs, as police bribes are less effective at avoiding unwanted attention in the United States. U.S. apartment brothels typically have small promotional expenses associated with flyers or postcards, whereas in Europe and Asia, brothels are easier to see or access through hotels, taxi drivers, or walking the streets.

Massage parlors in the United States are primarily filled with East Asian slaves. I have only included revenues for the incremental purchase of sex, not the cost of a full massage and sex services.

Tables B.20–B.21: The primary modes of slave trading from East Asia and Mexico to the United States are noted. For Mexico, most trafficking to the United States is conducted by segmented units, each of which receives a payment from a brothel owner, as opposed to an overall purchase price for the slave. A small number of operations are vertically integrated, wherein the slave traders manage each step in the process and deliver victims to a brothel that they might own in full or in part. There would not be a final purchase price in this scenario, only the overall expense of the trafficking.

Table B.25: The government-mandated daily wage for carpet weaving is fifty rupees, ($1.10); however, for bonded laborers, half the day-wage is almost always deducted as debt repayment. The carpets are typically sold at approximately ten dollars (450–500 rupees) per square foot on the wholesale market. Depending on the location, retailers can charge four to ten times this number. There are three common sizes of carpets: two feet by five feet, five feet by eight feet, and twelve feet by fifteen feet. The smaller carpets take two people about five to six days to weave. The medium-sized carpets take three people about two to four weeks to weave. The largest carpets take five people up to two months to weave.

Table B.26: There are over thirty thousand brick kilns in South Asia—twenty thousand in India—in which over two million people toil. Most brick kilns are medium sized, which means they operate with approximately fifty bonded laborers. Each medium-sized kiln is capable of molding, drying, and baking up to five hundred thousand bricks per month. The roles of the bonded laborers are highly segmented. At a medium-sized kiln one finds brick molders (*pathera*), who mold the clay bricks and dry them in the sun for three days; loaders (*kumhar*), who carry the unbaked dry bricks to the kilns; stackers (*beldar*), who stack the bricks and coal inside the kiln in alternating layers, topped with sand or coal ash; arrangers (*papaswala*), who work alongside the stackers and arrange layers of soil between the bricks before the burning process; firemen (*jalaiwala*), who watch over the kiln twenty-four hours a day to ensure its internal temperature is maintained at 1,000 degrees centigrade for fifteen days; and unloaders (*nikasiwala*), who remove the baked bricks at the end of the firing cycle and stack them for transportation. The fired bricks emerge in different grades. Some are high quality, some are cracked or otherwise defective. Better-grade bricks command a top price of 2.5 rupees each, while lower grade bricks are sold for 1.5 rupees.

In addition to the above laborers, each medium-sized kiln typically has two foremen and an accountant. The foremen monitor work and mete out punishment. The accountant keeps track of the number of bricks baked and sold at each grade level and also manages the debits and credits of the bonded laborers. Payments of government wages ($1.29 per day) are provided every two weeks, excluding debt deductions.

Aside from labor, equipment, and a government royalty for land used, the largest expense for a kiln operator is fuel. Diesel fuel is required to operate the pump that transports water to the dirt pits and several tons of coal are required to maintain the seething temperature across an oven four hundred feet in diameter. Fuel costs are unavoidable, which is why minimized labor expenses boost profits. Taxes are also minimized by virtue of bribes to local magistrates, as well as cooked books on the number and type of bricks sold.

Table B.27: *Batterias* may have forced laborers, debt-bondage slaves, or both. These laborers work in hellish conditions, heating wood in ovens at extreme temperatures with minimal oxygen to transform wood into charcoal. Lungs filled with soot, devastating burns, and physical beatings at the hands of merciless *gatos* (managers) ensure the work is completed. The environmental damage is considerable, as the laborers clear-cut dozens of trees per cycle to produce the charcoal. The low number of slaves required—fourteen per thirty ovens—and the high price of charcoal on the wholesale smelting market ensure compelling returns.

Table B.28: Coffee-bean production involves two harvests per year; thus, the spreadsheet represents harvest rather than monthly economics. Large up-front costs might include land, fertilizer, and processing machines. To simplify, I have assumed that the plantation utilizes only forced laborers, when many might be in debt bondage. Spot prices vary from year to year, so I have tried to assume a conservative mean.

Coffee production is labor intensive and involves heavy exposure to toxic pesticides. The grueling first step involves hand-picking each individual flush once the coffee plants begin to bear fruit. Flushes ripen at different times, so the laborers must retrace the same row of coffee plants multiple times. Processing the flushes involves separating the coffee bean from the pulp, either by machine or by hand. Beans must then be sorted by type, color, and suitability for production. After sorting, beans are dried in the sun for up to two weeks. Once dried, the beans are packed in sixty-kilogram sacks and sold to wholesalers. To ensure that slaves do not attempt to escape, many slave owners slice the feet of their slaves with razor blades each morning.

Appendix C
Selected Human Development Statistics

TABLE C.1
Selected World Demographics, 2006

	Total Population (millions)	Population Density (people per square kilometer)	Population Under 18 (millions)	Percent under 18	Percent of Population Urbanized	Women as Percent of Labor Force	Life Expectancy at Birth (2005)	
							Women	*Men*
Albania	3.2	116	1.1	35	44	41	76.7	71.0
Moldova	4.3	129	1.1	26	46	49	71.3	63.9
Central and Eastern Europe	**406.2**	**141**	**108.0**	**27**	**63**	**46**	**72.4**	**68.8**
India	1,090.5	368	420.0	39	28	32	65.0	61.8
Nepal	25.8	176	11.9	46	15	41	62.0	61.2
South Asia	**1,468.5**	**298**	**584.6**	**40**	**28**	**33**	**64.5**	**61.4**
Burma	49.5	70	14.4	29	29	40	63.1	57.5
Thailand	62.8	121	19.2	31	32	46	73.8	66.3
East Asia and Pacific	**1,958.2**	**117**	**593.8**	**30**	**41**	**45**	**73.4**	**68.0**
Nigeria	135.8	150	63.6	47	47	37	43.6	43.1
Sub-Saharan Africa	**665.5**	**30**	**340.1**	**51**	**36**	**42**	**42.0**	**41.4**
Mexico	101.7	54	39.8	39	75	33	77.5	72.6
Latin America and Caribbean	**537.8**	**27**	**197.1**	**37**	**77**	**35**	**74.0**	**70.7**
United Kingdom	59.3	246	12.4	21	89	45	80.6	76.0
Italy	57.6	196	9.8	17	67	39	83.1	74.6
Netherlands	16.5	479	3.5	21	66	41	81.1	75.7
United States	301.0	32	76.4	25	80	46	80.0	74.6
Industrialized countries	**953.6**	**—**	**207.4**	**22**	**76**	**42**	**81.2**	**75.0**

TABLE C.2

Selected Economic Indicators

	Per Capita Income, 2006 (U.S. dollars, PPP[1])	GDP Per Capita Growth, 1990–2005 (percent)	Average Annual Rate of Inflation, 1990–2005 (percent)	Central Government Expenditure, 1992–2004 (percent)				Population Living under $2 per Day, 2005 (percent)
				To Health	*To Education*	*To Defense*	*To External Debt*	
Albania	4,878	*5.0*	*29*	*4*	*2*	*4*	*3*	*12*
Moldova	1,979	*–5.3*	*79*	*4*	*5*	*2*	*10*	*64*
Central and Eastern Europe	**7,850**	***–0.5***	***102***	***4***	***5***	***9***	—	***34***
India	3,389	*4.2*	*7*	*2*	*2*	*15*	*18*	*80*
Nepal	1,490	*2.1*	*7*	*5*	*18*	*8*	*6*	*83*
South Asia	**2,997**	***3.7***	***7***	***2***	***2***	***15***	***16***	***78***
Burma	1,620	*1.5*	*25*	*3*	*8*	*29*	—	*82*
Thailand	8,190	*2.8*	*3*	*8*	*17*	*6*	*16*	*33*
East Asia and Pacific	**5,675**	***6.0***	***6***	***1***	***8***	***11***	***11***	***50***
Nigeria	1,154	*0.0*	*23*	*1*	*3*	*3*	*12*	*91*
Sub-Saharan Africa	**1,950**	***0.4***	***38***	—	—	—	***10***	***76***
Mexico	9,903	*1.5*	*16*	*5*	*25*	*3*	*21*	*26*
Latin America and Caribbean	**8,060**	***1.3***	***44***	***6***	***16***	***4***	***31***	***25***
United Kingdom	30,921	*2.5*	*2*	*15*	*4*	*7*	*0*	*< 1*
Italy	28,320	*1.5*	*3*	*11*	*8*	*4*	*0*	*< 1*
Netherlands	31,789	*2.1*	*2*	*10*	*2*	*4*	*0*	*< 1*
United States	41,684	*2.1*	*2*	*22*	*2*	*25*	*0*	*< 1*
Industrialized countries	**32,148**	***1.8***	***2***	***15***	***4***	***10***	***0***	***< 1***
World	**9,045**	***1.5***						

[1] Purchasing power parity.

TABLE C.3

Selected Education and Gender Equality Indicators

	Adult Literacy Rate 2000 (percent)		Primary School Attendance, 1996–2005 (percent)		Ratio of Female to Male Earned Income
	Male	*Female*	*Male*	*Female*	
Albania	*92*	*77*	—	—	0.56
Moldova	*100*	*98*	*86*	*87*	0.65
Central and Eastern Europe	***98***	***95***	***79***	***77***	**0.60**
India	*68*	*45*	*80*	*73*	0.38
Nepal	*59*	*24*	*79*	*66*	0.51
South Asia	***66***	***42***	***78***	***71***	**0.42**
Burma	*89*	*81*	*82*	*82*	—
Thailand	*97*	*94*	—	—	0.61
East Asia and Pacific	***93***	***81***	**—**	**—**	**0.62**
Nigeria	*72*	*56*	*64*	*57*	0.41
Sub-Saharan Africa	***69***	***53***	***60***	***56***	**0.40**
Mexico	*93*	*89*	*97*	*97*	0.38
Latin America and Caribbean	***90***	***88***	***92***	***92***	**0.38**
United Kingdom	*99*	*99*	*99*	*99*	0.62
Italy	*99*	*98*	*99*	*99*	0.46
Netherlands	*99*	*99*	*99*	*99*	0.53
United States	*99*	*99*	*99*	*99*	0.62
Industrialized countries	**—**	**—**	**—**	**—**	**0.60**

Sources: United Nations Children's Fund 2005; United Nations Development Program 2005; Organization for Economic Cooperation and Development 2007; World Bank, online statistics database, available at http://econ.worldbank.org.

Notes

1. Sex Trafficking: An Overview

1. Rig Veda, "Rudra-Brahmana Hymn," tenth mandala, sixty-first hymn.

2. By freedoms I do not mean the right to vote, freedom of assembly, or the promotion of a free press, all of which are democratic qualities that have spread alongside the process of globalization. Rather, I mean the more individualized notion of freedom as the "real opportunity that we have to accomplish what we value" (Sen 1992: 31). Sen's notion of freedom posits that each individual in a society possesses certain "primary goods," including the "rights, liberties and opportunities, income and wealth, and the social bases of self-respect" (81) required to achieve what he or she values—precisely what globalization has eroded for many populations, and thereby eroded individual freedoms and contributed to the phenomenon of contemporary slavery.

3. The definitions of human trafficking in most countries suffer similar confusion. In the United States, where trafficking is the "recruitment, harboring, [or] transportation" of a person "*for the purpose* [my emphasis] of subjection to involuntary servitude, peonage, debt bondage, or slavery," (Trafficking Victims Protection Act, 2000, sec. 103 (8)(b)), the government has tried to clear the confusion by stating separately that movement need not occur for trafficking to occur (United States State Department 2007: 7, 31); however, the awkward wording nonetheless connotes movement for the purpose of exploitation, obfuscating the essence of the crime.

4. Even worse, 2.4 million (22 percent), died during the journey. See Hochschild 2005: 32.

5. Throughout this book, I use the terms "slave trade" and "sex slavery" to refer to the movement and exploitation components of sex trafficking. However, in some cases, the term "sex trafficking" is linguistically preferable, as when used as a verb. It would be awkward to say, "Jane Doe was slave traded to Italy," as opposed to "Jane Doe was trafficked to Italy."

6. The most comprehensive campaign underway to end poverty and redress a host of other global human-development deficiencies is embodied in the Millennium Development Goals of the United Nations. In 2000, the United Nations enumerated eight goals: eradicate extreme poverty and hunger; achieve universal primary education; promote gender equality and empower women; reduce child mortality; improve maternal health; combat HIV/AIDS, malaria, and other diseases; ensure environmental sustainability; and develop a global partnership for development. It aimed to achieve these goals by 2015. As of 2007, each goal was substantially off target (see http://www.un.org/millenniumgoals). The most crucial component of these plans consists of foreign aid promised by twenty-two rich countries under the Organization for Economic Cooperation and Development (OECD). Each of these nations pledged 0.7 percent of their gross national incomes (GNI) from 2000 to 2015 to direct aid to poor countries, but only a handful of the countries have consistently met the mark. In 2005, the United States was third from last, with 0.22 percent of its GNI donated to foreign aid overall (see OECD 2007).

In addition to improving key human-development deficiencies, it is crucial for the systemic asymmetries constituent to the process of economic globalization to be remedied to reduce global poverty levels. Massive trade imbalances related to tariffs, safeguards, antidumping duties, agricultural subsidies, and other trade mechanisms cost developing economies more than three times what is given to them in development aid each year (see Stiglitz 2006: 78). Insurmountable debt loads continue to transfer much-needed capital from poor nations to rich ones, and a lack of equitable access to markets and sustainable profit participation in global industry exacerbate poverty levels and motivate the mass migration trends that slave traders exploit with ruthless precision.

7. UNHCR 2007: 7.

8. Ibid.: 7, 11.

9. Data related to human trafficking are inherently imprecise due to the clandestine nature of the crimes and the broad overlap with smuggling and migration. To advance the process, I have attempted to formulate a transparent framework from which to generate key sex trafficking metrics, particularly those required to conduct a comprehensive business and economic analysis of the industry. More refined methodologies will no doubt be formulated, but the following is intended as a good place to start.

To calculate the number of sex trafficking victims in each region, I began by calculating the number of sex slaves, for which I applied a bottom-up approach to key countries, then extrapolated for a regional number (a more refined approach might analyze all countries). For example, in Western Europe, I analyzed Italy, Germany, the Netherlands, France, and the United Kingdom in detail, then extrapolated for the remainder of Western Europe. North America and South Asia were the only regions in which I was able to analyze each country.

Taking Italy as an example, I began with the total number of prostitutes, for which I was given estimates of thirty-eight thousand to eighty thousand, depending on the source (academic, government, and nongovernment). Prominent Italian academic Francesco Cachediti provided the low-end number, which included only those prostitutes who could be seen and counted. The high number (from several NGOs) accounted for the fact that up to one-half of prostitutes operate behind closed doors. I calculated a number closer to a low end: fifty thousand.

From this number, I ascertained the ratio of prostitutes who are sex slaves. Again, the estimates in Italy vary: one out of ten to seven out of ten. From an economic standpoint, the ratio is bound to be higher than lower because the retail price of a sex slave is almost always less than that of a prostitute, as the former is unpaid and kept in conditions that require minimal expense. Because most customers gravitate toward a less expensive version of the same product, sex-slave establishments slowly take over the market in any area. Based on my field observations and subsequent calculations, I settled on a ratio of one out of three prostitutes in Italy as sex slaves, or 16,500 total. Performing a similar analysis for the other West European countries mentioned above, I extrapolated for the entire region to arrive at one hundred eighty thousand total sex slaves in Western Europe.

In calculating the number of annual sex trafficking victims as well as slaves who were escaped, freed, or deceased, I used two key drivers: the total number of sex slaves and the average duration of enslavement. I calculated the average duration of enslavement based on several hundred victim interviews and victim case studies. In reality, the range in each region varies from a few months to a decade or more, but settling on conservative averages allows for important calculations, including the monthly churn rate of sex slaves in each region.

In a business context, the churn rate is defined as the percent of an average subscriber or audience base lost each month. The monthly churn rate I calculated for sex slaves in South Asia is 2.5 percent; in East Asia and Pacific, 2.7 percent; in Western Europe, 3.1 percent; in Central and Eastern Europe, 3.3 percent; in Latin America, 3.1 percent; in the Middle East, 3.4 percent; in Africa, 2.7 percent; and in North America, 3.3 percent. The churn rate for South Asia means that 2.5 percent of the sex slaves in a given month are not slaves at the end of that month, either because they escape, are freed, or perish. This churn rate implies the average duration of enslavement of a sex slave in South Asia is approximately 3.3 years. The Middle East has the highest churn rate, at 3.4 percent per month, or approximately 2.5 years enslavement. Numerous factors affect the duration of enslavement, including the modality of entry, the quality of social services, and the level of law enforcement and judicial corruption. Applying the churn rate allows for calculations of the number of slaves lost in a year, which can be netted against new sex trafficking victims for a total number of slaves the following year.

If the number of sex slaves and average duration of enslavement in a region are known, and if one assumes a zero percent growth rate (no one is arguing that sex trafficking is diminishing), then one can calculate a bare minimum number of annual sex trafficking victims required to keep the market at the same size. Applying the zero-growth number to each region results in a total of five hundred thousand sex trafficking victims per year. A maximum of six hundred thousand accounts for the top level of growth I can justify.

10. Beginning in 1998, numerous governments, UN bodies—United Nations Children's Fund (UNICEF), United Nations Interregional Crime and Justice Research Institute (UNICRI), United Nations Development Fund for Women (UNIFEM), and United Nations Office on Drugs and Drime (UNODC)—and international governmental agencies began producing estimates of annual human-trafficking victims. These estimates ranged from five hundred thousand by UNIFEM to four million by USAID. The estimates have been declining over time, and in the last few years, most organizations have relied on data provided either by the United Nations or the U.S. State Department. The UNODC has assumed the primary role of assessing human trafficking data and trends for the United Nations; in 2006, it ceased offering estimates until more analysis could be conducted (see UNODC 2006: 45). A separate UN initiative called the UN Global Initiative to Fight Trafficking (UN.GIFT) is also working on comprehensive trafficking data (see http://www.ungift.org), though none have yet been provided. At present, the U.S. State Department offers the primary human trafficking statistics; however, no transparency on the methodology utilized has been provided.

11. United States Department of State 2007: 8. When I attempted to ascertain the methodology utilized via discussions in 2006 with top staff at the State Department's Office to Monitor and Combat Trafficking in Persons, no one was able to provide me with the information.

12. International Labour Organisation 2005: 55.

13. In reality, this disaggregation is not always the case. Many movers belong to the same network that the exploiters do. This vertical integration is found more often in Europe than Asia, where organized crime groups are more heavily involved in human trafficking. However, agents in an organization who are responsible for recruitment and transportation are still paid for their work, and that payment includes a profit margin above the pure expense of recruitment and transportation. Payments to traffickers in the same organization might be higher or lower than payments to third-party traffickers. To simplify, I have assumed all payments are made to third-party traffickers, though at depressed margins of 45 to 60 percent. These margins are in many cases lower than reality, as demand for new slaves from brothel owners can lead to bidding wars at sex-slave buyers' markets.

14. Numerous articles have appeared on the subject: see, e.g., Christian Miller, "Iraq's Foreign Laborers Face Exploitation, Death," Los Angeles Times, October 12, 2005; David Phinney, "Labor Trafficking in Iraq," April 22, 2006, available at http://www.davidphinney.com/pages/2006/04/labor_trafficik.php;

Cam Simpson, "U.S. Tax Dollars Tied to Human Trafficking, Report Alleges," Chicago Tribune, June 6, 2006; Cam Simpson, "Officer Says Iraq Firms Were Slow to Return Passports," Chicago Tribune, June 22, 2006.

15. I say "almost always" because during the twenty-five years after World War II, centrally planned economies outgrew and were more stable than were capitalist economies. The Soviet economy grew 3.35 percent per year from 1948 to 1973, while the economy of the U.S. grew 2.45 percent per year during that same period and the economy of the United Kingdom 2.42 percent (Maddison 2006: 643). Health care, mortality rates, and literacy were also superior in socialist countries during this period.

16. Stiglitz 2003: 142.

17. The global economic integration that commenced in the 1990s was more accurately the recommencement of the global economic integration that began in 1896 but was abruptly interrupted in 1914 by World War I, followed by the Great Depression, World War II, and the rise of socialism. This original economic globalization from 1896–1914 was similarly catalyzed by advancements in communications (telegraph and telephone) and transportation (railroad, steam engine, and internal combustion engine), as well as the adoption of the gold standard, which provided stability and predictability to international commerce. Unprecedented levels of trade, labor immigration, and global economic integration were similarly predicated on the accretion of many unsustainable ills, including a new wave of colonial conquest in Africa and Asia, the disintegration of traditional livelihoods and societies, and the unequally distributed benefits of globalization in favor of the rich at the expense of the poor.

18. For more information on the profitability of Old World slavery See Bales 1999: 16; see the same work for a broader discussion on the comparability of contemporary slavery and nineteenth-century slavery. An excellent account of the economic history of nineteenth-century slavery in the United States can be found in Ransom 1989. For a comprehensive study of the early history of slavery, see Meltzer 1993.

19. For example, the cost of airline travel decreased 90 percent from 1930 to 2000 (Frieden 2006: 95).

20. Quoted from Frieden 2006: 229.

21. Along with the World Bank, the IMF was born at the end of World War II at the United Nations Monetary and Financial Conference in the Mount Washington Hotel at Bretton Woods, New Hampshire. One of the chief topics was avoiding another Great Depression, which during the 1930s had led to unprecedented levels of global unemployment and poverty. At the conference, the British economist John Maynard Keynes argued that the lack of global aggregate demand led to global economic downturns, and that governments should stimulate demand to avoid these downturns. The IMF was created and charged with preventing another global depression by pressuring countries that were not doing their part to maintain global aggregate demand. If necessary, the IMF would provide loans to those countries to do so.

22. Calculated from Maddison 2006: 489.

23. Calculated from Ibid.: 185.

24. Calculated from Ibid.: 183.

25. Calculated from Ibid.: 489.

26. Calculated from Ibid.: 183.

27. The standard metric for assessing poverty levels is that those who subsist on incomes of less than two dollars per day are living in poverty, and those who subsist on incomes of less than one dollar per day are living in extreme poverty. At present, over 2.6 billion people, or 40 percent of the planet, subsist on less than two dollars per day. Under the policies of economic globalization, the number of people living in poverty increased by approximately 25 percent from 1990 to 2000.

28. UNDP 2005.

29. The massive increase in debt obligations was also a result of an increase in the real value of loans due to currency devaluation and interest-rate increases.

30. Other factors in addition to IMF economic policies are considered to have played a part in the East Asian economic crisis of 1997. Some of these factors include: the collapse of the Mexican peso in 1994, which eroded confidence in developing-country currencies worldwide; the increase in interest rates in the United States during the 1990s, which drew capital away from East Asian currencies; and increasing economic competition from China, the currency of which was kept artificially low in relation to the U.S. dollar, rendering its goods less expensive. For a detailed discussion of the East Asian financial crisis, see Agenor, et al. 1999.

31. Quoted from Frieden 2006: 352–353.

32. In 1936, Keynes wrote, "The modern capitalist is a fair-weather sailor. As soon as a storm rises, he abandons the duties of navigation and even sinks the boats which might carry him to safety by his haste to push his neighbor off and himself in" (See Keynes 1997: 380). Truer words could not be spoken about the behavior of modern capitalists during the Asian economic crisis six decades later.

33. Calculated from Maddison 2006: 552–553.

34. Thailand's economic stability can be traced back almost one thousand years. The early kingdoms of the modern Thai people—Dvaravati (eleventh to twelfth centuries), Sukothai (twelfth to thirteenth centuries), Ayuthaya (fourteenth to sixteenth centuries), and Chakri (seventeenth to eighteenth centuries)—were among the most prosperous of their time. Thailand was historically more prosperous than its Mekong subregion neighbors primarily because it was never conquered or colonized by a foreign power. By contrast, every other Mekong subregion country was colonized by the British or French. While centuries of colonial oppression and post-independence instability weakened the economies of these countries, present-day Thais enjoy almost 2.5 times the per capita income of their neighbors.

35. Globalization apologists cite the fact that in the last twenty years, the percentage of people living in extreme poverty has decreased, even though the total

number has increased. However, if one accounts for the fact that two dollars today is worth considerably less than two dollars ten or fifteen years earlier, both the percent and total number of people in the world living in poverty has increased as a result of economic globalization. Assume that the two-dollar metric started in 2000. Assume India's inflation rate has been 5.0 percent per year from 2000 to 2007. The over eight hundred million Indians who lived on fewer than two dollars per day in 2000 must be compared to the number of Indians who lived on less than $2.81 in 2007. Based on my own calculations, the number and total percent of Indians subsisting on incomes beneath this level are greater than the number and total percent living under the two-dollar level in 2000. Similarly, the number and total percentage of people in the world living on an inflation and purchasing power parity–adjusted daily metric in 2007 are greater than the number and total percentage living on fewer than two dollars per day in 2000. Because inflation consists in large part of price increases associated with the skyrocketing wealth of upper classes, the poor have borne the brunt of eroding real incomes, in both poor and rich countries. In the United States, real wages of the middle and lower classes have stagnated for the past two decades (Stiglitz 2006: 10). Across the world, the richest five hundred individuals have a combined income greater than that of the poorest 416 million (UNDP 2005: 4). This means that for every one dollar these poorest people earn, the richest earn $832,000. Such disparities in wealth are utterly unsustainable and immoral.

36. UNDP, April, 2005.

37. As part of its National Literacy Decade (2003–12), the United Nations also noted that two-thirds of the over eight hundred million illiterate adults in the world are females and that a lack of education is a key factor in promoting poverty, higher HIV infection rates, and vulnerability to exploitation and trafficking. For more detail, see UNESCO's website on the United Nations Literacy Decade, available at http://www.unesco.org/education/litdecade/.

38. World Bank 2007: 13.

39. UNIFEM 2005: 2.

40. Guilmoto 2007: 15.

41. The Pre-Natal Diagnostic Technique Act was passed in 1994, prohibiting doctors from using prenatal diagnostic techniques to determine the sex of a fetus. Though widely publicized at the time, a lack of resources, corruption, and loopholes have resulted in only one conviction since the act was passed (Guilmoto 2007: 15).

42. Asia Development Bank 2003: 49.

43. UNIFEM 2005: 3.

44. Ibid.: 1.

45. World Health Organization, online web statistics, available at http://www.who.int/en.

46. In India, *dalits* are typically enslaved as bonded laborers or forced laborers, but almost never for sexual exploitation because other Indians see them as untouchable.

47. In addition to these specific market forces, classical economists have argued that the supply of a product alone creates its own demand. As John Stuart Mill explained, "[that] which constitutes the means of payment for commodities . . . is, simply, commodities . . . A general excess of supply, or excess of all commodities above the demand, so far as demand consists in means of payment, is thus shown to be an impossibility . . . It is evident enough, that produce makes a market for produce, and that there is wealth in the country with which to purchase all the wealth in the country" (Mill 2004: 522–523). Per Mill's reasoning, a massive increase in the supply of potential slaves would inherently create a substantial, if not equal, increase in demand for slaves.

48. From the consumer's perspective, sex trafficking could be construed as the version of prostitution that maximizes pleasure, violence, and debauchery. It could also be considered as maximizing profit, as it minimizes costs.

49. Unless otherwise stated, all per capita figures are purchasing power parity (PPP)–adjusted numbers.

50. Considering demand for sex services in relation to the number of hours of labor required to make the purchase is appropriate because, as Adam Smith relates, "Labour . . . is the real measure of the exchangeable value of all commodities" and "the real price of every thing, what every thing really costs to the man who wants to acquire it, is the toil and trouble of acquiring it" (*Inquiry*, book 1, chapter 5, 43).

51. Keynes 1997: 96.

52. I have used the arc elasticity of demand formula: $((p1+p2)/(q1+q2)) \times (Dq / Dp)$.

53. Keynes 1997: 96.

54. A more classical articulation of the relationship between supply and demand can be found in Keynes 1997, which describes supply and demand in their relation to full employment. Aggregate supply $(Z)=ø(N)$, where $N=$employment. Aggregate demand $(D)=f(N)$. So long as $D>Z$, the employer will have an incentive to increase N to the profit maximizing point where $D=Z$. In the case of the "employer" of sex slaves, the slave owner would add slave employees so long as $ø(N)<f(N)$. Because $ø(N)$ is a minimal number (primarily because sex slaves are almost entirely unpaid), and because $f(N)$ is an inherently greater number (that is, the retail price of sex is always greater than the unit operating costs of slave labor), D would always be greater than Z, so the demand for sex slaves by a slave owner would be almost limitless. Put another way, the more slaves a brothel owner can get his hands on, the more profits he can enjoy. The only way to decrease slave-owner demand would be to increase $ø(N)$ or to lower the profits for each marginal increase in (N). If $ø(N)$ increases, the only way for a slave owner to maintain the same relation between $ø(N)$ and $f(N)$ would be to increase the retail price of his product. As demonstrated by the principles of the elasticity of demand, any increase in the retail price of a sex act would decrease consumer demand.

55. United States Department of Justice 2006: 8.

56. Investigations and court cases can also last years, and not all traffickers convicted from 2001 to 2005 committed crimes during that same time period.

By assuming that traffickers only committed crimes in the year convicted, the conviction rate of 3 to 4 percent is a considerable overstatement, though it provides a more conservative metric from which to make other calculations.

2. India and Nepal

1. *Paan* is a palate cleanser that typically includes a mixture of various spices, fruits, sugar, betel nut, and sometimes tobacco, wrapped in a betel leaf.

2. HIV claims the lives of countless prostitutes and sex slaves each year, and unprotected sex with prostitutes is the single largest contributing factor to India's rapidly growing HIV problem. Assuming 1.5 million prostitutes in India, nine hundred thousand (60 percent) would be HIV positive. If each prostitute provided sex to ten men per day and the infection rate were one in five thousand (.02 percent), then each day, one thousand eight hundred men in India would become infected with HIV as a result of sexual intercourse with a prostitute. For each .01 percent increase in the infection rate, an additional nine hundred men per day would be infected.

3. Tamang is the dominant ethnicity of the Nepalese in the Sindhupalchok region.

4. *Dalits* are among the poorest, least educated, most disenfranchised, and most exploited people in India. The very term *dalit* is rooted in the Sanskrit word "dal," which means "suppressed," "crushed," or "oppressed."

5. A little over one-half the children in rural India and Nepal are married while they are still children, and almost all are teenage girls married to much older men. In India, such marriages are protected by the Sharda Act (Child Marriage Act), which makes it legal for a man to marry a child once she is fifteen years old. This act was passed to establish a higher age than most Indian girls had reached when they married.

6. At a shelter in Allahabad operated by a priest named Father Raymond, I met thirty-four boys who were rescued from carpet-loom enterprises. They had been trafficked, starved, tortured, and coerced to work eighteen or more hours per day. Because the looms were located inside shacks with little ventilation, the high level of particulate matter from thread dust resulted in severe respiratory ailments. Many children also had scars from beatings as well as injuries suffered from the sharp claw tool they used to push the thread down the loom, which they regularly mishandled due to fatigue from sleep deprivation.

7. Bonded labor planted a firm foot in India, thanks in large part to the country's historical caste system. During ancient times, castes were grouped into four major *varnas,* or types. In descending order of prominence, the *varnas* were: *brahmin* (scholar, priest), *kshatriya* (king, warrior), *vaishya* (trader, landowner), and *shodra* (craftsman, service provider). Castes are no longer as integral to South Asian society as they once were, but some legacies persist, including the fact that hundreds of millions of poor untouchables, such as the *dalits,* are excluded from the caste system altogether.

The Indian Constitution outlawed bonded labor in 1950, but the first significant national act to abolish bonded labor—the Bonded Labor System Abolition Act—did not appear until 1976. The 1976 act prescribed steps to be taken once a government official identified a bonded laborer, including cancellation of the debt and grants of up to ten thousand rupees ($222) for the purchase of necessary assets (livestock, equipment) to generate income. In 1986, the Child Labor and Juvenile Justice Act was passed to prevent the exploitation of children for bonded and forced labor. After an initial flurry of activity, government apathy and head-shaking levels of corruption have rendered the laws impotent. A bonded laborer named Satish told me that he did not even bother with the rehabilitation programs under the 1976 act: "If we apply for these grants, the landowner bribes the local official and takes the money for himself." Some landowners even conjure laborers out of thin air, register them, and abscond with the grant money. In other cases, corrupt local officials deduct processing fees so that almost no money ends up in the laborer's hands. To date, only a few offenders have been convicted under either act.

8. In 1776, Adam Smith wrote, "Wherever there is great property, there is great inequality. For one very rich man, there must be at least five hundred poor, and the affluence of the few supposes the indigence of the many" (Smith 2003: 903). In Mahi village, the ratio of the indigent to the affluent was 1,250 to one.

9. *Lakh* is a term for 100,000 in South Asia. One hundred thousand Nepalese rupees is about $1,425.

10. Beginning in 1989, Nepalese citizens began demanding democratic reforms after centuries of monarchic rule, under the banner of the Jana Andolan, or People's Movement. The government responded to nonviolent protests in February 1990 with bullets, arrests, and executions. Riots continued, and on April 9, 1990, King Birendra lifted the ban on political parties. Elections and fragile coalitions followed for six years, but ongoing corruption inspired a guerrilla war against the government beginning in 1996, dubbed the Maoist insurgency. Democracy in Nepal was dealt a further blow on June 1, 2002, when Crown Prince Dipendra gunned down King Birendra, Queen Aishwarya, and himself. The king's brother, Gyanendra, immediately seized power and has since ruled with despotic efficiency. Under international pressure, the first democratic elections in seven years were held on February 7, 2006, though less than 10 percent of the country voted due to boycotts and violence. Roiling internal conflict has continued, fueling the flow of migrants and trafficking victims to India.

11. In October, 2005 two amendments were proposed to stiffen penalties related to trafficking crimes, including escalation of the fine for owning a brothel from 2,000 ($44) to 100,000 rupees ($2,222) and a new fine of 10,000 rupees ($222) for purchasing sex from a prostitute. As of December, 2007 neither had passed.

12. India and Nepal consulted each other in drafting the legislations, though many of the final stipulations and penalties ended up being quite different.

13. See Nepal Office of the Attorney General 2005 and 2006.

14. Abortion was illegal in Nepal until 2002. At present, it is only permitted under circumstances involving rape or a credible risk to the life of the mother during childbirth.

3. Italy and Western Europe

1. Before this time, trafficking victims were treated under immigration laws, specifically the Aliens Law 286/98 and laws relating to sexual exploitation and other forms of slavery: articles 600–604 of the Italian penal code.

2. The foreign nationals of the following countries are allowed to engage in prostitution (with valid residence permits) and work for an employer: Austria, Belgium, Cyprus, Czech Republic, Denmark, Estonia, Finland, France, Germany, Greece, Hungary, Iceland, Ireland, Italy, Latvia, Liechtenstein, Lithuania, Luxembourg, Malta, Norway, Poland, Portugal, Slovakia, Slovenia, Spain, Sweden, and the United Kingdom.

3. Under Article 250a of the Dutch penal code, it remains illegal to force a person to engage in prostitution, traffic a person for the purpose of prostitution, or force a prostitute to surrender income from sex work. These laws were updated in 2004 with Article 273a to provide stiffer jail terms, of up to twenty years, as well as a maximum fine of forty-five thousand euros. Despite the rigorous penalties, fines are rarely more than a few thousand euros, and prison terms are rarely greater than three years.

4. Dutch Ministry of Foreign Affairs 2004: 2.

5. Ibid.: 5.

6. Ibid.: 6.

7. Dutch Ministry of Foreign Affairs 2005: 23.

8. Ibid.: 5.

9. Ibid.: 31.

10. Ekberg 2004: 1187.

11. Ibid.: 1202.

12. United States Department of State 2005: 8.

4. Moldova and the Former Soviet Union

1. International Center for Women's Rights Protection and Promotion 2005: 34.

2. Ibid.: 37.

3. White passports are reentry permits commonly provided to asylum seekers or refugees to allow them to travel internationally.

4. United Nations Fund for Agricultural Development 2007: 2.

5. World Bank 2005: 135.

6. The articles in the Moldovan penal code stipulate U.S. dollar fines because the lei suffers considerable inflation.

7. Sachs 2005: 149.

5. Albania and the Balkans

1. Fox 1989: 38.
2. Ibid.: 22.
3. Ibid.: 40.
4. Ibid.: 26.
5. Ibid.: 52.
6. Ibid.: 132–133.
7. Ibid.: 132.
8. Most recently in U.S. State Department 2007.
9. Human Rights Watch 2002: 4.
10. Ibid.: 15–19.
11. Ibid.: 66.
12. Ibid.: 67.
13. Amnesty International 2004: 5.
14. Ibid.: 6.
15. From transcripts of interviews conducted by Terre des Hommes, 2004.
16. See Republic of Albania 2005.
17. Calculated from Vatra Psycho-Social Center 2002, 2003, 2004, and 2005.

6. Thailand and the Mekong Subregion

1. In Australia, Thai sex slaves are euphemistically termed "contract girls" because they ostensibly sign work contracts before traveling to Australia, after which they are coerced into prostitution.

2. Like India, China has a severe sex-ratio imbalance, with anywhere from one hundred ten to one hundred thirty females per one hundred males, depending on the province. Accordingly, it can be difficult for a Chinese male to find a Chinese female to marry. Females from several neighboring countries are imported to fill the gap.

3. The most commonly quoted passage involves the imagery of a chariot that carries individuals to *nirvana,* in which the Buddha explains to his top disciple Ananda: "And be it woman, or be it man for whom such a chariot doth wait, by the same care into *nirvana's* presence shall they come" (Bikku 2002, *Connected Discourses, samutta nikaya* I.5.6).

4. Theravada Buddhists maintain that the Buddha refused to ordain women as nuns and only agreed after lobbying from Ananda. Though the Buddha acceded, he added eight precepts that nuns must follow on top of the two hundred twenty-seven prescribed for monks (later, the number for nuns grew to three hundred thirty-one). Theravada scholars point to this and other anecdotes to justify the spiritual inferiority of women.

5. The most important include the 1997 Measures in Prevention and Suppression of Trafficking in Women and Children, the 2003 Child Protection Act, the

1998 Labour Protection Act, the 1996 Prevention and Suppression of Prostitution Act, and the 2003 Witness Protection Act.

7. The United States

1. CAST internal database; please contact the organization for access.

2. Quoted from "Lucita" narrative recorded by CAST; available by contacting the organization.

3. Bales and Lize 2004: 26.

4. Ibid.: 38.

5. United States Department of Justice 2006: 10.

6. Bales and Lize 2004: 39.

7. Ibid.: 38.

8. There are a few documented cases of trafficking across the U.S.-Canada border through the twenty-eight thousand acres of the St. Regis Mohawk Territory. Because the territory straddles the border, questions of jurisdiction arise and border enforcement is often spotty, further complicated by the Mohawks' claims of sovereignty. According to a statement provided by Louis F. Nardi, director of the Smuggling/Criminal Organizations Branch of the U.S. Immigration and Naturalization Service, to the U.S. House of Representatives on March 18, 1999, at least 3,600 individuals were smuggled by Chinese organized crime groups into the United States through this territory during 1997 and 1998. Despite efforts to crack down, slave-trading operations through the territory continue.

9. United States Department of Justice 2006: 29.

10. Kwong 2001: 241.

11. United Nations Fund for Agricultural Development 2007: 10, 14.

12. As I have discussed in previous chapters, loose borders are also problematic, as slave traders can conduct business more easily or allow migrants to transport themselves before recruiting them into exploitation. This is one of the reasons why I have argued that the best way to eradicate the sex trafficking industry is to focus on slavery, and less so on slave trading.

13. United States Department of Justice 2006: 11.

14. United States District Court, Eastern District of New York, Cr. No. 04–140(S-1)(FB).

15. According to the TVPA (103[8]), severe forms of trafficking are: sex trafficking in which a commercial sex act is induced by force, fraud, or coercion, or in which the person induced to perform such an act has not attained eighteen years of age; or the recruitment, harboring, transportation, provision, or obtaining of a person for labor or services, through the use of force, fraud, or coercion, for the purpose of subjection to involuntary servitude, peonage, debt bondage, or slavery.

16. Unlike trafficking laws in most countries, the potential fines in the United States are unlimited, though they have primarily ranged from ten thousand to one hundred fifty thousand dollars per victim.

17. Cam Simpson, "Officer Says Iraq Firms Were Slow to Return Passports," *Chicago Tribune*, June 22, 2006.

18. The full name of the PROTECT Act is the Prosecutorial Remedies and Other Tools to End the Exploitation of Children Today Act of 2003.

19. Clark pleaded guilty, though he reserved the right to challenge the constitutionality of the PROTECT Act, arguing "that Congress exceeded its power to enact criminal laws that do not involve interstate commerce and that criminalizing activities in a foreign country violate due process and international law." Clark's appeal is pending (United States Department of Justice 2006: 36.)

20. See TVPA 107(e).

21. Data from World Bank, online statistics database.

22. United States Department of Commerce 2006: 47–48.

23. Calculated from data gathered from the U.S. Department of Labor, National Compensation Survey, available at http://www.bls.gov/ncs/home.htm.

24. Dwyer 2005: 2, 8.

8. A Framework for Abolition: Risk and Demand

1. UN.GIFT could meet the role if it is sufficiently funded and open to the types of assertive measures discussed in this chapter—or measures designed to achieve similar ends.

2. Separately, I have composed a business plan of what the coalition might look like, including details of personnel allocation, infrastructure and regional presence, strategy for advocacy and deployment of tactics, and a ten-year budget. The funding required is $355 million per year ($65 million for the first unit, $290 million for the second). This budget assumes that 87.5 percent of monies are applied directly towards abolitionist programs. Three hundred and fifty-five million dollars per year ($131 per trafficked slave) may sound like a prohibitive sum, but it is not. The United States spends $1.5 billion per day on defense. Three days of this budget would fund coalition activities for twelve years. Alternatively, the IMF might provide the funding. Given that the IMF perpetrated policies that directly contributed to the mass vulnerability of millions of individuals to trafficking and slavery, the organization might redeem itself by funding a coalition dedicated to undoing a portion of the harms it caused.

3. A few simplifying assumptions must be made. First, in the formula for the cost of being caught, I have treated the prosecution and conviction probabilities as independent even though there are any number of real-world conditions that might render them dependent (and thus far more difficult to calculate). Second, properly calculating the probability of being prosecuted would require quantifying the total number of trafficked sex slaves in a country, multiplying this result by the number of forced sex acts that those slaves perform in any given year (total number of criminal acts); then dividing the number of trafficked sex slaves and sex acts associated with the prosecutions in that country, in that year,

by this result. The denominator in this case would be an astronomical number, rendering the prosecution probability meaningless. In addition, new slaves are trafficked each year, each representing additional criminal acts. To simplify, one can assume that once an individual is enslaved, all future criminal acts are a result of the initial enslavement. The total number of criminal acts in a year would thus be defined as the number of trafficked sex slaves in a country in that year plus new victims trafficked into the country in that year. This may heavily understate the number of criminal acts, but it allows for a more meaningful analysis. One might object to this methodology by pointing out that some of the individuals prosecuted are solely slave traders and some are solely slave owners, and that by combining the two I have overstated the prosecution rate. Combining the two, however, seems to be a reasonable assumption to make in the interests of overstating the prosecution rate, thereby providing a more conservative analysis.

4. Table A.3 calculates the EV of brothel sex slaves in each region. For simplicity, I have applied these numbers as the EV of the average sex slave rather than calculating EVs for all modes of sex slavery in each region and deriving a weighted average EV for sex slavery from those numbers.

5. Another reason that the real risk of sex trafficking must be elevated is that "the chance of gain is by every man more or less over-valued, and the chance of loss is by most men under-valued" (see Smith 2003: 149). In other words, sex slave owners will inherently undervalue the risks associated with their crimes and overvalue the already enormous profits; hence, those risks must be made all the greater to have a tangible profit-compromising and real-world prohibitive effect.

6. The prosecution and conviction rates are calculated estimates that include a few assumptions. First, I have counted new victims in the country to or within which they are trafficked. Second, regional averages for the number of traffickers or slave owners per prosecution hover around two to three per case, whereas averages for the number of victims per trafficker or slave owner in prosecuted cases were twice as high in Western Europe as in South Asia, due to the higher level of organized-crime involvement in the former. Because Moldova and Albania are primarily origin and transit countries, I have included in the denominators of each of those the number of estimated 2006 trafficked sex slaves as well as the estimated number of new sex trafficking victims from 2002 to 2006, around the time when each country first passed trafficking laws. Nepal could be included in this same logic, but I believe that its domestic sex slave market is large enough to justify similar treatment to other destination countries. The conviction rates include defendants who settled before going to trial, where such data were available.

7. It could be argued that shutting down sex slave operations will decrease the supply of sex slaves to consumers, allowing slave owners that are still in operation to raise retail prices. However, doing so would decrease demand by consumers, who are fundamentally motivated by minimal retail price, so in either case, demand for sex slaves would decrease.

Appendix A

1. International Labour Organisation 2005: 10.

2. Shankardass 1990: 298.

3. For each type of slavery and each industry in which slaves are exploited, I applied weighted averages of revenue and net profit margins to calculate global average metrics. For example, to arrive at $1,810 as the global weighted average revenue for bonded labor/debt bondage, I assumed that approximately 89 percent of bonded laborers and debt-bondage slaves are in South Asia allocated to the following industries: brick kilns (15 percent), carpet weaving and other manufacturing (25 percent), and agriculture, such as rice and sugar cane (60 percent). Of the remaining bonded labor and debt-bondage slaves, I assumed one-half are in Latin America and one-half in Africa. In Latin America (Brazil, Peru, Bolivia), I calculated weighted averages based on charcoal camps (10 percent), cattle farms (30 percent), and agriculture, such as tobacco and sugar cane (60 percent). In Africa (Ivory Coast, Kenya, Uganda), I calculated weighted averages based on agriculture, such as coffee and cocoa (90 percent) and conveyance (10 percent). There are a small number of debt-bondage slaves in other regions, but these fit within the mean economics of those considered. I conducted a similar exercise for forced labor, a small percentage of which include child military slaves who generate no actual revenues, thereby slightly lowering the weighted average revenue number.

4. UNODC 2007: 170.

Appendix B

1. I calculated operating expenses, such as food, medical costs, and rent, based on price points in the red-light areas or areas in which I found sex-slave establishments. Interviews with sex slaves and experts at local anti-trafficking NGOs also provided information on the levels of food, clothing, and medical expenses accrued, as well as wages for staff, such as cashiers and guards.

Works Cited

Agenor, Pierre Richard, Marcus Miller, David Vines, and Axel Weber, eds. 1999. *The Asian Financial Crisis: Causes, Contagion and Consequences.* Cambridge: Cambridge University Press.

Amnesty International. 2004. *So Does It Mean that We Have the Rights? Protecting the Human Rights of Women and Girls Trafficked for Forced Prostitution in Kosovo.* London: Amnesty International.

Asia Development Bank Staff. 2003. *Combating Trafficking of Women and Children in South Asia: Regional Synthesis Paper for Bangladesh, India, and Nepal,* Manial, Asia Development Bank, April.

Bales, Kevin. 1999. *Disposable People.* Berkeley, CA: University of California Press.

Bales, Kevin, and Steven Lize. 2004. *Trafficking in Persons in the United States: A Report to the National Institute of Justice.* University, MS: Croft Institute for International Studies.

Bikku, Bodhi. 2002. *The Connected Discourses of the Buddha: A New Translation of the Samyutta Nikaya.* Boston: Wisdom Publications.

Dutch Ministry of Foreign Affairs. 2004. *Dutch Policy on Prostitution.* The Hague: Dutch Ministry of Foreign Affairs.

Dutch Ministry of Foreign Affairs. 2005. *Trafficking in Human Beings: Fourth Report of the Dutch National Rapporteur.* The Hague: Dutch Ministry of Foreign Affairs.

Dwyer, Paul E. 2005. *Salaries of Members of Congress: A List of Payable Rates and Effective Dates, 1789–2006.* CRS Report for Congress 97-1011 GOV. Washington, DC: Congressional Research Service.

Ekberg, Gunilla. 2004. "The Swedish Law that Prohibits the Purchase of Sexual Services: Best Practices for Prevention of Prostitution and Trafficking in Human Beings." *Violence against Women* 10, no. 10 (October 2004): 1187–1218.

Frieden, Jeffrey A. 2006. *Global Capitalism: Its Fall and Rise in the Twentieth Century*. New York: Norton.

Fox, Leonard, trans. 1989. *The Code of Lekë Dukagjini/Kaunui I Lekë Dukagjinit*. Shtjefën Gjeçov, New York: Gjonlekaj Publishing Company.

Guilmoto, Christophe. 2007. *Characteristics of Sex-Ratio Imbalance in India, and Future Scenarios*. Paris: United Nations Fund for Population Activities.

Hochschild, Adam. 2005. *Bury the Chains*. New York: Houghton Mifflin.

Human Rights Watch. 2002. *Hopes Betrayed: Trafficking of Women and Girls to Post-Conflict Bosnia and Hercegovina for Forced Prostitution*. New York: Human Rights Watch.

International Center for Women's Rights Protection and Promotion. 2005. *La Strada, Trafficking in Persons in Moldova: Trends and Recommendations*. Chisinau: International Center for Women's Rights Protection and Promotion.

International Labour Organisation. 2005. *A Global Alliance against Forced Labor*. Geneva: International Labour Organisation.

Keynes, John Maynard. 1997. *The General Theory of Employment, Interest, and Money*. Amherst, NY: Prometheus Books.

Kwong, Peter. 2001. *Global Human Smuggling: Comparative Perspectives*, Baltimore, MD: Johns Hopkins University Press.

Maddison, Angus. 2006. *The World Economy*. Vols. 1 and 2. Paris: Development Center Studies, OECD Publishing.

Meltzer, Milton. 1993. *Slavery: A World History*. New York: De Capo Press.

Mill, John Stuart. 2004. *Principles of Political Economy*. Amherst, NY: Prometheus Books.

Nepal Office of the Attorney General. 2005. *Annual Report*. Kathmandu: Nepal Office of the Attorney General.

Organization for Economic Cooperation and Development (OECD). 2007. *OECD Factbook 2007: Economic, Environmental, and Social Statistics*. Paris: OECD Publishing.

Plan International. 2005. *Growing Up in Asia: Plan's Strategic Framework for Fighting Child Poverty in Asia*. Bangkok: Plan International.

Ransom, Roger L. 1989. *Conflict and Compromise: The Political Economy of Slavery, Emancipation, and the American Civil War*. Cambridge: Cambridge University Press.

Republic of Albania: Council of Ministers. 2005. *Albanian National Strategy For Combating Trafficking in Human Beings: Strategic Framework and National Action Plan: 2005–2007*. Tirana: Dajti 2000 Printing House.

Sachs, Jeffrey. 2005. *The End of Poverty: Economic Possibilities for Our Time*. New York: Penguin Press.

Sen, Amartya. 1992. *Inequality Reexamined*. Cambridge, MA: Harvard University Press.

Shankardass, Rani Dhavan. 1990. "Debt Bondage: The Survival of an Ancient Mechanism." In *India: Creating a Modern Nation*, ed. Jim Masselos, pp. 287–312. New Delhi: Sterling Publishers, 1990.

Smith, Adam. 2003. *An Inquiry into the Nature and Causes of the Wealth of Nations*. New York: Bantam Dell.

Stiglitz, Joseph. 2003. *Globalization and its Discontents*. New York: Norton.

Stiglitz, Joseph. 2006. *Making Globalization Work*. New York: Norton.

United Nations Children's Fund (UNICEF). 2005. *The State of the World's Children: Childhood under Threat*. New York: UNICEF.

United Nations Development Fund for Women (UNIFEM). 2005. *Not a Minute More*. New York: UNIFEM.

United Nations Development Program (UNDP). 2005. *Human Development Report*. New York: UNDP.

United Nations Fund for Agricultural Development (UNIFAD). 2007. *Sending Money Home: Worldwide Remittances to Developing Countries*. Rome: UNIFAD.

United Nations High Commissioner for Refugees (UNHCR). 2007. *UNHCR Statistical Yearbook: 2006*. Geneva: UNHCR.

United Nations Office on Drugs and Crime (UNODC). 2007. *2007 World Drug Report*. Vienna: UNODC.

United Nations Office on Drugs and Crime (UNODC). 2006. *Trafficking in Persons: Global Patterns*. Vienna: UNODC.

United States Department of Commerce. 2006. *Income, Poverty, and Health Insurance Coverage in the United States: 2005*. Washington, DC: United States Department of Commerce.

United States Department of Justice. 2006. *Report on Activities to Combat Human Trafficking: 2001–2005*. Washington, DC: United States Department of Justice.

United States Department of State. 2003. *Trafficking in Persons*. Washington, DC: United States Department of State.

United States Department of State. 2004. *Trafficking in Persons*. Washington, DC: United States Department of State.

United States Department of State. 2005. *Trafficking in Persons*. Washington, DC: United States Department of State.

United States Department of State. 2006. *Trafficking in Persons*. Washington, DC: United States Department of State.

United States Department of State. 2007. *Trafficking in Persons*. Washington, DC: United States Department of State.

Vatra Psycho-Social Center. 2002. *The Girls and the Trafficking*. Annual report. Vlora: Vatra Psycho-Social Center.

Vatra Psycho-Social Center. 2003. *The Girls and the Trafficking*. Annual report. Vlora: Vatra Psycho-Social Center.

Vatra Psycho-Social Center. 2004. *The Girls and the Trafficking*. Annual report. Vlora: Vatra Psycho-Social Center.

Vatra Psycho-Social Center. 2005. *The Girls and the Trafficking*. Annual report. Vlora: Vatra Psycho-Social Center.

Wilson, H. H., trans. 1977. *Rig Veda Samhita*. New Delhi: Nag Publishers.
World Bank. 2005. *Global Economic Prospects: Economic Implications of Remittances and Migration*. Washington, DC: World Bank.
World Bank. 2007. *Global Monitoring Report: Confronting the Challenges of Gender Equality and Fragile States*. Washington, DC: World Bank.

Laws and Treaties

Most laws and articles cited below were provided to me in hard copy and translated form by local colleagues. United Nations treaties and United States laws can be found online.

Albania

Albanian Criminal Code, Article 110.
Albanian Criminal Code, Article 114.
Albanian Criminal Code, Article 128.
Albanian Criminal Code, Article 298.

India

Bonded Labor System Abolition Act, 1976.
Child Labor and Juvenile Justice Act, 1986.
Domestic Violence Act, 2006.
Immoral Trafficking and Prevention Act, 1986.
Indian Criminal Code, Article 376.
Narcotic Drugs and Psychotropic Substances Act, 1985.

Italy

Abolizione della Regolamentazione della Prostituzione e Lotta Contro lo Sfruttamento della prostituzione Altrui, Italian Law 75/1958.
The Aliens Law, Italian Law 286/98.
Measures Against Trafficking in Human Beings, Italian Law 228.

Moldova

Moldovan Criminal Code, Article 165.
Moldovan Criminal Code, Article 206.
Moldovan Criminal Code, Article 220.

Nepal

Human Trafficking Control and Punishment Act, 1986.
Human Trafficking Control and Punishment Act, 1999.

Netherlands

Dutch Penal Code, Article 250a.
Dutch Penal Code, Article 273a.

Sweden

Law that Prohibits the Purchase of Sexual Services, 1998:408.

Thailand

Child Protection Act, 2003.
Labor Protections Act, 1996.
Measures in Prevention and Suppression of Trafficking in Women and Children, 1997.
Prevention and Suppression of Prostitution Act, 2003.

United Nations

International Convention on Elimination of All Forms of Discrimination Against Women, 1985.
Observance by United Nations Forces of International Humanitarian Law, 1999.
Protocol to Prevent, Suppress, and Punish Trafficking in Persons, Especially Women and Children, 2000.
Universal Declaration of Human Rights, 1948.

United States

Controlled Substances Act, USC 21, 1996.
PROTECT Act, U.S. Public Law 108-021, April 13, 2003.
Trafficking Victims Protection Act, U.S. Public Law 106-386, October 28, 2000.
Trafficking Victims Protection Reauthorization Act, H.R. 2620, January 7, 2003.
Trafficking Victims Protections Reauthorization Act, H.R. 972, January 4, 2005.

Index

Page numbers in italics refer to figures and tables.